KT-483-124

LITERARY LIAISONS

LITERARY LIAISONS

Auto/biographical
Appropriations
in Modernist
Women's Fiction

LYNETTE FELBER

NORTHERN ILLINOIS UNIVERSITY PRESS / DEKALB

© 2002 by Northern Illinois University Press

Published by the Northern Illinois University Press, DeKalb, Illinois 60115

Manufactured in the United States using acid-free paper

All Rights Reserved

Design by Julia Fauci

Library of Congress Cataloging-in-Publication Data

Felber, Lynette, 1951–

Literary liaisons : auto/biographical appropriations in modernist women's writing / Lynette Felber.

    p.   cm.

Includes bibliographical references (p.) and index.

ISBN 0-87580-301-6 (alk. paper)

1. American fiction—Women authors—History and criticism. 2. Modernism (Literature)—United States. 3. Women and literature—United States—History—20th century. 4. Women and literature—Great Britain—History—20th century. 5. Autobiographical fiction, American—History and criticism. 6. Autobiographical fiction, English—History and criticism. 7. English fiction—Women authors—History and criticism. 8. Modernism (Literature)—Great Britain. 9. Couples in literature. 10. Self in literature. I. Title.

PS374.M535 F45 2002

813'.5209112'082—dc21

  2002067179

KING ALFRED'S COLLEGE
WINCHESTER

813·09
/ FEL   KA0276984K

To my mentors

Contents

Illustrations

Preface

If we cannot write books about ourselves then I ask about whom may we write them?

—Radclyffe Hall, lecture to the English Club

It is a truth universally acknowledged that unhappy relationships are the stuff of literature. Reciprocated love, reconciliation, and happy marriage serve only to end a story. Some of the most intriguing stories are those produced in the aftermath of the volatile, conflicted relationships of lovers who are also writers. In recent years biographical revelations about writing couples have even threatened to obscure the posthumous literary reputations of those exposed. Sylvia Plath's battle with Ted Hughes, for example, resurfaced when he published poems about her—thirty years after her death. A recent popular biography exposed the hypocrisy of France's foremost feminist, Simone de Beauvoir, who introduced her female lycée students to Jean-Paul Sartre and ultimately shared her lover with them. Literary battles and scandals reach the mass media because they appeal to our voyeuristic curiosity about the autobiographical truths lurking behind every work of fiction, disclaimers notwithstanding.

Such conflicted autobiographical stories are the subject of this book, stories told by five modernist women writers about their intimate-professional relationships. This book takes something from two biographical traditions: the single subject and the relational subject, the couple or family. It focuses on women who refused to be mere subordinate facilitators; they insisted on their identity as writers, deserving publication, professional respect, and recognition. Yet, in common with the relational tradition, this book emphasizes the woman's experience within the writing couple. The stories told by Anaïs Nin, Rebecca West, Zelda Fitzgerald, Radclyffe Hall, and H.D. are also relational with each other since they shared a common temporal setting in the early postsuffrage period. The texts resulting from their relationships offer variations on a recurrent theme: the woman writer's anger at being denied subjectivity in a literary liaison. By placing the autobiographical fiction of these writers in a common theoretical framework—at once feminist, Lacanian, Kristevan, and genre-based—and by placing the texts in contact with each other through a shared context, I hope to bring to attention neglected works that deserve a place in the modernist canon, as well as to bring to light unacknowledged connections between these five women and their partners.

Acknowledgments

I would like to acknowledge my own professional connections. This work is the product of neither a literary liaison nor a coauthorship; at the same time, as with most academic projects, a number of people quietly and generously contributed their knowledge and skills during its long gestation period. A chance comment by Ellie Ragland-Sullivan after an M/MLA conference session suggested my eventual Lacanian emphasis on the mirror stage. Ruth Hoberman was an early source of encouragement and suggestions about interesting lesser-known writers to investigate. Harriet Kramer Linkin was always a responsive listener and a superb source of cyperspace dialogue. I would like especially to thank Mary Lincoln, director of Northern Illinois University Press, for her support and patience during the long period it takes to bring such a project into print. My department chair Mary Helen Thuente and my colleague John Minton, who replaced me as editor in chief of *Clio* during a sabbatical leave, were also instrumental to the completion of this project. In the English Department office, Elaine Weber deserves a hearty thanks for putting up with my distraction from my duties as editor; Gladys Thiele and Jennifer Langley contributed in myriad ways.

As this work went through evolutions and drafts, a number of helpful anonymous readers also became much-appreciated facilitators and muses. One particular specialist referee made so many astute suggestions that she served as teacher, mentor, and editor as well. A discerning reader might recognize her voice as a near collaborator, particularly in the introduction and the final section of chapter 5. She knows who she is, and I want to express my deepest gratitude for her generous contribution.

Research on this project was supported by a Purdue Research Foundation Summer Faculty Grant in 1995 and a sabbatical leave from Indiana University–Purdue University Fort Wayne in 2000–2001. My research was also supported by a travel-to-collections grant from *Tulsa Studies in Women's Literature*. I would like to thank *Tulsa Studies* editor Holly A. Laird for her support as well as her reading of an early draft of the manuscript. Always gracious and helpful, managing editor Linda Frasier facilitated my plans for the visit and my application for the grant. At the Tulsa University McFarlin Library, home of the largest collection of Rebecca West's papers, Lori N. Curtis, head of Special Collections, and Gina L. B. Minks, Special Collections librarian, deserve many thanks for their assistance in using the collection, along with Lisa Inman and Milissa Burkart for their help. For her hospitality and sustenance in Tulsa I thank Sharry White, innkeeper at the Cottage Inn.

At Indiana University–Purdue University Fort Wayne, I owe a debt of thanks to those who provided years of document deliveries, particularly Cheryl Truesdell and Christine Smith, as well as Maureen Gaff, Jennifer Pidd, Mark Schobert, Lisa Wall, and Mark Watrous. English liaison librarian Sue Skekloff was a valuable resource at several crucial times over years of research.

The University of Tulsa McFarlin Library and the agency pfd, on behalf of the West estate, graciously grant permission for my quotations from Rebecca West's notes, letters, and papers in the Tulsa Special Collections. The photograph of Zelda and F. Scott Fitzgerald is provided courtesy of the Papers of F. Scott Fitzgerald, Manuscripts Division, Department of Rare Books and Special collections, Princeton University Library. Two portions of chapters were previously published, and permission to reprint is granted by *Tulsa Studies in Women's Literature* for "The Three Faces of June: Anaïs Nin's Appropriation of Feminine Writing" and by *Frontiers* for "Mentors, Protégés, and Lovers: Literary Liaisons and Mentorship Dialogues in Anaïs Nin's 1931–34 *Diary* and Dorothy Richardson's *Pilgrimage*."

Finally, I am grateful to Garrett and Steven for their teasing, and laughter, and humor.

LITERARY LIAISONS

"Books Not of the Imagination"

No character in this book is wholly fictitious
—Sackville-West, *The Edwardians*

Literary liaisons, relationships between individuals who are both writers and lovers, offer opportunities and conflicts surpassing those offered by mere literary friendships or ordinary love affairs.[1] Combining a mutual professional interest with the power struggle often present in romantic relationships, the interactions of the couple traverse the border between public and private. For the partners examined in this study, the common interest in literature produced alliances that resembled mentorships, sometimes approaching collaboration but never quite coauthorship, within which the women struggled to find artistic identity. The struggle for identity—as well as the frequent, resultant hierarchy in the professional and romantic dimensions of these liaisons—suggests that the underlying paradigm is that of the Lacanian subject/Other. A recurrent preoccupation in the autobiographical fiction of the women in these literary liaisons is the difficulty of acquiring the status of subject within the writing couple.

The texts selected for this study (primarily novels) were all produced by modernist women writers involved in relationships with other writers during the period from World War I through the 1930s, though many of the texts were published long after the affairs were over. Anaïs Nin had relationships of various kinds, both sexual and platonic, with many writers, including Antonin Artaud, Lawrence Durrell, Edmund Wilson, and Gore Vidal. Chapter 1 focuses on her 1931–1934 *Diary* (1966), on *House of Incest* (1936), and on the diary that was published posthumously as *Henry and June* (1986), all of which, as autobiographical fiction, focus on the period of her extramarital affair with Henry Miller—a relationship in which the partners were preoccupied with Nin's emerging identity as a woman writer. The subject of Chapter 2, Rebecca West's unfinished and posthumously published novel *Sunflower* (1986), fictionalizes the transition from her

ten-year (1913–1923) affair with H. G. Wells to an abortive relationship with Lord Beaverbrook. Chapter 3 provides an analysis of Zelda
Fitzgerald's *Save Me the Waltz* (1932), which reflects her literary and
marital conflicts with F. Scott Fitzgerald. Chapter 4 analyzes Radclyffe
Hall's contribution to autobiographical fiction, *The Forge* (1924), a
novel in which a heterosexual couple enact in coded fashion a conflict between vocation and love that is informed by Hall's long-term
relationship with her lesbian partner, Una Troubridge. Chapter 5 examines H.D.'s prolific fiction written in reaction to a series of homosexual and heterosexual literary liaisons. The focus is on *Bid Me to Live*
(1960), a novel set in World War I that fictionalizes several literary relationships, including her marriage to Richard Aldington and her infatuation with D. H. Lawrence.

Some of these writers' texts take the form of the roman à clef, a
novel that faintly disguises actual people, and are used for social criticism. West's novel, for example, in its parodic characterization of
Wells and his masculinist values, is deployed as retaliation against
male dominance. Hall codes her autobiographical relationship as
heterosexual and thereby critiques the consequences of patriarchy
for the woman artist.[2] Some of these writers depict their liaisons
(even those that were heterosexual) in plots that use the fictionalization to displace male hegemony with woman-to-woman bonds.
Fitzgerald disguises her writing conflict with her husband and displaces Scott's centrality by providing her protagonist with a female
mentor and assigning vocations other than writer to the couple's fictional counterparts. Nin's strategy for writing her conflict is to create
a bisexual love triangle within which she and her lover vie to create
the authoritative portrait of his wife.

Most of these writers are known to the educated public, but they
are generally renowned for works other than their autobiographical
fiction. West, for example, is best known for her journalism. The recent Balkan conflict has restored interest in her voluminous *Black
Lamb and Grey Falcon* (1941). H.D. is revered for her mythical modernist poetry. Nin, now that her 1970s cult status has abated, is often
known among general readers for her erotica. Her reputation has
been enhanced by the controversy surrounding the first NC-17-rated
film, *Henry and June*, based on her posthumously published diary.
Ironically, several of these writers are known primarily for their association with their more celebrated partners, who thwarted, from the
outset, the publication and reception of the autobiographical texts
they inspired. The powerful Lord Beaverbrook, for example, let it be
known that he would cause serious trouble if West tried to publish a
novel in which he was fictionalized. Aldington's ambivalent efforts
to help H.D. publish *Bid Me to Live* in Britain may actually have forestalled its publication. F. Scott Fitzgerald tried to stop Zelda from

publishing *Save Me the Waltz,* intervening with her publisher and the psychiatrists who controlled her literary production while she was a resident of Henry Phipps Psychiatric Clinic. Some of the texts produced as a result of the liaisons were commercially successful, Nin's *Diary,* for example. Some, such as H.D.'s *HERmione* and *Bid Me to Live,* have entered the canon of women's studies. Others remain noncanonical, such as Hall's *The Forge,* which is overshadowed by her more celebrated novel, *The Well of Loneliness,* the subject of a notorious censorship trial in 1928.

My focus on autobiographical fiction depicting literary liaisons foregrounds a polemical but as yet unexplored subgroup of the novel that vexes distinctions between fiction and autobiography. If the boundary is a site of contestation, then fictional autobiography—inhabiting the intersection of fiction and nonfiction and traversing the limits of the imagined and the real— self-consciously occupies the metaphorical territory that Gloria Anzaldúa has termed the "borderland." The lack of critical attention accorded these texts, despite the reputations of their writers and despite the distinctive subgroup of modernist writing they represent, inspires a primary objective of this study: to juxtapose noncanonical fictional autobiographies as a project of feminist and modernist recovery. In a recent collection of essays theorizing women's autobiography, editors Sidonie Smith and Julia Watson identify fictionalized autobiography as a neglected area of study and ask: "What does it mean for readers to blur the distinction, to read novelistically?" (38). I would recast their question to emphasize the writer's act of fictionalization: What does it mean when a writer blurs this boundary? The five women authors studied in this text eschew the fixed stasis implicit in autobiography (the writing of a lived life) for fictional depiction (the writing of a narrative that can, theoretically, change from version to version, as H.D. most aptly demonstrates, even when the protagonist appears to be the same). Thus, these modernist women sometimes move away from a unified, singular identity to explore a kind of destabilized, multiple, various subject.

This fiction often foregrounds the conflicts of heterosexual liaisons as a contested site of literary production, but lesbian relationships, or those that are to some degree homosocial, also play an important role in the texts as they provide an alternative to the heterosexual hegemony against which these women were writing. In much of this autobiographical fiction, the woman in a heterosexual relationship initiates her struggle for artistic identity as she rebelliously defines herself against her partner and his masculine aesthetic. In several of the texts, however, woman-to-woman relationships provide a sense of identity for the narrators, a discovery of self. It is important to note, as Bonnie Zimmerman explains, that "a woman's identity is not defined only by her relation to a male world and male literary tradition[,] . . . that powerful bonds between women are a crucial factor in women's lives, and that the sexual and emotional orientation of a woman profoundly affects her consciousness and thus her creativity" ("Never Been" 201). The "orientation" of the lesbian during the modernist period appears to have produced other kinds of fiction than liaison novels ("coming out" novels, for example) in order to deal with the issue of identity.

It is, in point of fact, difficult to find modernist examples of fictional autobiography in which lesbians are represented as partners in a writing couple, that is, where both are represented as writers.[3] Although I am reluctant to generalize in such terms, the modernist literary-liaison novel appears to comprise a subgroup with a manifest content that is gendered primarily heterosexual. By this I do not mean that these women were exclusively or consistently heterosexual; indeed, their biographies and my analyses suggest otherwise. However, the texts analyzed foreground heterosexuality because they were written as a reaction against a heterosexist and patriarchal construction of the literary and romantic relationship during a historical period when homosexual content in fiction was only just beginning to become explicit. At the same time, these writers present an illuminating array of alternatives in their fiction. Watson finds it useful to juxtapose texts by women of different sexual orientations: "Reading women's autobiographies of lesbian and heterosexual orientations, declared or not declared, against one another may help to frame a politics of reading that undoes their simple opposition" (141). Another major goal of this study, then, is to explore a continuum of sexual orientations for women within writing couples rather than isolate the lesbian from the heterosexual woman writer or vice versa.

One can read the story of West's relations with H. G. Wells and Lord Beaverbrook against the (only slightly obscured) lesbianism of Hall's *The Forge* and peel back the layers of H.D.'s autobiographical fictions, which challenge the categories of lesbian and heterosexual by positing variously oriented sexual-romantic relationships for the same autobiographical subject. One text depicting lesbian collaboration, H.D.'s *Tribute to Freud*, fleetingly poses an alternative to the subgroup of heterosexual liaison autobiography (see Chapter 5). The absence of plots depicting fictional lesbian writing couples might in part be explained by the social taboo on homosexual content (which would account for Hall's coded version), but it exists also because, during the modernist period when these novels were written, lesbians had not yet (and perhaps still have not) been constructed in our society as couples. Nin's *Henry and June* (1986) and H.D.'s *HERmione* (1981) come the closest to a lesbian writing couple; they receive some consideration in this study but are not foregrounded because the act of writing plays a fairly insignificant part in their narratives.

The primary texts, selected from British and American fiction written in the 1920s and 1930s, comprise a distinct subset of autobiography with special relevance to the expanding Anglo-American modernist canon. In 1988 Sandra Gilbert and Susan Gubar described the phenomenon of "scribbling sibling rivalry . . . between mutually admiring pairs" in which "each half of the pair recorded anxieties, or at least reservations, about the other" (*No Man's Land* 1:149). Despite the seeming coherence of this phenomenon, it has not yet been studied in any intensive, concentrated manner. The probable reasons for the emergence of such a permutation of autobiography in the 1920s and 1930s may be contextualized within the culture of the era, and within the modernist literary movement, specifically. These women were seduced not only by their lovers but also by the promise of freedom that resulted from the first-wave feminist movement. For West this promise first took the form of turn-of-the-century feminism for which she was a teenage activist; for Zelda Fitzgerald the promise was symbolized by the flamboyant, independent flapper; Hall cultivated the image of the mannish lesbian, publishing *The Well of Loneliness*, the novel that marked the coming-out of lesbian fiction; H.D. and Nin were drawn into expatriate circles in Europe, tantalized by the freedom and intellectual stimulation accorded the bohemian artist. Each woman found herself in one or more nonegalitarian, often extramarital, relationships—in which she ended up serving as Other for a male partner (Hall excepted), at the expense of the very subject status she had sought as a writer. The literary liaisons studied thus represent thwarted desire and the disappointment of a failed idealized relationship, in which a woman desired equality in both the personal and public spheres, as both lover and writer.

In its most idealized form, the dual personal/professional paradigm seems to pose an answer to the problem of heterosexual hegemony under patriarchy. In the Victorian era there was a precedent for the egalitarian personal/professional ideal in the Elizabeth Barrett–Robert Browning relationship. Barrett Browning added love and marriage to her achievement as a poet, in which capacity her reputation originally obscured that of her husband; she serves as a model in particular because she was first known and loved for her writing. Her poetry was the preliminary attraction for Robert Browning, who wrote in the letter that inaugurated their famous courtship: "I love your verses with all my heart, dear Miss Barrett."[4] In the early twentieth century the promise of this Victorian egalitarian ideal was intensified.

The idealization of the Victorian Barrett-Browning relationship recurs as a motif in the modernist literary liaisons. H.D. was attracted to Ezra Pound, according to Janice Robinson, because of "an idealistic notion of a poetic relationship modeled on the marriage of Robert and Elizabeth Browning" (42). Radclyffe Hall and Una Troubridge viewed the Barrett-Brownings as a model couple of the romantic literary order. Troubridge's biography of Hall describes how "John [Hall] evolved the idea that after the war, if and when we returned to Italy, we would try to obtain a lease of their apartment. She would say thoughtfully: 'I think I should like to work in the rooms where Robert and Ba were so happy together'" (177). On her deathbed Hall wanted to hear the poems of Robert Browning and Elizabeth Barrett Browning (Cline 53). After Hall's death Troubridge had the quotation "And if God Should Choose I Shall / But Love Thee Better After Death" from Elizabeth Barrett Browning's sonnet cut into the marble grave slab, with her own name below the inscription and Hall's name above (Cline 372).

In contrast to the idealized story of Elizabeth Barrett, many of these moderist women adapt the Pygmalion myth as a more realistic paradigm for their liaisons because, in most tellings, this story embodies a heterosexual and hierarchal artistic conflict within a couple. West and Zelda Fitzgerald, for example, found themselves dominated by partners (H. G. Wells and F. Scott Fitzgerald) who had already made significant names for themselves as writers. H.D. and Nin, on the other hand, were involved with men who were as much emerging writers as they (Pound, Aldington, and Miller). H.D. transforms the myth, however, in order to examine the lesbian partners' contested desire to be the mentor figure, Pygmalion, rather than the protégée, Galatea. Although Hall was the dominant artist in her relationship with Troubridge, she fictionalizes the relationship from the point of view of a woman subordinated in marriage to a male writer (the predominant perspective of the fiction studied). Since these texts were conceived or produced in the modern postsuffrage era, this inequality may be surprising. As Gilbert and Gubar characterize this era, "men and women in the twentieth century were more than ever before joined in literary enterprises. They were friends, peers, colleagues, coeditors—readers and revisers of each other's work" (*No Man's Land* 1:149). Although this new freedom made potential peers of female and male writers, the women actually found it most difficult to achieve power in the realm over which, ironically, they would seem to have had the most control: their intimate relationships. For these authors, the literary liaison is a site where a woman writer's identity is enacted, contested, and finally empowered or suppressed, in close conjunction with romantic hierarchy.

The emergence of the liaison novels, often experimental in form and subject, in the 1920s and 1930s suggests a link with the flowering of modernism. William Spengemann defines autobiography itself as specifically modernist in spirit; he sees experiments with autobiography as a part of the historical modernist movement, which has "a tendency to assume fictive forms in the modern era" (xiii). Sabine Vanacker also remarks on "a marked interest in the autobiographical position" within modernism (112). She reconsiders the place of gender in the connection between modernism and autobiography, noting that "modernist women wrote alternative autobiographies" and that much "autobiographical writing by women takes place against the back-

ground of an ongoing discussion with . . . fictive identity as pro-
pounded by a male voice" (117). "Making it new," the writers involved
in these liaisons envisioned themselves as partners in defiance of literary strictures and social mores. As such, the liaisons were sites of rebellion, where, for the woman, an alliance against the literary establishment often evolved, analogously, into a rebellion against her partner.
Thus the proliferation of literary-liaison fiction may be related to the
backlash against the first feminist movement, as outlined by Gilbert
and Gubar in *No Man's Land* (1:89).[5] This backlash is also noted by historian of sexuality Sheila Jeffreys, who documents a movement against
"independent women, spinsters and lesbians" in the 1920s. She points
out that the sexual liberation movement of that era was more geared
toward fostering male heterosexual pleasure (168 and elsewhere).[6] Lillian Faderman hypothesizes that stories about lesbians, such as D. H.
Lawrence's *The Fox*, were published in the 1920s with a moralistic,
condemnatory intent (351). Interpretations of this period as gendered
and reactive have recently come under criticism, however; it is clear
that this view is but one interpretation of women's position in relation
to modernism and the male literary establishment.[7]

This study explores the conflicts that create antagonism within the
literary liaison and the relation of these conflicts to artistic production. Some biographers have emphasized the romantic dimension of
the relationships I view as antagonistic. For instance, my assessment
of the Nin-Miller alliance, grounded in her fictionalizations, is less romantic and decidedly less positive about mutual influence than Noël
Riley Fitch's account, grounded in personal recollections of Nin's contemporaries ("Literate Passion"). Is the difference to be found in
source materials or in the perspective of the interpreter? The "sex war"
persists, however, and even predominates as an explicit subject of discussion in the literary-liaison autobiographical fiction, even the fiction authored by Hall.

Fictionalized autobiography allows a writer to work through a
highly conflicted relationship by creating or re-creating it, reimagining
intimate portions of the subject's life, often in fiction that makes the
relationship public through the roman à clef. To fictionalize and thus
publicize a relationship might be viewed as an act of dubious ethical
conduct—a kind of exposure, or exploitation, betrayal, or even theft.
Fiction created from shared autobiographical material complicates the
issue of literary rights. To whom do the rights to a mutually experienced relationship belong? The material that arises from a couple's relationship vexes notions of individual ownership, libel, and appropriation. To "appropriate" means "to take *exclusive* possession" (*Webster's
Ninth New Collegiate Dictionary;* my emphasis). Linda Hutcheon notes
that the Latin etymology of "appropriation" is "*proprium,* property—
that which belongs to one person" (107). Beaverbrook's purported

threat to West shows that he thought libel could be charged, even though the experience they shared was also hers, and he had no interest in putting it to paper himself. F. Scott Fitzgerald argued in his dispute with Zelda that he held exclusive rights to all shared autobiographical material, from which she was excluded by virtue of his established success as a writer. When autobiographical material is shared, however, can one individual's rights be isolated and privileged over the partner's? Legal charges of libel often hinge on truth, malice, and damage—all problematized when mutually owned autobiographical material is fictionalized by one partner.

Another definition of the verb "to appropriate" is "to set apart for or assign to a particular purpose or use" (Webster's). Literary appropriation in these texts often directs the material appropriated against the person from whom it was seized. When appropriating an autobiographical relationship for fiction, writers make significant and revealing aesthetic choices. Curiously, the writers in this study rarely idealize either the relationship or the self in their fictive treatments. West, for example, makes her fictionalized self a successful but seemingly obtuse actress instead of a writer; Hall's character is a pompous, dilettantish writer. My own choice of the word *appropriation* may seem to focus not only on the reactive but also on the adversarial—the nasty underside of a relationship dealing with the struggle for power instead of the romance and affection emanating from a love affair. This lexical choice is premeditated, however, since I foreground the act of productive antagonism whereby women writers in a patriarchal society try to seize agency through authorship for what is, by right, at least partly their own.

By writing her intimate life as it overlaps with the life of another, an author, a public self she knew in private, the woman in a writing couple transgresses the boundary between public and private spheres. Nancy K. Miller notes that the "decision to go public is particularly charged for the woman writer," pointing to the "reticence about naming names" (48). Contributing to this gendered argument, Domna Stanton finds that "conflicts between the private and the public, the personal and the professional" are characteristic of "autogynographical narrative" (13). In the transformation of personal autobiography into public fiction, an individual male partner is often charged with the collective crimes of patriarchy. Fictionalizing their personal struggles, the writers inscribe their rebellion against the culture in which they lived and wrote. The women writers in this study, finding equal partnership difficult to attain within their relationships, act through fictional autobiography to create an alternative textual version of the relationship, an appropriation from property jointly owned. They break with the conventions that Phyllis Rose attributes to conventional biography: instead of the "individual subject" ("Biography" 115), these women begin with the couple; instead of the chronology beginning at birth and proceeding to death, the temporal boundaries of the liaison provide a fictional chronology.

Fictionalized autobiography may thus be a kind of hypotext or *apophrades:* a text that relates to a previous model (the real-life relationship) in such a manner as to suggest, in retrospect, that the appropriating writer actually authors the prior text (the relationship itself).[8] In a type of re-vision, these autobiographers appropriate what was already their own but may not have been as they wished. To write the relationship is to seize control as a writer, a creator of stories. The writer of fictionalized autobiography not only controls the fiction (the writing process and the product) but also controls, as a lover, life-after-the-fact (the retrospective function of autobiography)—gaining a kind of control or subjectivity that was never achieved in life. Similar to the sequel or to the remake of a film, fictional autobiography is created in relation to a previous story and has the potential to obscure or distort the original, publicly as well as privately. In contrast to the sequel writer, however, the fictional autobiographer has no obligation to re-create the original or its emotional impact. The partner, who in the relationship may have played the role of subject, is now cast in the role of character, the protagonist's (and the author's) Other, fictionalized into this status through the writer's act of dominance and control. In the process of appropriation, the partner's role as speaking subject (someone who produces speech) is transformed into spoken subject (something to be perceived or consumed).

• • •

My approach to the five writers and their texts is generally more multifaceted than thesis-driven, so the remainder of this introduction is divided into four sections. The first section introduces the Lacanian paradigm of the mirror stage, which, I argue as my primary thesis, represents the relations between self and Other and underpins the fictional autobiographies to be studied here. Drawing comparisons between the original mirror-stage experiences and the adult reenactments occurring in the literary-liaison texts, I delineate a common pattern in the representations. I endeavor to keep the model fluid enough, however, to foreground the differences and idiosyncracies of each account (including the possible creation of an alternative female world, often via a feminine language or *écriture féminine*).

The second section examines how fictionalized autobiography is "different" for female subjects than for male subjects. In arguing that women's autobiographies differ from men's, feminist critics (myself included) risk charges of essentialism. Yet the designation "woman autobiographer" is necessary to considerations of gender and genre. Delineation of any group requires a degree of nominal essentialism, which Diana Fuss (*pace* Locke) terms "a linguistic convenience, a classificatory fiction we need to categorize and to label" ("Reading" 99), and which is also useful to discuss women as a group in a certain time and place. This is not the same as the reductive, fixed essentialism that has vexed those feminists who insist on a binary opposition between essentialism and constructionism, thus pitting a biological gender difference against one created by and within society.[9]

The third section further considers autobiographical fiction as a genre. I conceptualize fictionalized autobiography as a crossing of the border between fiction and autobiography. Because this border creates a fluctuating intersection, I find it more productive to explore than to define the characteristics of fictional autobiography. These texts have enough in common that it is useful to group and juxtapose them, but they are too diverse and variously experimental for strict genre classification, and this work is not conceived as a taxonomical study.

The fourth and final section comprises my review of previous research. Many prior studies of writing couples have been biographical in focus, privileging biography over fiction and often relegating the women to secondary status as writers. My comparison of the present literary, feminist study with previous research is thus often focused on the selection, approach, and treatment of other studies.

THE ADULT REENACTMENT OF THE LACANIAN
MIRROR STAGE AND THE WOMAN SUBJECT AS ARTIST

Writers in a literary liaison are in love with each other and in love with language. Either refusing or unable to disengage the personal from the professional, the partners often seem attracted to each other first because of the language the other writes. Lacanian theorist Juliet Flower MacCannell explains that "it is by means of language that desire for the other is transformed into love of the other" (46). For the most part the focus of this study is on the postromantic stage of the relationship, a time when the previous merging of personal and professional interests is interrogated and reevaluated. This postromantic focus helps explain why these accounts are pessimistic about the possibility of egalitarian relationships; they articulate disappointment following (in most cases) the failure of the relationship. The literary liaisons studied here take the form of adult reenactments of the Lacanian mirror stage, an early formative experience that in the fictionalized versions is centered around entrance into the world of professional written language and acquisition of an artist identity.[10] The reenactments depicted share with the infant mirror-stage experience an emphasis on individual identity, a jubilant but false anticipation of unity, an ensuing experience of distancing and separation, and a feeling of loss.

In the original mirror-stage experience, an infant metaphorically confronts the reflected self in a mirror and first conceives of the self as separate from the mother/world. Self-recognition is effected through reflection: it "is the mirror image in which the subject initially 'finds' its identity" (Silverman, *Semiotics* 176). In the adult reenactment, the lover functions as the mirror, providing the reflection of identity. Just as the mirror stage marks the child's "acquisition of an identity . . . the genesis of a sense of self or personal unity" (Grosz, *Lacan* 32), through the reenactment of this process within the literary liaison, the adult woman writer seeks an independent artistic identity. It is therefore significant that the relationships that serve as the focus of this fiction were generally youthful, marking the beginning of the woman's identification of herself as a writer. The woman subject confronts an Other whom she initially needs for her identity as a writer—but who ultimately thwarts such an identity by his (sometimes her) own wish for centrality and for control of the partner's production. The significance of the original mirror stage for the adult woman is not merely as a passage (a temporal or temporary experience) but as an enduring location and permanent split within the psyche—thus Lacan's pun on the French *stade* as both a temporal experience, a "stage" or phase, and a place, a "stadium" (*Écrits* 5).

The writer's search for her own identity in the lover/Other is somewhat narcissistic: "The lover is a narcissist with an *object*" (Kristeva, "Freud and Love" 250). Kaja Silverman emphasizes that "since others will be loved only if they are believed to be capable of completing the subject, desire must be understood as fundamentally narcissistic" (*Semiotics* 177). Although the term *narcissism* might seem pejorative, the process described (that of finding the self in the other) is a contradictory impulse that represents a desire both for relation and for independence. The post-mirror-stage loss creates a desire for wholeness—the loss of the feeling of oneness with mother and world creates a desire for unity—but the "One that is sought in love is really one's own unity" (Lee 181). In the adult reenactment, the "jubilant activity" that Lacan describes as the infant's deceptive perception of self-as-other (*Écrits* 1) is reiterated through an enthusiastic, albeit narcissistic, commitment to the loved one. The Other provides, nevertheless, only an illusion of unity and truth:

> Subjects in language persist in their belief that somewhere there is a point of certainty, of knowledge and of truth. When the subject addresses its demand outside itself to another, this other becomes the fantasied place of just such a knowledge or certainty. Lacan calls this the Other—the site of language to which the speaking subject necessarily refers. The Other appears to hold the "truth" of the subject and the power to make good its loss. But this is the ultimate fantasy. (Rose, "Introduction II" 32)

To write the relationship, therefore, is to presume, seek, and inscribe a wholeness that cannot be found in the subject, much less in the Other.

The experience of being part of a couple resembles the prior unity of the mother-child dyad, not only because the lover replaces the mother in the adult relationship but also because both the initial mirror stage and the reenactment of the fictionalized liaisons ultimately entail the dissolution of a relationship. The centrality of the mother in this fiction has, for the daughter, its origin in the woman-woman bond that preceded the mirror stage. Julia Kristeva's work, especially her concepts of the *chora* and the presymbolic mother, are suggestive for the mother-daughter relations that play such an important part in these autobiographical fictions. Kristeva's *chora* designates the premirror state, a place of "nonexpressive totality" that "precedes evidence, verisimilitude, spatiality, and temporality" (*Revolution* 25, 26). The *chora* "underlies figuration, and thus specularization, and is analogous only to vocal or kinetic rhythm" (26).

In several of the fictions examined herein, a woman protagonist, frustrated with her experiences in patriarchy, figuratively takes her search for a writer's identity back to the *chora.* This temporary retreat resembles the hypothetical or actual separation from men/patriarchy that feminists sometimes propose. As a therapeutic interval, for example, Luce Irigaray describes such a retreat as a tactic whereby women "keep themselves apart from men long enough to learn to define their desire . . . to forge for themselves a social status that compels recognition" ("This Sex" 33). The search for the powerful mother is motivated by a retrospective conceptualization, Kristeva explains, revealing "a belief, ultimately maintained, that the mother is phallic, that the ego—never precisely identified—will never separate from her, and that no symbol is strong enough to sever this dependence" (*Revolution* 65). The desire for this reunification reflects the wish for the original dyadic unity. Marcia Ian elucidates: "The so-called phallic mother . . . symbolizes . . . the specific fantasy of corporeal completeness (the symbolic reunion with mother), which Freud claimed lurked deep in every psyche as an innate idea" (xi). At the same time, the search for this ambiguously gendered fantasy figure defies the gendered limitations of reality (to be *either* man *or* woman) and embodies, in the postulation of a powerful role model, the contradictory desire for post-mirror-stage relation and autonomy.[11]

The post-mirror-stage daughter wishes to regain connection with her mother; the woman artist in a similar way desires the close intimacy, the dyadic connection, of the presymbolic (simultaneously both pre- and nonverbal) and also the expression of the symbolic (verbal), a paradoxical endeavor. The *chora* is a source of "poetic language" (the title of Kristeva's 1974 study), a site that exposes contradictory impulses. The mother the writer/artist seeks there as an alternative mentor and role model is *nonverbal*, yet the artist desires to *articulate* the emotions elicited by this realm. In the fictionalized accounts, therefore, the protagonists often experiment with alternative forms of "language" (such as dance, hieroglyphics, or synesthesia) that anticipate the contemporary French feminists' designation of an *écriture féminine*, a sensual, gendered language. In the texts by Nin, Fitzgerald, and H.D., the daughter tries to serve as mediator and articulator for this paradoxical, nonverbal language and for the choric drives.

The proposition of an *écriture féminine* or a *parler femme* is a significant departure from and revision of Lacan. The French feminists playfully advocate a feminine language that represents and celebrates the female body, particularly its multitudinous sexual potential and its capacity for *jouissance* (according to Irigaray the female body is the "sex that is not one" both because of women's many erogenous zones and because of women's marginalization as the unseen sex). Such writing is not relegated exclusively to women writers and has been attributed to male writers including Joyce, Artaud, and Genet. Hélène Cixous, usually credited with the manifesto for this writing (in "Laugh of the Medusa"), points out that writing itself may be gendered female, whatever the sex of the writer: "the fact that a piece of writing is signed with a man's name does not in itself exclude femininity" ("Medusa" 52). The texual features associated with an *écriture féminine* are nontraditional and nonlinear. Ann Rosalind Jones draws from Luce Irigaray's concept of "feminine subjectivity" to define *écriture féminine* as characterized by "double or multiple voices, broken syntax, repetitive or cumulative rather than linear structure, open ending" (88), although she does not fully endorse the notion of such a language. Other textual features are suggested by Julia Penelope Stanley and Susan J. Wolfe (Robbins) as deriving from a "female consciousness," which takes the form of "an unrelenting language of process and change" ("Feminist Aesthetic" 66) and a "syntactic structure [that] must accommodate itself to the shifting perspective of the writer's observing mind" (67).[12]

Critics have found the concept of *écriture féminine* particularly useful to describe the features of modernist and experimental texts. Although this linguistic inscription of the female body has been rejected by many feminists as essentialist, other feminists point out that *écriture féminine* is merely a descriptive device to name a hypothetical, fictitious sex, a technique that resists the values of patriarchy. Such a naming, then, is constructed rather than biological or innate. The attribution of an *écriture féminine* to fiction written during the 1920s and 1930s anticipates the contemporary French feminists and presents an alternative to the language of patriarchy, the "symbolic," the conventional language of the status quo. Applying the name *écriture féminine* to fiction written during this time is to describe a self-conscious effort to write beyond the social reality of the early postsuffrage era.

In the autobiographical fictions examined in this study, the woman comes to a realization that the unity of the couple is illusory, which foreshadows a realization that the unity of the self is also illusory, and that the ideals of unity and equality often resolve themselves into hierarchy instead. Irigaray's poetic allegory of the mirror stage explores the implications of the mother-daughter bond and the origin of the subject/Other relationship: "And the one doesn't stir without the other. But we do not move together. When the one of us comes into the world, the other goes underground. When the one carries life, the other dies" ("And the One" 67). The subject/Other relationship is itself associated with loss and with longing to regain what has been lost. Through the reenactment of this experience of loss, the woman artist seeks "a promise or anticipation of (self)mastery and control" in relation to the identity of the other (Grosz, *Lacan* 32). Such adult reenactment, moreover, is complicated by gender difference. The nurturing dyadic relationship is a lost ideal, and when the Other being sought is a patriarchal male, some degree of hierarchy is inevitable. The adult woman's reenactment of the Lacanian mirror stage thus also prefigures the (proto)feminist realization that she is Other in patriarchy, and that the positions of male and female in such a society are hierarchized.

The distancing in the latter part of the mirror stage (the distancing from one's mother that is essential to see one's own individual image) resembles the distancing represented in most of these textual accounts—and also the double distancing that occurs in the fictionalizing of autobiography (life written retrospectively by one member of a couple). This separation is necessary for an author to attain subject status. The price of the distanced, distinct self, however, is all too often the subordination of the Other, male or female. The liaison fiction examined is rebellious writing that situates the self in relation to an Other, who in real life occupied the place of the subject. These women writers move the partner (the former subject) to a position of fictional subordination to the self (the current writer-subject, previously the Other). Yet, the texts generated by these liaisons present only qualified optimism concerning the possibility of freeing the self from the obsessive need for an Other (and for the unity represented by the relationship). Equality between partners, when it is achieved, is usually successive rather than simultaneous; it is unstable, transitory, and difficult to sustain. Even when the authors or the protagonists are themselves unable to move beyond the traumatic mentorship experience, however, the fictionalized autobiographies often suggest strategies for moving beyond a unitary self, through role-playing, cross-identification, multiple variations on an autobiographical story, and so forth—strategies that acknowledge the split subject of the post–mirror stage. The fragmented self posited by Lacan and his successors is often viewed in a negative light because it embodies loss; yet this precarious location of the subject (the "I") is a place of contradiction that portends great possibilities, multiplicity, and potentiality.[13]

Lacan's theories are useful for analysis of writing couples because of his emphasis on subjectivity, the speaking subject, and the connections between language and identity. The literary liaison is a fruitful site that represents the intersection of language (essential for the writer) and the acquisition of subjectivity within a relationship. Emile Benveniste points out that language facilitates subjectivity because it "puts forth 'empty' forms which each speaker, in the exercise of discourse, appropriates to himself and which he relates to his 'person,' at the same time defining himself as *I* and a partner as *you*" (227). No subject can be a subject for itself, however. The Other is essential to the subject's identity as speaker: one is active, through speaking; the other is constructed, by spoken discourse. Language is associated inherently with the mirror stage because, as Julian Henriques explains, "it is the entry into language which is the precondition for becoming conscious or aware of oneself as a distinct entity within the terms set by pre-existing social relations and cultural laws" (213). Representation, or language, is thus also a means of coping with and compensating for the post-mirror-stage loss of wholeness. The conflict over identity and language is a recurrent scene in these fictions because linguistic representation is essential to subject status: "As words displace the original object, we see the first step in the process of repression which forms the unconscious; entry into language inaugurates the production of subjectivity" (Henriques et al. 215). In the liaison fictions examined, linguistic expression is sometimes displaced and represented by an artistic context other than writing, as in the novels by West and Zelda Fitzgerald. For the protagonists in the fiction of Nin, Hall, and H.D., the process of recasting autobiographical experiences takes the more direct form of the women's dialogues with lovers and mentors about aesthetics and about their roles as writers. A frequent theme in these Pygmalionesque conversations is the woman's rebellion against her partner's conception of art and the artist, or against the limitations placed by the lover on her ability to create.

This overview of the way the literary liaisons reenact the Lacanian mirror stage necessarily glosses over a multitude of variations and permutations. Although there are striking parallels in the quests undertaken and the frustrations experienced by the women writers examined, my approach is cumulative and prismatic: each experience adds another perspective to the common desire for subject status within a relationship. Lacanian-inflected constructs are most visible in the chapters on Zelda Fitzgerald and H.D. In contrast, the chapters on Nin and West are more pervasively informed by Kristeva and, to some extent, Freud. Hall's use of a coded (ostensibly heterosexual) lesbian couple somewhat confounds application of gendered psychoanalytic theory. My approach to her work is more eclectic than for the others. The juxtaposition of these diverse texts brings into relief distinctive issues (such as lesbianism and collaboration) and various solutions to inequality (such as feminine language, binary portraits, and so on) that are represented in their fiction.

THE WOMAN SUBJECT AND FICTIONALIZED LITERARY LIAISON AUTOBIOGRAPHY

These fictional autobiographies depict formative, transitional relationships. They focus on the self within a relationship; they rebel against the previous subordination of the self; they often propose multitudinous selves; but what autobiographical self do they ultimately write? Recent theorists have seen the autobiographical self as "necessarily a fictive structure" (Eakin 3), which challenges both the notion of a fixed self and the possibility of objectively writing it. West goes further, calling *biographies* "books not of the imagination." Her definition ambiguously evokes imagination after it has already been prefaced with a negation, suggesting biographies may be fiction at the same time she denies this possibility. West elaborates, "Just how difficult it is to write biography can be reckoned by anybody who sits down and considers just how many people know the real truth about his or her love affairs" ("Skepticism" 115). West's ambivalent formulation and her stipulation about "the real truth" reveal her skepticism about biography, interrogating the truth of the genre either as fiction or as nonfiction, a skepticism that may have contributed to her writing of fictionalized autobiography. The aesthetic choices made in fictionalizing do not necessarily reveal Truth. The literary liason writers' self-reflexivity shows that they are simply writing a truth, an alternative to the "real" story, itself disputed and ultimately unseizable. Avrom Fleishman links autobiographical skepticism to Georges Gusdorf and the "French tradition from Montaigne," which reveals "an underlying linkage between subjective truth and epistemological doubt" (8). Fictional autobiographers construct the subject and create an illusory wholeness that neither they nor their subjects could achieve in real life. Lacan's metaphoric, punning descriptions of the formation of subjectivity similarly presume a constructed—a social and linguistic—self. "The 'I', then, is not a given at birth but rather is constructed, assumed, taken on during the subject's problematic entry into the Symbolic" (Fuss, "Reading" 106).

Feminist critics' efforts to define the "difference" of women's autobiography are informed both by notions of a constructed self and by skepticism concerning the truth of biographers and autobiographers. Leigh Gilmore coins a useful new term, "autobiographics," to describe women's autobiographical techniques, many of which are evident in the fictional autobiographies discussed herein: "an emphasis on writ-

ing itself as constitutive of autobiographical identity, discursive contradictions in the representation of identity (rather than unity), the
name as a potential site of experimentation rather than contractual
sign of identity, and the effects of gendered connection of word and
body" (42). In her fictions H.D. links writing to identity through recurrent phrases such as "[s]he herself was the writing" or "the story
must write me," emphasizing the acquisition of a writer's identity
through the process of writing. Nin presents "discursive contradictions" as she emphasizes the multiplicity of her selves. She refuses to
distinguish between her true autobiographical story and the fictional
lives she creates, earning herself the epithet of "liar." (And the charge
by recent biographers and critics that Nin lied because she fictionalized her diary has seriously damaged her posthumous reputation.)
Hall also exploits such contradictions, as she fictionalizes her story of
lesbian love through a heterosexual paradigm, disrupting correspondences between the "real" autobiographical story and the fictional account. The professional names these writers chose to assume—West,
that of a character in Ibsen's play *Rosmersholm;* Hall, a masculine version of her inherited name; H.D., a name bestowed on her writer self
by Ezra Pound; and Nin, her maiden name—are sites of experimentation with identity, crossing the borders of patriarchal conventions to
create alternatives to biographical reality.[14]

The alternate stories told by fictionalized autobiographies present
gendered adaptations of the Künstlerroman (the novel about a quest
for artistic identity), telling emblematic tales of the woman writer's relationship with patriarchy. Recently, feminist critics have expressed
concern about the construction of patriarchy as a "universalizing concept" (Butler 35), and Lacan's paradigm of the mirror stage has been
similarly disparaged as phallocentric, universalizing, and ahistorical.
Feminists who adapt Lacan, however, recognize that his theories,
though produced by and within a patriarchal social order, help us understand the internalized mechanism of this very order. Grosz notes
that Lacan "proposes a theory of the socio-linguistic genesis of subjectivity which enables male and female subjects to be seen as social and
historical effects, rather than as pre-ordained biological givens" (*Lacan*
148). Silverman describes the mirror stage itself as "an event which is
in some way culturally orchestrated" (*Semiotics* 161). MacCannell explains that, for Lacan, "human experience is structured by the culture
into which it is born" (79). Warnings about essentialism and universalizing are themselves historically generated and must be contextualized in a specific time and place. Clearly patriarchy is not identical in
all cultures and eras, nor in all manifestations of a particular culture.
Perhaps we should think about "patriarchies" in the plural, just as we
define various "feminisms." Although some think we may now be en-
tering a new (post)feminist era, the modernists in this study wrote

their autobiographical fiction in the days of early postsuffrage feminism. Coming to view the male lover who hindered her writing as an agent and a representative of patriarchy was a logical first step for a woman writer of this period. And a woman who characterizes her husband metaphorically as the phallus, a "bulbous vegetable . . . a turnip" in her fiction (H.D., "Hipparchia" 14), most certainly reveals a universalizing impulse, in her choice of imagery at any rate. At the same time, H.D. and West demonstrate that there are different representations and degrees of patriarchy as they place their protagonists in relations with multiple, contrasting, male mentor-lovers in order to foreground variations (and exceptions).

The women's struggles depicted in this book not only mirror the public conflicts of women writers in the 1920s and 1930s, they also reveal how difficult and devastating such struggles are when they occur in the emotionally charged personal and private arena. Although they might be judged not sufficiently feminist by contemporary standards, these women are forerunners of contemporary feminists in their efforts to place themselves imaginatively not only against but also beyond patriarchal restrictions.[15] Lacan's paradigm of the mirror stage, focusing as it does on identity achieved as a result of separation from a loved one and ambivalent, conflicted desires for unity and autonomy, seems particularly relevant to these women's difficult post-suffrage-era transition encompassing new expectations, and to their strenuous efforts to achieve equality and subject status in a literary establishment still dominated by patriarchy.

The woman who fictionalizes a liaison writes in a different autobiographical tradition from that devoted to the cogito, the self-sufficient ego. Through the woman writer's fictionalized, emblematic struggle with patriarchy, these texts provide an alternative to the autonomous autobiographical project defined in traditional, "masculine" terms. Defining an alternative to the public, societal context for the self, Susan Stanford Friedman emphasizes the personal, relational aspect of women's autobiography, in opposition to the conventional, autobiographical emphasis on an individual: "The very sense of *identification, interdependence,* and *community* that Gusdorf dismisses from autobiographical selves are key elements in the development of a woman's identity, according to theorists like Rowbotham and Chodorow. Their models of women's selfhood highlight the unconscious masculine bias in Gusdorf's and other individualist paradigms" ("Autobiographical Selves" 38). Gabriele Griffin asks why critical studies of autobiography, even by feminists, focus on the "single writing woman" rather than the "relational self" (52). Griffin posits, as one explanation, the conventional presupposition that "Autobiography is supposed to be the story of the narrating self. Autobiography is not *alter*biography or the story of the relationship between one self and another" (52). The liaison fiction examined here, in contrast, creates just such "*alter*biographies," rewriting experience via the interaction of a created persona or personae with a fictive Other. For Nin, West, Fitzgerald, Hall, and H.D., to describe oneself relationally is an inevitable first step in self-creation. These literary liaisons are microcosms of women's struggles in patriarchal society, in which these writers disclose and reject their internalized subordination by the Other.

The liaison fiction thus revises a lived narrative in order to reject prior subordination. Phyllis Rose points out that conventional biography reifies hegemony; it is "a tool by which the dominant society reinforces its values" ("Biography" 114). Mary Mason characterizes women's autobiography by its very emphasis on otherness or alterity: "One element, however, that seems more or less constant in women's life writing—and not in men's—is the sort of evolution and delineation of an identity by way of alterity" (41). Many of the women writers examined here (Nin most notably) explore their alterity through experiments with a writing they perceive as "feminine."[16] In writing fictionalized autobiography, these five modernists disrupt the usual relation between the privileged (male) subject and the Other (woman). By presenting the self within an autobiographical relationship, the current writer-subject and the prior lover-subject contest each other for a fluctuating primacy; the usual hierarchy and hegemony of biography are destabilized while the equation of narrator and single subject in the "autobiographical pact" is violated through fictionalization.

The fictionalized autobiographies are in many ways works of rectification as well as retribution for marginalization, and one important way to rectify the lived relationship and recast the subordination of the self is through parody. For Nin and West in particular the interactions (re)produced in the fictional autobiographies reveal a productive antagonism and an aesthetic opposition; the women's resistance and rebellion surface in the sexual language of their fiction and their sometimes parodic depiction of their lovers-mentors and/or their lovers' texts. Parody is a form that is "transformative," that creates a "differentiation" from the original or "model" (Hutcheon 38). Thus, parody may facilitate or represent a writing beyond patriarchy. Although theorists of parody (Hutcheon most notably) foreground textual parodies of literary and artistic texts and these liaison fictions do indeed contain some parodies of the lovers' texts, most of their parody works to (con)textualize the lover and the relationship—to make a fiction out of an autobiographical subject, to transform the original into text. This parodic transformation may function as textual retribution, but the results are not always angry or destructive. As Hutcheon points out, parody can take many forms and convey various attitudes: "this [parodic] irony can be playful as well as belittling; it can be critically constructive as well as destructive. The pleasure of parody's irony comes not from humor in particular but from the degree of engagement of the reader in the intertextual 'bouncing' (to use E. M. Forster's famous term) between complicity and distance" (Hutcheon 32).

The liaison texts, though various in tone, often explore the woman's own complicity with previous marginalization. Her anger, though directed primarily at the partner, is also directed at herself and at society, recognizing that she was duped by an illusory romantic ideal. The intertextual relationship is (retrospectively) analytical, a kind of coming-to-terms with or working through loss and disappointment. And the very attention bestowed upon the original, as Hutcheon notes of textual appropriation, "must implicitly place a certain value upon the original" (107). It might seem that parodic fictionalizations will always stand in a subordinate position to the originals, thus replicating the situation that provoked the parody. Yet parody may also transcend the original, and these writers eschew subordination by creating an asymmetrical parody of the "original" lover rather than of his work.

AUTOBIOGRAPHICAL FICTION AS GENRE

Most novels are to some degree autobiographical; their authors' claims range from Henry Miller's seemingly guileless insistence that his protagonist (named Henry Miller) is himself to Flaubert's elusive cross-gendered claim that Madame Bovary "c'est moi." A central difficulty in studying fictionalized autobiography is that it represents a subset at the intersection of two of the broadest, most all-encompassing genres—autobiography and the novel—each with its own challenges for definition. If the novel and autobiography are blurred genres in and of themselves, their intersection produces an even less distinct category: "Autobiography . . . merges with the novel by a series of insensible gradations" (Frye 307). Despite this amorphous merging of genres, and in contrast to Northrop Frye, Philippe Lejeune insists on distinguishing between autobiography and the novel. He defines autobiography as a *"[r]etrospective prose narrative written by a real person concerning his own existence, where the focus is his individual life, in particular the story of his personality"* (4).[17] Unusual among critics of autobiography, Lejeune makes provision for autobiographical novels as

> all fictional texts in which the reader has reason to suspect, from the resemblances that he thinks he sees, that there is identity of author and *protagonist,* whereas the author has chosen to deny this identity, or at least not to affirm it. So defined, the autobiographical novel includes personal narratives (identity of narrator and protagonist) as well as "impersonal" narratives (protagonists designated in the third person); it is defined at the level of its contents. Unlike autobiography, it involves *de-*

grees. The "resemblance" assumed by the reader can be anything from a fuzzy "family likeness" between the protagonist and the author, to the quasi-transparency that makes us say that he is the "spitting image." (13)

Lejeune distinguishes the autobiographical novel from the parent group of autobiography because "it involves *degrees*" of resemblance: "Autobiography does not include degrees: it is all or nothing" (13). This distinction disavows, however, the creative, artistic, and fictive elements that comprise all narratives, historical as well as biographical. Yet Lejeune's point about degrees of resemblance is nevertheless useful. Obscuring the distinction between "personal" and "impersonal" narratives, liaison fiction ranges from the implied "transparency" in Nin's *Diary* to the cryptic "family likeness" of H.D.'s "Hipparchia," in which the autobiographical subjects are displaced into a quasi-historic narrative about ancient Rome.

Furthermore, Lejeune's "autobiographical pact" problematically distinguishes between kinds of intent: "What distinguishes autobiography from the novel is not an unattainable historical exactitude, but only the sincere *project* of recapturing and understanding one's own life. It is the existence of such a project that matters, and not an ultimately impossible sincerity" (Lejeune quoted in Fleishman 17).[18] Such an intent clearly does underpin the liaison fiction, although the writer's actual honesty and motivation in fictionalizing the lover may be suspect. The ultimate sincerity of an autobiographical project is indeed impossible to measure; it is not "reliably ascertainable" (Fleishman 18). Nin, for example, has been widely attacked for her dishonesty in using her diary to present a carefully constructed self. Yet can a woman who devoted her life obsessively to the diary, as a therapeutic project and for self-understanding, really be charged with insincerity because she failed to dissect herself as brutally as her most critical biographer, Deirdre Bair? Suzette Henke explains that Nin spent "most of her adult life as both fiction writer and autobiographer, articulating various versions of personal trauma in novels, diaries, and short stories that served as elaborate exercises in 'scriptotherapy'—the practice of writing out and writing through traumatic experiences in the mode of therapeutic reenactment" ("Life-Writing" 84). Indeed, liaison autobiography may, in its fundamental difference from both biography and single-subject autobiography, interrogate the very possibility of sincerity, attempting as it does to tell the stories of two individuals within a couple from the point of view of one of the partners.

A relationship belongs to both partners, but the act of taking possession is inherently asymmetrical: the appropriating author writes fictionalized autobiography in depicting herself or himself, and fictionalized biography in depicting the partner. There is asymmetry involved also in the roles played by biographer and autobiographer. Conventionally, the biographer is granted more authority than the autobiographer because a distanced second party is presumed to achieve greater objectivity than the participant; the writer's depiction of the partner would thus have greater credibility than the autobiographical treatment of the writer-subject. In literary-liaison autobiographies, however, the writer nevertheless plays both roles simultaneously: I use the term *auto/biography* to signal this asymmetry.[19]

There is also asymmetry in the distinctive generic blend, the combination of fiction and the (purported) nonfiction of auto/biography. Generally, when autobiographical material is presented as fiction, no one expects fidelity to reality. The responsibility of fidelity to truth is assumed in biography, and, because the liaison novels also contain the fictionalized biographies of the authors' partners, their possible objections always hover behind the texts. The asymmetry inherent in fictionalizing a liaison entails an appropriation of the lover through fiction that is a more polemical act than writing one's own life. Such asymmetries constitute a defining feature of this subset of modernist autobiography, producing the reactive dimension of the texts and, I propose, excluding most collaboration, even for those writers who collaborated with other writers or in other endeavors. For example, as an editor, H.D. collaborated extensively with her lesbian partner, Bryher (Annie Winifred Ellerman), and with Amy Lowell, yet H.D. asked Lowell to act in her place as editor in revising Aldington's work, because "she could not speak freely *as a poet* to her husband" (Marek 108; my emphasis).[20] Fictional auto/biography cannot comprise a distinct genre in itself but, rather, forms a subgroup at the intersection of two particularly amorphous genres, autobiography and novel, that exaggerates and amplifies novelists' usual propensity to draw upon their own experience. As Fleishman puts it, "there where living was, let writing be" (33).[21]

My approach is a blend of feminist and Lacanian-inflected psychoanalytic theory, close textual reading, and interpretive biography; it is not intended as biography, yet it deploys biographical material with the objective of analyzing literary texts so highly auto/biographical that biography cannot be ignored. The "New Critics," by prohibiting any evidence external to the literary text, created a schism between biography and literary criticism that has yet to be thoroughly bridged, although cultural studies has provided a justification and some models for this reconnection. Excellent, often multiple, biographies and biographical treatments have been published for all of the writers treated in this study and for most of their partners. There are also editions of published correspondence, and some interesting but idiosyncratic personal recollection biographies and autobiographies. I am heavily indebted to the biographers, particularly in the introductory biographical sections of each chapter. Previous studies of the liaison texts have chosen to view them primarily as either biography or auto-biography, rather than as fiction, and their generic blurriness may evoke this propensity.

PREVIOUS STUDIES OF WRITING COUPLES, COLLABORATION, AND MENTORSHIP

In this study I focus on writing couples and auto/biographical fiction; I touch on collaboration, coauthorship, and mentorship; and I include five writers and their many partners. These emphases intersect with many previous studies, yet this study resembles none of them closely. Therefore, my review of prior research responds to the approach and selection of authors more than to the studies' often only tangentially related arguments.

Four books published in the 1980s and 1990s emphasize the relational context in which creativity is cultivated: they pave the way for couples autobiography, and for studies devoted to collaborative writing and coauthorship. The first is a significant inaugural study, *Mothering the Mind: Twelve Studies of Writers and Their Silent Partners*, an essay collection edited by Ruth Perry and Martine Watson Brownley, which points to the contribution of writers' "silent" partners. The introduction establishes the importance of a personal connection that nourishes creativity, referring to D. W. Winnicott's emphasis on the necessary "presence of another (who reflects the self to one)," the other who is essential to "the capacity to be alone" (Perry and Brownley 7). Several of the fifteen relationships described, drawn from the English Enlightenment through the twentieth century, are those of writing couples (or partnerships where both individuals are writers), but the collection's main focus is on the asymmetrical function of "(m)othering" the primary artist by a subordinate, nurturing partner—sometimes literally a mother. Jack Stillinger, in *Multiple Authorship and the Myth of the Solitary Genius,* also explores the effect of facilitators: he challenges the idea that writers work autonomously. Primarily interested in male partnerships from the Romantic period through the present, Stillinger does not limit himself to couples but, rather, theorizes a broad concept of authorship; his concept of "multiple authorship" includes editors' contributions to texts. In an appendix, for example, he lists "instances of unacknowledged multiple authorship," including H.D.'s contribution to Bryher's *Two Lives,* Pound's editing of H.D.'s poems, and F. Scott Fitzgerald's "use" of Zelda's diaries and letters.

Significant Others: Creativity and Intimate Partnership, edited by Whitney Chadwick and Isabelle de Courtivron, like Stillinger's book contests the notion that art is created only by individuals. A collection of essays for a general rather than a scholarly audience, the work examines couples who were simultaneously lovers and professional colleagues. The couples are of many nationalities, from the late nineteenth through the twentieth century. The study includes essays on artists as well as writers and explores relationships that were productive though not always egalitarian: "most of the artists and writers concerned have not escaped social stereotypes about masculinity and femininity and their assumed roles within partnership," although "many have negotiated new relationships to those stereotypes" (8). Primarily biographical, this collection focuses on the "realities of exchange and influence" (11), emphasizing reciprocity between the partners rather than an asymmetrical facilitation of one partner's work by the other's. An essay by Noël Riley Fitch examines "The Literate Passion" of the Nin-Miller alliance.

Literary scholars have been slow to acknowledge the pervasiveness of collaboration, but this practice has been the focus of research in composition and professional writing for more than two decades.[22] *Singular Texts/Plural Authors: Perspectives on Collaborative Writing* by Andrea Lunsford and Lisa Ede is one of the best-known studies of collaboration. Generating their data through surveys circulated in the workplace, the authors are concerned with collaboration in the office and classroom rather than within fiction-writing couples. The study nevertheless suggests what might actually transpire in writing situations, for couples or for a group of writers (dialogic or hierarchical modes of collaboration, for example).

Four recent books use a cultural studies approach (combined with various other perspectives) to the phenomenon of writing couples or coauthorships—partnerships that may be romantic, platonic, or simply ambiguous in orientation. As a result of the emphasis on collaboration and coauthorship, the authors often treat the partners as a unit. These studies focus mostly, as I do, on one sex, a group of either female or male writers; the sexual orientation of the writers is often a major criterion for their selection. Holly Laird's *Women Coauthors* shares with my study an emphasis on women writers, an emphasis on autobiography, as well as a Freudian/Lacanian approach. However, where I emphasize the separation of the mirror stage, she foregrounds a revision of Lacanian desire, "constituted by the gap between subject and (m)other" (18), that brings the partners together. Reconsidering "hierarchical power differentials" (6), Laird postulates a collaborative desire: "a process of reciprocally operating power exchanges between two desiring subjects who are attracted as much (or more) by their affinities and contiguity as by what they may have to gain from each other" (14). She regards the texts resulting from "partial collaborations" and coauthorship as the "realization of [the] relationship" (2, 5). Laird views her work as a feminist project of recovery, bringing to light previously unknown texts; she examines such neglected coauthorships as H.D.'s collaborations with Freud and Bryher. Other examples, drawn from the Victorian period through the twentieth century, include Harriet Taylor and the Delany sisters. Emphasizing women writers, the study nevertheless includes several male coauthors. Bette London's *Writing Double: Women's Literary Partnerships* also selects primarily women writers, with a special interest in the practice of spiritual mediums. Spiritualists' methods such as automatic writing comprise a "discourse about the practice and problematics of authorship," about collaborations in particular (170). Her examples of "literary partnerships," from the Brontës to Yeats, illustrate primarily productive, egalitarian alliances, though she does note some of the same cross-gendered conflicts I have found. She finds that "cross-gender writing relationships" frequently include "women's authorial contributions" to canonical male writers' texts (19), an activity the women writers I study come eventually to reject.

Victor Luftig's *Seeing Together: Friendship between the Sexes in English Writing from Mill to Woolf* adopts a primarily Foucauldian cultural-studies approach. Luftig examines heterosexual couples who sometimes veer from platonic friendship to sexual engagement. He interrogates the concept of friendship to find that "the labels and demarcations that distinguish courtship and ordinary working relations, for instance, are less absolute than the commonplace idioms suggest" (3). Beginning in the Victorian era, Luftig traces the vexed boundary between professional and personal relationships through the postwar period. Wayne Koestenbaum's *Double Talk: The Erotics of Male Literary Collaboration* challenges the concept of friendship by focusing on male collaborators and coauthors who were in no sense public or romantic couples. He finds the partners often take on a third party to form a triangle of displaced desire. Koestenbaum adapts the homosocial bonding within mixed-sex triangles postulated by Girard and Sedgwick to focus on overtly heterosexual male partners, many of whom were well known and almost equal in stature—Wordsworth and Coleridge, for example. The partnerships are taken from the Romantic through the modern eras, and they covertly use a woman/text to engage in displaced, "metaphoric sexual intercourse," symbolic homosexual relations. Koestenbaum calls their acts of collaboration "double talk" because they simultaneously "express homoeroticism" and "strive to conceal it" (3). Both Koestenbaum and Laird share my interest in the texts resulting from a relationship, though they conceive of productive alliances rather than the antagonism I define as a force to generate literary texts.

These various studies generally focus either on facilitative (but silent) partners or on coauthors who are considered partners in some sense of the term. I generally foreground *one* productive but still marginalized partner within the relationship. When previous studies have focused on one writer, it has traditionally been the canonical partner (except when both are noncanonical), and this is especially true when the approach is primarily biographical. John Tytell's *Passionate Lives: D. H. Lawrence, F. Scott Fitzgerald, Henry Miller, Dylan Thomas, Sylvia Plath—In Love* treats F. Scott Fitzgerald and Henry Miller, two partners of the women writers I discuss, as modern Romantics. Although his concern is with male writers, he too finds a desire for women's equality motivating these relationships: "These writers' beliefs broke through inherited assumptions about sexual hierarchy, and they intuitively sought out mates who they felt were spiritual equivalents. In their work, they tried to chart the changing relations between the sexes. In their actual lives, they were victims of a liberation more easily imagined than realized" (4). I view my project as a supplement and a corrective to the approach taken by Tytell and others who focus on the canonical writer within a couple. For example, Tytell describes Nancy Milford's biography *Zelda* as "a genre that approaches the artist through his wife" (314), a dismissive categorization of a book that unequivocally establishes Zelda Fitzgerald as its titular subject.

Louise DeSalvo is one of the few biographical critics to disdain the often idealized or romanticized approach to writing couples and to examine the channeling of residual resentment in conflicted partnerships, such as Leonard Woolf's resentment toward Virginia Woolf. Her *Conceived with Malice*—a work that includes an account of Miller and his wife, June—provides an original perspective, revealing that a writer's autobiographical "revenge" need not focus exclusively on a writing partner (DeSalvo 9).[23] DeSalvo defines a larger or more diffuse kind of target (for example, Djuna Barnes's retaliation against her family). The main focus is on twentieth-century writers.

The paradigm central to my thesis—the Lacanian mirror-stage formation of self/Other—has much in common with mentorship as it implies hierarchy and a formative but transitional relationship. The most detailed discussions of mentorships have traditionally focused on men, although some feminist research, particularly in business, has begun to study cross-gendered mentorships. Kathy Kram's *Mentoring at Work* emphasizes the private sector but is useful to discussion of literary liaisons because of its conceptualization of mentor relationships and its chapter on cross-gender mentorships. Daniel Levinson's *The Seasons of a Man's Life*, a study of male mentoring, is unexpectedly relevant to the women writers I discuss because one of the four professions he studies is that of novelist. The literary liaisons often follow the evolution of mentorship that he outlines.[24]

In the later stages of literary mentorships, as reflected in many of the auto/biographical fictions, the women's comments to and about their partners' efforts to mentor them become increasingly bitter and combative. It is not only that mentorships "evolve over time," as protégé and mentor assume different roles and satisfy different needs at various career stages (Kram 63), but it is also possible that the protégé will become an equal of the mentor, or even a mentor him- or herself. The final phase of a mentorship is normally characterized by disillusionment and the eventual end of the involvement: either the mentor or the protégé may be the first to become disaffected, and at some point the latter must gain a sense of individual authority (Levinson 100–101, Philip-Jones 114, Sheehy 35).[25] Romantic literary partnerships may be especially conflicted because they merge and intensify the dynamics of two similar processes: both mentorships and love relationships may end in "admiration and contempt, appreciation and resentment, grief, rage, bitterness and relief" (Levinson 334).

Two recent studies focus on the mentor and protégé within literary couples exclusively. In the introduction to the collection *American Literary Mentors,* editors Irene C. Goldman-Price and Melissa McFarland Pennell generalize that, although mentoring is ideally a "nurturing" process, "emotions [such as jealousy, domination, or sexual desire] complicate matters" (4). In *Erotic Reckonings: Mastery and Apprenticeship in the Work of Poets and Lovers,* Thomas Simmons uses the paradigms of Mentor (in the Odyssey) and Abelard and Héloïse to analyze the mentorships of poets, including H.D. and Pound. Simmons finds the eroticism within the relationships to be particularly relevant to their dynamics: "the kind of devotion one finds even in a nonsexual mentor-apprentice relationship suggests the erotic force behind this mode of self-creation" (17). Moreover, although the role of mentor is assigned to the male partner in two of the heterosexual couples he discusses (a recurrent pattern in research on cross-gendered mentorships), in the case of Louise Bogan he assigns the role of mentor to the woman and the role of apprentice to the male.

The literary texts I have selected, however, more often incorporate the myth of Pygmalion than that of Mentor and Ulysses, perhaps to contest (as George Bernard Shaw does) the dominance of the Ovidian Pygmalion. The literary liaisons resemble mentorships largely because they occurred early in the writers' careers. The women often moved on to other long-term relationships—sometimes more socially conventional (West's marriage to banker Henry Andrews) and sometimes less socially conventional (H.D.'s lesbian alliance with Bryher) than the affair or marriage. Most of the texts in this study are in some sense the children of divorce, ambivalent products of passionate but terminated relationships. The actual appropriation (the act of writing) generally took place when the relationship was ending or had ended, because these stories could not be written until they had been lived and finished; the writers exorcise their connection by working through the past and thus provide the final break with the affair.

Two studies produce generic and/or author intersections with my project. The first is Suzanne Nalbantian's *Aesthetic Autobiography,* one of the few studies to discuss autobiographical fiction as a genre, and an exception to the prevalent biographical focus. Nalbantian includes a chapter on Nin and shares my interest in the transformation of life into the autobiographical novel. Fictional autobiography, for Nalbantian, is not a subgroup but a relation—a "sister genre"—to autobiography (1). Her view of this genre is much more fixed than mine, and she can therefore claim that literary critics "have not come to terms with the autobiographical novel as a genre with its own autonomous structures and concerns" (41). The second study is Suzette Henke's *Shattered Subjects: Trauma and Testimony in Women's Life-Writing,* which shares with this study common subjects Nin and H.D., as well as an emphasis on "life-writing," a feminist psychoanalytic approach, and a focus on the process of working through. Henke emphasizes the healing effect of "scriptotherapy" for more physically inflicted psychological traumas (incest, breast cancer, stillbirth, racism) than the psychologically scarring emotional conflicts I foreground.

Whereas previous studies of writing couples sometimes feature Nin and H.D., this project is unique in its selection and juxtaposition of British and American women writers from the 1920s and 1930s. Its asymmetrical emphasis on one partner's appropriation of shared auto/biographical material provides a distinct perspective from the more symmetrical formulation of books focusing on collaboration and coauthors. Moreover, my selection and analysis of texts resulting from liaisons, a literary focus, set it apart from biographical and cultural studies approaches to writing couples.

. . .

The chapters that follow are not arranged chronologically—in terms of either the writers' lives or the publication of their fiction—but rather they trace different kinds of mentorships and affiliations, the writers' variously successful (more often unsuccessful) efforts to combine romance and writing. Nin's liaison with Henry Miller provides a useful starting point because her multiple versions of the liaison story focus on writing and the woman writer's identity conflicts. Nin's account of her relationship with Miller, told primarily in an elusively categorized genre that purports to be autobiographical nonfiction, contains many direct statements that clearly delineate patterns and problems against which the subsequent liaison stories may be counterpointed. Nin began her liaison with Miller in her early thirties, while married to Hugh Guiler (indeed, she married again without divorcing him), discovering her vocation as writer and experimenting with a subterranean cross-class lifestyle that was, at the time, adventurous for a woman. Although Nin's morality was unconventional and she circulated in a bohemian artistic subculture, her liaison with Miller defines many features of a traditional, hierarchical cross-gendered mentorship—a model that Nin and the other women writers discussed in subsequent chapters both reject and revise. The relationship was characterized by a high degree of authority conferred on the male mentor by virtue of his age and gender. She ultimately outgrew her need for this mentor, and their relationship evolved (as many mentorships do) into an enduring nonromantic friendship. Nin was somewhat atypical in her status as Miller's financial patron, although patronage, in terms of both financial and emotional support, figures to some degree in all of the relationships I study.

Chapters 2 and 3, dealing with West and Fitzgerald, foreground mentorships between young women and established or emerging literary giants, supplying a different kind of obstacle to the women's progress to literary independence: the partner's literary authority resides not only in his gender but in his status as a respected author. West and Fitzgerald began their liaisons when they were scarcely out of their teens, and each gave birth to a child by the time she was twenty-one. Their novels focus on the dissolution of a first love. Most significantly, *Sunflower* and *Save Me the Waltz* add another dimension to Nin's accounts not only as they suggest additional alternatives to cross-gendered mentorship but also as they move away from the genre of purported nonfictional autobiography to autobiography presented as fiction. These two writers displace and reenact their mentorship traumas, but the novels' fictional protagonists may more fully extricate themselves from their mentor-lovers than their real-life prototypes ever did.

The final two chapters present the least traditional kinds of mentorships through protagonists who more fully explore the woman-woman bond as an alternative to the hierarchical self/Other dyad. Chapter 4, in drawing upon Hall's lesbian relationship with Una Troubridge, foregrounds accommodation as a solution. Rather than simply fictionalizing her most serious long-term relationship in *The Forge*, Hall uses the device of a heterosexual couple. She thus transforms autobiographical details to produce a coded version of her relationship with Troubridge, who displaced Hall's first partner, Ladye (Mabel Veronica Batten), after she died of a stroke in 1916. *The Forge* is the only novel in the study that depicts a real-life relationship that continued throughout the life of the writer (though Hall's romantic attention was distracted from Troubridge to another lover during her final years). H.D.'s first literary liaison, with Ezra Pound, began when she was only fifteen; her marriage to Richard Aldington, the relationship that figures most prominently in *Bid Me to Live*, began when she was twenty-seven and was definitively ended when she gave birth to a child fathered by another man at the age of thirty-three. She engaged in a series of homosexual and heterosexual liaisons of various literary significance even after she had entered a more enduring relationship with Bryher. Because H.D. wrote numerous fictional versions of her traumatic relationships with Aldington and Lawrence, while hinting at her subsequent relationship with Bryher, Chapter 5 explores perhaps the largest number and most fluid variations and alternatives to traditional mentorships. I conclude with this chapter because it is the only one to depict a kind of proto-literary coauthorship (between H.D. and Bryher), providing a glimpse of a more egalitarian literary liaison.

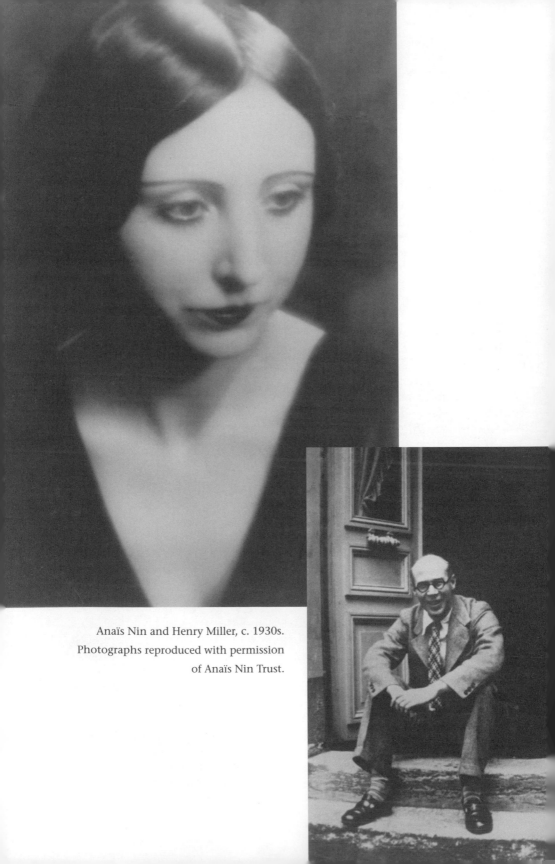

Anaïs Nin and Henry Miller, c. 1930s.
Photographs reproduced with permission
of Anaïs Nin Trust.

CHAPTER ONE

The Many Faces of June
Anaïs Nin's Appropriation of Feminine Writing

To write as a woman, and as a woman only.

—Nin, *Diary*

In 1931 Anaïs Nin and Henry Miller, two fledgling writers, would seem to have had the potential for a literary liaison based on professional equality. Yet as a younger woman involved with an older man, Nin found herself in a relationship embodying many of the perils of cross-gendered mentorship. The hierarchy of authority and experience that mentorships normally entail may well intensify if the protégée is female and the mentor is both older and male. As the protégée finds her own identify as a writer, the inegalitarian configuration is likely to produce tension, infusing both the mutual professional interest and the romance. Nin's relationship with Miller establishes the pattern of a woman seeking equality within a loving relationship only to discover herself in conflict (and often rivalry) with a lover who entertains different ideas concerning her role as writer. Nin's developing objective was to create a feminine aesthetic, a goal that seems counterproductive within a cross-gendered mentorship, especially with a mentor so little concerned about feminine selfhood as Miller. Arguing for a valorization of the feminine, Nin claims that women must change both themselves and society in order to achieve liberation, but that "to become man, or like man, is no solution" ("Notes on Feminism" 28).

Nin's mentorship battle with Miller began with her efforts to define herself in opposition to the male Other, but in the process she discovered a more conciliatory role as aesthetic mediator between the sexes.[1] Miller parodied Nin's texts, yet as she gained confidence in her writing she reciprocated by appropriating not only Miller's sexually explicit subject matter but also his primary and obsessive subject, his second wife, June. The fictionalization of this femme fatale was a site for Nin to explore her own developing authorial identity as she enacted her desire for subject status through efforts to capture or possess June in a self-perceived, self-defined feminine language. In her multiple, revised versions of this material, Nin does not conform to rigid literary categories; her innovative experimental forms challenge the boundaries of established genres. Her genre-crossing is evidence of the kind of double "both/and" thinking that DuPlessis describes as feminine, expansive in contrast to a masculine "either/or" ("Etruscans" 276). Nin ultimately moves from a fairly traditional role within a cross-gendered mentorship to a rebellious, gendered concept of the artist. Although her self-proclaimed purpose is to write as a woman, she mediates between what are conventionally perceived as masculine and feminine languages: her efforts show her also writing women for men.

THE SEARCH FOR A MENTOR

The early pages of Nin's 1931–1934 *Diary* show her clearly in search of a mentor. Her sessions during this period with two psychoanalysts, René Allendy and Otto Rank, were ostensibly undertaken to resolve her traumatic relationship with her father, but they were largely devoted to discussion of her development as a writer, and a major conflict in her analysis was the choice between being "a non-neurotic woman or a neurotic artist" (Niemeyer 69). The first phase in acquiring a writer's identity was accomplished through a romantic mentorship that eventually convinced Nin she could indeed be both woman and artist. It was circumstance that brought Nin to a literary mentorship with Miller, however. The living artist she most admired at this time was Djuna Barnes—but Barnes did not respond to Nin's admiring letters and was probably too eccentric and independent to function as a role model or mentor. Indeed, she was furious when Nin named a character in *Cities of the Interior* "Djuna," fictionalizing and appropriating her identity. Nin was introduced to Miller by Richard Osborn, a lawyer friend of Miller's she had consulted about the copyright for her book on D. H. Lawrence.

When they met on December 5, 1931, neither Nin nor Miller was established as a writer. Miller had been writing since 1924 but had published only a few short pieces (Nin, *Passion* xi); Nin was awaiting the publication of her first book, *D. H. Lawrence: An Unprofessional Study* (1932). Miller was twelve years older than Nin, the usual age difference for a mentor—not old enough to be a father figure but often a "half generation" older than the protégé (Levinson 99). Miller was far from ideal as teacher or mentor, but for the most part he took her seriously as a writer. Nin reports in her *Diary* that one would-be mentor, Allendy, called her a *"petite fille littéraire"* (*Diary* 114), an ingenue playing out literary fantasies. Another potential mentor, Edmund Wilson, told her that he wanted to marry her so that he "could teach [her] how to write" (Stern 155).[2] Miller also assumed a condescending role at times, but he was more helpful than Wilson. Miller was unable to sponsor her, since he was himself without influential contacts at the beginning of their mentorship, but he saw himself as a teacher, working to develop her writing skills. At one point he stated, "you will soon exhaust all I have to teach you" (*Diary* 88), and in a letter to Nin he characterized his editorial role as a "maestro" working on her manuscripts (Nin, *Passion* 223). She already had access to the artistic world because of her family's musical connections, but he introduced her to the bohemian Parisian demimonde.

Within their early literary partnership, Miller and Nin often adopted the hierarchical roles of editor (primarily Miller) and patron (primarily Nin), more than those of collaborators or coauthors. A distinctive feature of the Nin-Miller alliance is that almost from the start it was the woman who assumed the potentially powerful role of patron, a permutation of the usual power balance in cross-gendered mentorships.[3] When Miller had difficulty getting *Tropic of Cancer* published, Nin interceded to underwrite its publication (Nin, *Passion* xv). As the wife of a banker, Nin was able to offer Miller protection and a kind of sponsorship, the usual function of the mentor rather than the protégé. Miller also tried to get her diary published by subscription, placing an advertisement in *The Booster* in 1937. Although he did attract the interest of T. S. Eliot, the project was never realized.[4] Women who are not writers frequently assume the role of patroness in relation to male artists, and in the 1930s Nin's financial and social class standing clearly facilitated this relation. Nin was not content to be merely a patron to the artist, however; she desired the latter role for herself. Nin rebelled against her role as protégée after Miller purportedly stole ideas for his own work from her unpublished diary. She claimed that her objective in the prose poem *House of Incest* was to write "as a woman, and as a woman only" (*Diary* 128). Throughout her career Nin and her circle claimed she was writing a new feminine prose.

This tactic might be dismissed as merely a marketing technique, typical of the kinds of promotion in which Nin and Miller engaged. For example, Miller's public pronouncement that Nin's diary provides "the first female writing I have seen," revealing "the opium world of woman's physiological being, a sort of cinematic show put on inside the genito-urinary tract" ("Être" 289), seems designed to associate her work with the commercial success of his own Rabelaisian excesses in *Tropic of Cancer*. Similarly, Nin's assertion in a postscript to the reprinting of *Delta of Venus* that she was "intuitively using a woman's language, seeing sexual experience from a woman's point of view" (*Delta* xvi), was probably motivated by a desire to promote and legitimate her erotica. Her book sales in the 1970s suggest that the marketing of a feminine writing, coinciding with the woman's liberation movement of the late 1960s and early 1970s, was indeed astute merchandising. Yet in the wake of the recovery of "lost" and "minor" women writers such as Kate Chopin or Zora Neale Hurston and their inscription into a new feminized canon, Nin herself has been denied entry. By choosing to cultivate the identity of a feminine writer, Nin may have relegated herself to the status of a vogue or coterie writer and contributed to her own literary marginality both with male critics, for whom *feminine* is a term of denigration or condescension, and with feminist critics, who in the 1980s and 1990s often dismissed the self-proclaimed feminine writer as essentialist.[5] Whereas most of the other women writers in this study seem to be edging into the canon (and some of their texts are now part of *a* modernist and/or women's studies canon), Nin's reception is still largely polarized between uncritical admiration and harsh often moralizing denigration. By foregrounding her generic innovation, especially in work begun much earlier than it was actually published, I hope to contribute not only to a reevaluation of Nin but also to an emerging but still underdeveloped scholarly analysis of her texts.

INFLUENCE, ATTEMPTED COLLABORATION, AND PARODY

Nin's accounts of mutual influence in her liaison with Miller are somewhat inconsistent, probably reflecting changes in their relationship, her increasing success and confidence in herself, and her ultimate realization that gender was crucial to her role as writer. Early accounts, particularly the novella "Djuna" (1939) and *Nearer the Moon,* depict Nin and Miller in a brief honeymoon period, working productively together. Valerie Harms's study of the Nin papers at Northwestern University establishes that Miller copiously annotated Nin's early drafts with criticisms and revisions. In 1933 Nin initially claimed, "We have much influence over each other's work, I on the artistry and insight, on the going beyond realism, he on the matter, substance, and vitality of mine. I have given him depth, and he gives me concreteness" (*Diary* 166). Miller introduced Nin to new kinds of subject matter ("substance"), which she then incorporated into her diary and fiction. One conspicuous example of this subject matter is the erotic scene in her 1931–1934 *Diary* where the lovers visit a brothel at 32 rue Blondel. The episode also appears in *Henry and June* (which contains scenes that were expurgated from or altered in the diary published during Nin's lifetime), but in this work she is accompanied by her husband, Hugh Guiler, rather than by Miller. Although her friendship with Miller probably inspired the actual visit, in the *Diary* as originally published she not only shields her husband's identity by substituting Miller in the scene but also gives the experience an appropriateness it may have lacked in real life (that she be initiated by the licentious "gangster writer").

Nin's subsequent writing and publishing of erotica was a move prompted by her association with Miller, yet she believed her writing in this genre was distinctly "feminine."[6] In a preface to her erotica, which was written for a collector in the 1940s but unpublished until the 1970s, Nin claims: "Rereading [the erotica] these many years later, I see that my own voice was not completely suppressed [by the male erotic tradition]. In numerous passages I was intuitively using a woman's language, seeing sexual experience from a woman's point of view" (*Delta* xvi). The combination of erotic subject matter influenced by Miller and her own "feminine" rendering is evident in *The Delta of Venus* and to a greater degree in *Henry and June*, as Nin herself noted while the unexpurgated diary was still unpublished (*Delta* xvi).

Despite her earlier claim of mutual influence, in 1968 Nin denied the influence of Miller and other male writer-friends on her early development:

> I worked out my problems as a woman writer, as a writer of poetic fiction, within the diary. I never remember appealing for help in these matters. I did have discussions with Henry Miller and Lawrence Durrell, but they undermined my confidence, usually, and the diary helped me recover my equanimity and integrity. I was young and surrounded by mature, educated writers, and could easily have been swamped, overwhelmed by them and influenced to imitate them. (*Novel of the Future* 146)

Her correspondence with Durrell shows her, as early as 1939, rejecting some of his suggested revisions: "you ought really to let me take my chance, let me pay for my weaknesses, defects. You cannot write my book for me" (*Nearer the Moon* 303). Nin's shifting descriptions of her literary relationships with male writers may exemplify a contrast between the positive feelings of the early stages of a mentorship and her retrospective reevaluation years later. Kram describes the "cultivation stage" as "typically the period least fraught with conflict or uncertainty," whereas there is an increasing conflict and rebellion in the separation and redefinition stages (55).

Conflict is evident fairly early in this mentorship. As a literary product of their relationship, Nin and Miller created parallel texts in which they developed a pattern of intertextual appropriation and parody (a pattern also present in the West-Wells liaison). These texts reflect the emerging ambivalence in their relationship, expressed indirectly through textual caricature and parody. Their efforts to collaborate produced highly emotional, somewhat vindictive results. Nin responded angrily to Miller's opportunistic recycling of passages she had deleted from *House of Incest* into a work he published entitled

Scenario. The book was conceived as a collaboration in which each would write "individually," as well as together, about various films (Stephenson, editor's note 88). When the work was published in 1937, the finished product emerged as Miller's parody—even caricature—of Nin's original. In her diary she wrote:

> I hate *Scenario* and I never had the courage to tell Henry. It is the worst and basest product of our association and collaboration. In his hands all my material was changed, the very texture of *House of Incest* was changed. He wrote *Scenario* but the ideas were mine, all of them. He only added Henry-like touches: doves coming out of asses, skeletons, noise, and things I don't like, loud and filmlike, the opposite of *House of Incest.* . . . A monstrous deformed bastard child born of our two styles and a caricature of mine. (*Nearer the Moon* 107)

A pattern of textual retribution—accomplished sometimes via parody, sometimes by theft or appropriation of material—recurs with significant variations in this liaison.

Through parody, a manifestation of influence, each partner extended the personal relationship and its conflicts into literary texts. The relations of these texts create what Hutcheon (after E. M. Forster) terms "intertextual 'bouncing'" (32), an interaction between texts that, with eventual publication, takes the private into the public. The intertextual relationship of two passages from works written during the time of their liaison, Nin's *House of Incest* and Miller's "Into the Night Life," exposes a literary collaboration in which a parodic imitation expresses ambivalence, even antagonism. In the original text Nin writes:

> The rooms were chained together by steps—no room was on a level with another—and all the steps were deeply worn. There were windows between the rooms, little spying-eyed windows, so that one might talk in the dark from room to room, without seeing the other's face. The rooms were filled with the rhythmic heaving of the sea coming from many sea-shells. (*Incest* 51)

Nin's description reflects a surrealistic emphasis (circa 1930s) on symbolic, psychological imagery. In his parodic piece "Into the Night Life," Miller imitates Nin's simple diction and her symbolically suggestive imagery; he also exaggerates her staccato style:

> There are chains binding me to the bed. The chains are clanking loudly, the anchor is being lowered . . . . There are three rooms, one after the other, like a railroad flat. I am lying in the middle room in which there

is a walnut bookcase and a dressing table. The old hag removes her wrapper and stands before the mirror in her chemise. She has a little powder puff in her hand and with this little puff she swabs her armpits, her bosom, her thighs. ("Night Life" 157)

Like Nin, Miller is influenced by surrealism, as shown in his juxtaposition of incongruous images. But he does not take seriously Nin's earnest effort to create a symbolic text through an interior suggesting the psychoanalytic process of communication with the unconscious. Stylistically, his short, choppy sentences mimic Nin's rhythm and short, declarative sentences.

In addition to the parodic tone and the replacement of Nin's mysterious romantic house with a banal railway flat, Miller incorporates other, more ludicrous reflections of *House of Incest.* In the rest of the piece, Miller's narrator with holes in his side resembles Nin's skinless, ultrasensitive Modern Christ; the dancing narrator "with a parasol over [his] head" corresponds to Nin's celebratory dancer with no arms. As with Nin's prose poem, the images are drawn from dreams; there is a lack of causality. In Miller's sketch, however, the dreamlike exaggeration produces parody, and Nin's sensual, suggestive images are transformed into the mundane: he describes a hag who "swabs" her armpits; in a subsequent passage a watch is attached to a dressing table with prosaic black tape, and horsehair sprouts from the chins of gathered relatives. When the narrator subsequently begins to embellish his dance and "snort like a bull . . . prance like a fairy . . . strut like a peacock" ("Night Life" 158), it is clear that Miller's exuberant persona has broken out. The partners' literary styles were certainly not complementary. Furthermore, in his novels as in the passage above Miller continued to depict women (here the hideous primping hag) from a perspective that can only be called masculinist, in the most pejorative sense of the word.

Nin was offended by this piece, though it must be said, in all fairness to Miller, that the *précieuse* style of her prose poem makes it vulnerable to parody. At the same time, in creating his parody, Miller implicitly acknowledged her status as writer, finding her worthy of imitation. Not only does parody appropriate a writer's property, "it is also true that any concept of textual appropriation must implicitly place a certain value upon the original" (Hutcheon 107). Miller's parody belittles Nin's writing style (a recurrent issue within their mentorship), but it also grants her status as a writer who merits recognition. Rather than retaliate with her own parody of Miller's writing, however, Nin appropriated his literary subject, his wife, using the June portraits to develop a critique of the masculinist values underpinning his aesthetic practice. The parodic and parallel texts embody self-exploration for the individual writers and a sort of metadiscourse, communicating with the other intimate feelings about their relationship and roles as writers.

EXPERIMENTATION AND THE QUARREL OVER GENDERED AESTHETICS

The many rewritings of the June story, the multiple versions of the autobiographical love triangle, reflect Nin's experimentation with genre. Although her primary genre is the diary, it is variously edited, and she also cultivates the June portraits in story or novella form as well as in the prose poem: each explores—and blurs—the distinction between nonfiction and fiction in her writing (much to the dismay of some of her biographers). Nin's literary critics evaluate the innovation of the edited, fictionalized diary in divergent ways, ranging from praise for its novelty and craft to condemnation for its confusion of fiction with fact. Erica Jong maintains that Nin creates "a kind of writing which hybridizes autobiography and fiction" (213). Evelyn Hinz views the diaries as artfully composed to exhibit a thematic progression from the development of the artist in the first volume to the artist as public figure in the fourth (*Mirror and Garden* 97–116). Joan Bobbitt, however, objects to a "calculated artistry," which contradicts Nin's ideals of spontaneity and "artistic truthfulness" (269). She concludes that, problematically, "[n]ot only does it resemble fiction, it *is* fiction" (270).

Nin's bold fictionalization of autobiography has undermined her posthumous literary reputation. Recently it has elicited a new round of disparagement, as biographer Deirdre Bair claims that "Anaïs Nin 'lied'." Establishing this perspective on the second page of her introduction (*Nin* xvi), Bair sets up the biography with an ethical judgment that ignores the generic innovation of Nin's tactic. Generic experimentation is a major part of Nin's gendered aesthetic, however. Nin might be regarded as a woman autobiographer who uses the subversive techniques Gilmore defines as "autobiographics" (see my Introduction); Nin's purported untruthfulness might also be valued for its creation of "discursive contradictions in the representation of identity (rather than unity)" (Gilmore 42). Rather than be named a liar, Nin might instead be evaluated as a woman autobiographer who gestures toward a postmodern view of the self.

Bobbitt criticizes Nin's "calculated artistry" in presenting the edited diary as nonfiction; but it is more productive to consider the selective, edited diary as fiction, and the diary's narrator—as well as the narrator of *House of Incest*—as textual personae, named Anaïs Nin in the diaries, unnamed in the prose poem. Some critics also attribute the craft of her diaries to Nin's editors. Miller, for example, tried to rewrite *House of Incest* but gave it up as "presumptuous" (*Diary* 117).[7] That both the prose poem and the *Diary* were influenced by male editors and colleagues does indeed complicate discussion of gendered discourse in these texts. Nevertheless, Nin denied the influence of male colleagues on her early development as a writer (*Novel of the Future* 146); and as author, she is ultimately accountable for all versions of works published in her lifetime. Even if in a literal sense she is not the exclusive author of the text, she is the legal, public, and imputed author, granted ascribed authorship.

One might arrange Nin's works on a generic continuum with the least fictionalized (the unedited journal) at one end and the most fictionalized (the erotica) at the other.[8] Because of the early diary's focus on the Miller-Nin liaison and the generative relation of the genre to her other writing, the emphasis here is on her first published diary; several generic variations on the same material from Nin's oeuvre show that those variations are nevertheless significant and mutually informing. In deliberate opposition to those critics who attack her diaries as nonfiction that constructs a false, egotistic, and idealized self, I treat the diaries, prose poem, and stories as autobiographical fictions. All the liaison fiction examined in this study violates to some degree Lejeune's autobiographical pact. Nin's fiction approaches the problems of fictionalizing literary relationships from a different angle, however. Whereas writers of a roman à clef present an autobiographical relationship as fiction, Nin presents it as nonfiction. Her choice to name the genre of her major achievement a diary rather than a journal reflects an indifference to factual—rather than inner or unconscious—truth and a desire to gender her work as feminine.

Many critics have lauded and romanticized Miller's support of Nin's diary, in the process ignoring her accounts of his ambivalence toward it. For example, Nin's editor Gunther Stuhlmann describes Miller as "a devoted editor and critic of her work," who "never flagged in his passionate advocacy of what he consistently regarded as her major work: the enormous diary" (quoted in Nin, *Passion* xii, xv). Miller wrote a flattering, inflated introduction for the *Diary,* predicting that it would "take its place beside the revelations of St. Augustine, Petronious, Abelard, Rousseau, Proust" (*Diary* v). Yet he was ambivalent about the work, and frustrated with Nin's inability to move beyond it into fiction writing. Despite his enumeration of august male diarists and confessional writers, Miller's ambivalence about the diary is rooted in its genre. He alternately encouraged and discouraged her. He wrote to publisher William Bradley in 1933 to argue for the diary's publication and tried to publish it himself by subscription. But he verbally undermined these efforts: "I am aiming seriously at the destruction of this diary," he said (Nin, *Passion* 219), claiming: "Journal writing is a disease" (*Henry and June* 137).

As a friend, lover, and mentor Miller tried to be supportive of Nin's diary, but as with her fiction, which he tried to purge of its "femininities" (Nin, *Passion* 148), his reaction was tainted by ambivalence. In her letters she complains he is a less sympathetic reader of her work than she is of his. "You have it in for the diary," she tells him. "I won't send you any more pages" (*Passion* 219, 220). As early as 1933 she accuses him of getting pleasure from criticizing her: "Watch yourself a bit now, Henry, you're enjoying this dissection, you know, and you're getting heavy-handed" (220). Although she seemed to want to hear only praise from him (a reaction that recurred when she received professional reviews of her published works), she benefited from working *against* his criticism. In their correspondence Miller and Nin characterize their critical interchanges using metaphors drawn from fighting and wrestling. Miller claims to be toughening her up by his criticism, as a trainer prepares his prizefighter (Nin, *Passion* 220–25). Nin describes their productive antagonism as her "enameled style and [his] muscular one, wrestling, drawing sparks from one another" (119). Nin's struggle with Miller over an appropriate style and form for her writing was instrumental in her discovery and articulation of the aesthetic that earned her an international readership in the 1970s.

In viewing the diary as her primary work Nin privileges a culturally denigrated subgenre that is commonly relegated to the female. The "journal intime" in particular "may be more demonstrably 'feminine' in various ways than the novel" (Raoul 57), a personal genre written by and for women. So it is not surprising that Nin's male associates—Miller and her two analysts during this period, Rank in particular—tried to discourage her from continuing the diary. They argued that it diffused artistic energy which could have been channeled into her fiction. Rank wanted her to give up the diary and live by herself (Nin, *Diary* 280). Like a jealous lover he accused her of being "kept by the Diary" (289). Rank associates women's diaries with a realism he denigrates as lacking creativity. Of one of their sessions Nin reports: "Then we talked about the realism of women, and Rank said that perhaps that was why women had never been great artists. They invented nothing" (291). What was most troublesome to Rank, it seems, was the diary as a feminine form; since in his view women cannot invent, the diary cannot be art. Rank and Miller wanted Nin to leave the prosaic "feminine" diary to fulfill their image of her as a writer, a male subject using symbolic language. Nin at times conceded to her mentors' advice and made some attempts to direct her energy to fiction. But her struggle to retain the diary, a subgenre often considered feminine and stigmatized accordingly, was in fact a rebellious act of self-definition and identity. It is her work in this genre, not her fiction, that earned her fame and commercial success in the feminist-charged climate of the late 1960s and 1970s.

THE JUNE PORTRAIT IN PROSE: "DJUNA" AND THE DIARY

The multiple portraits of June that Nin creates in the novella "Djuna," in the first *Diary* volume published, in *House of Incest*, and in *Henry and June*, show her self-consciously experimenting with language she calls feminine. The interrelations of the portraits are complicated by discrepancies between the order of their composition and their dates of publication, as well as by the imbrication of material in Nin's works. The source material or intertext for all these variations (the Ur-text) is her lengthy unpublished diary (over 150 volumes). The June material is presented in the 1931–1934 *Diary* (published in 1966) and in *Henry and June* (published in 1986), both of which were edited and excerpted from the original diary. The volumes of the diary published in Nin's lifetime were edited to delete potentially libelous passages about her lovers, her husband, and others who did not want to be named. *Henry and June*, the posthumously published diary treating her liaison with Miller, was edited to restore most of the previously deleted passages focusing on Henry and June Miller and to exclude those already published in 1966. *House of Incest* appeared in 1936; Nin records her struggles with the composition of this prose poem in the first volume of the *Diary*, originally composed contemporaneously. The early phase of her encounter with Henry and June Miller was also published as a one-hundred-page story or novella entitled "Djuna" in the 1939 edition of *Winter of Artifice*.[9] These accumulated portraits revise the same material, over a period of more than thirty-five years, and work through the conflicts she experienced as she began to articulate a feminine aesthetic, a process that emerged from her conflicts with Miller.

Nin's earliest renditions of her liaison, written in the enthusiasm of the honeymoon phase of a mentorship, romanticize and eroticize the combination of writing and sex. In "Djuna," the shift from a quasi-professional friendship to an erotic affair is marked by a comment by Djuna (the Nin character), "And I thought we were in love with each other's writing!" spoken as they kiss and walk to Hans's (Miller's) room (12). Hans recounts his fantasy of women "not thrown on beds but on piles of manuscripts and open books" (28). In her jealousy of Johanna (the June character), Djuna wonders "if the full body of Johanna would triumph over all else, over understanding, over the ecstasies of our working together, over the double climaxes of body and mind burning in unison, over this double flame of creation and love" (18). The metaphoric, orgasmic association of writing and sex designates a mutual enhancement of the professional and the personal. The lovers' "double climaxes . . . burning in unison" suggest both the narcissism and the self-reflectiveness of an adult reenactment of the mirror stage.

In the first part of the story the narrator is not yet the autonomous "feminine" artist; she views herself as part of a dyad. Willing to subordinate herself as a woman she plays "at being the wife of a genius" ("Djuna" 23), and as a writer she describes her writing as "the wife of yours" (55). As Hans writes, she is impregnated; she feels his "book swelling up inside me like my very own child" (64). In her initial infatuation she willingly abdicates subject status in deference to the male subject: "I want to grant you all the privileges; you can be undivided artist and saint, hungry animal and clown!" (13). Yet even in this earliest version, the narrator sees the potential to collaborate with the other woman, the archetypal femme fatale, against their lover. As an artist, a "creator," she resolves to re-create "Johanna in Hans' mind" and to "poison him with the inextricable mixture of Johanna and myself" (20).

The June portraits, as they accrue, depict the narrator formulating alternatives to collaboration with the male writer-lover, and she moves to identify with the woman/Other. Nin used the June archetype (variously named) for many women characters in her fiction, but the focus in the following discussion is on the representative expository passages in Nin's initial portrait of June (the 1931–1934 *Diary*), the first account to reach a mass audience, recounting her response to their meeting and establishing the qualities of this enigmatic figure:

> Henry came to Louveciennes with June.
> As June walked towards me from the darkness of the garden and into the light of the door, I saw for the first time the most beautiful woman on earth. A startlingly white face, burning dark eyes, a face so alive I felt it would consume itself before my eyes. Years also I tried to imagine a true beauty; I created in my mind an image of just such a woman. I had never seen her until last night. Yet I knew long ago the phosphorescent color of her skin, her huntress profile, the evenness of her teeth. She is bizarre, fantastic, nervous, like someone in a high fever. Her beauty drowned me. As I sat before her, I felt I would do anything she asked of me. Henry suddenly faded. She was color and brilliance and strangeness. By the end of the evening I had extricated myself from her power. She killed my admiration by her talk. Her talk. The enormous ego, false, weak, posturing. She lacks the courage of her personality which is sensual, heavy with experience. Her role alone preoccupies her. She invents dramas in which she always stars. I am sure she creates genuine chaos and whirlpools of feelings, but I feel that her share in it is a pose. That

night, in spite of my response to her, she sought to be whatever she felt
I wanted her to be. She is an actress every moment. I cannot grasp the
core of June. (*Diary* 20)

This portrait emphasizes qualities of the femme fatale: June is an attractive but dangerous, predatory "huntress."[10] She is an enigmatic
menace, typical of the femme fatale archetype whose "most striking
characteristic, perhaps, is the fact that she never really is what she
seems to be. She harbors a threat which is not entirely legible, pre-
dictable, or manageable . . . a secret . . . which must be aggressively revealed, unmasked, discovered" (Doane 1).

While the beginning of the passage echoes the masculine perception of this literary archetype, and the threat of the huntress with
"even teeth" would appear to be castration, the passage presents a significant variation on the usual depiction of a male gaze fixed upon female object. The short declarative sentence-paragraph introducing the
portrait establishes that it is Miller, the male, who delivers the femme
fatale for Nin's *female* gaze. This perspective seems to have emerged in
revision; in the earlier "Djuna" the passage begins, "As she walked
heavily towards me from the darkness of the garden . . . " (67), without the introductory mention of Henry. What does it mean when the
gaze is female, when woman gazes upon woman? Film theorist Teresa
de Lauretis argues that "for women spectators . . . we cannot assume
identification to be single or simple. For one thing, identification is itself a movement, a subject-process, a relation: the identification (of
oneself) with something other (than oneself)" (*Alice Doesn't* 141). It is
significant that the female gaze seizing upon female image provides
an experience of identity and also difference, a discovery of self and of
Other. The female gaze differs from the male gaze/female spectacle in
both the identity (female sameness) and the (slighter, individual) *extent* of difference perceived.

Initially, the female narrator of the *Diary* participates in the male
attraction to the femme fatale, insisting on her own difference and
sharing the compulsion to "unmask" and expose June. The narrator
defines her function as an active translator of an inarticulate force:
"Poor June is not like me, able to make her own portrait" (*Diary* 16).
Together Nin and Miller ambivalently admire and fear the vortex of
June, for the "power accorded to the femme fatale is a function of
fears linked to the notions of uncontrollable drives, the fading of subjectivity, and the loss of conscious agency" (Doane 2). The femme fatale is primarily an archetype in male-authored fiction because she
represents "an articulation of fears surrounding the loss of stability
and centrality of the self, the 'I' ego. These anxieties appear quite explicitly in the process of her representation as castration anxiety"
(Doane 2). Drawn in by the attractions of the femme fatale, Nin

nevertheless differs from Miller in that she shares June's gender. Because her relationship with June is one of gender identification, Nin is not threatened by her in the same way as Miller. There can be no loss of "I" because there is no threat of castration, no Oedipal separation from the mother.[11]

Nin's representation of June differ's from the male strategy for dealing with the femme fatale because she emphasizes understanding. In the *Diary*, Nin insists that Miller asks the wrong questions about June, that he neglects to ask why she feels she must fabricate and lie. Nin tells him "perhaps you did not ask the correct questions of the Sphinx," and "I would not be concerned with the secrets, the lies, the mysteries, the facts. I would be concerned *with what makes them necessary*" (*Diary* 19; original italics). Hélène Cixous argues that man's view of woman as Sphinx is a strategy for keeping her outside the dominant culture: "And so they want to keep woman in the place of mystery, consign her to mystery, as they say 'keep her in her place,' keep her at a distance: she's always not quite there . . . but no one knows exactly where she is" ("Castration" 49). The male fascination with the femme fatale is rooted in paradox, in simultaneous and contradictory impulses: on one hand the compulsion to unmask her and on the other the knowledge that it is futile to do so. In contrast to the male gazer, when a woman is the onlooker, the process is not one of compensation and mastery over another but rather one of reconnection and mastery of self.

Even in the first version ("Djuna"), which foregrounds the narrator's collaboration with the male writer, Djuna emphasizes that it is *her* role to fuse with the third party (Johanna/June) in order to create her: "When Hans and I would lean over each other's work, to fill out her portrait, I would engrave the wonder of her everywhere, reveal it, so that he could never free himself of her. I would melt into Johanna so that he could not detect any more flaws in her; I would explain her lies and ennoble and embellish them. I would create a Johanna with Johanna's beauty and my own imagination and colors" ("Djuna" 18). Her creative mental powers enhance qualities Johanna already possesses, further entrapping Hans in a love triangle (that is somewhat softened and obscured in the subsequent *Diary* version). Kent Ekberg claims that the "triangular relationship" of Anaïs, June, and Henry is a "re-enactment of the Oedipal triangle that Nin confronts in her *Diary*" (4). This statement seems to suggest a Freudian interpretation, emphasizing the daughter's development as womanly seductress in relation to the father, and an autobiographical interpretation stressing Nin's traumatic childhood experience of being abandoned by her father. Yet Miller (the father figure) is secondary in this portion of the diary; although Nin places his appearance before the introduction of his wife, June quickly displaces him as the focus of the narrator's interest.[12]

It may be appropriate to view the *Diary* portrait of June as an account of female identity acquisition in relation to a mother figure, an illustration of the views of Nancy Chodorow and other feminist psychoanalysts and literary critics who focus on the mother-daughter dyad. Nin revives the memory of the forgotten mother through her encounter with June, and as she does so, the immediacy of Miller, the male lover, "suddenly fade[s]." The narrator establishes a direct and symmetrical relationship with June, who personifies an "image" she had previously "created" (*Diary* 20). This relationship, the revised mother-daughter dyad, emphasizes knowledge of self through the female Other, the inarticulate pre-mirror-stage (m)other. Nin's allegory of the woman writer's return to the unconscious, of her revitalizing connection with a powerful mother figure, resembles Kristeva's preverbal *chora* and the notion of the mother as a mediating force:

> The *chora* is a modality of significance in which the linguistic sign is not yet articulated as the absence of an object and as the distinction between real and symbolic. . . . The mother's body is therefore what mediates the symbolic law organizing social relations and becomes the ordering principle of the semiotic *chora*, which is on the path of destruction, aggressivity and death. (Kristeva, *Revolution* 26, 27–28)

In the *Diary* account, Nin learns from the encounter with the *chora*, with June, whose talk is "unconscious," an "underworld language."[13] The process of identification is clarified as Nin claims: "When I talk now, I feel June's voice in me" (*Diary* 27, 28, 29).

The diary passage (cited above) in which June is introduced anticipates Nin's aesthetic strategy as an artist mediating between the sexes. Claiming identification with the mother, Nin also provides a judgment of June, an activity characteristic of the male symbolic. Midway through the passage her emphasis shifts from admiration to rejection. Nin uses direct statement to pinpoint June's nature as "false, weak and posturing," and with the transitional sentence, "By the end of the evening," the narrator claims to have "extricated" herself from June's "power" (*Diary* 20).[14] This premonitory passage encapsulates the eventual reaction against June: the sequence ends with the narrator's judgment and rejection of June. In Lacanian terms, to define and to articulate June is to understand her, a stage in Nin's acquisition of language, the first manifestation of her subjectivity. The narrator's role in the *Diary* portrait of June vacillates between identification with the mother-figure and Lacanian conspiracy with the male in exposing her through the symbolic.

Nin characterizes Miller as a writing colleague in her *Diary*, but their multifaceted literary conflicts are nevertheless exposed. They quarrel about the proper genre for Nin's work, about their differing evaluations of the prose poem *House of Incest,* about ownership of their fictional portraits of June. Nin claims Miller "stole" from her then-unpublished diary and used her observations in his own depictions of his wife in *Tropic of Capricorn.* After discovering this, Nin writes: "And what have I left to work with? . . . What was left for me to do? To go where Henry cannot go, into the myth, into June's dreams, fantasies, into the poetry of June. To write as a woman and as a woman only" (*Diary* 128). Nin's accounts are defined against the realistic techniques of Miller's novel, yet she anticipates contemporary feminists such as Rachel Blau DuPlessis (see "Etruscans") in demonstrating that women speak two languages: the male discourse of the dominant culture and the feminine discourse that only women know as members of the majority "subculture." In a seeming contradiction, Nin articulates a purely feminine aesthetic while actually mediating between male and female literary traditions.

HOUSE OF INCEST: THE JUNE STORY AS PROSE POEM

Nin's deliberate cultivation of a feminine aesthetic as a means to distinguish herself from Miller's characteristic literary production represents both a personal and a professional step toward autonomy. Irigaray describes the motivation behind the acquisition of such an identity: "One must assume the feminine role deliberately. Which means already to convert a form of subordination into an affirmation, and thus to begin to thwart it" ("Power of Discourse" 76). In her efforts to find a style that was distinct from Miller's, Nin also inaugurates her lifelong project of writing against patriarchy, being male-identified, or "acting like men." In light of the French feminists' call for a writing that would inscribe the female body, Nin's oft-repeated assertions about writing "as a woman" deserve further consideration. Many of Nin's claims to be experimenting with a feminine writing were first made in reference to the portraits based on her encounters with June Miller. Her accounts of her efforts to capture the enigmatic June in writing read as a plea for a feminine discourse. Of all the writers in this study, Nin's fictionalization of the identity process is the least Lacanian, and it is most suggestively described using the concepts of Kristeva and other French feminist theorists. Through her experimentation with a self-proclaimed feminine language in the June portraits, Nin anticipates both contemporary arguments for an *écriture féminine* and feminist psychoanalytic revisions of the process whereby gender identity is formed.[15]

The writers' dialogues concerning *House of Incest* are initiated by Miller's complaints, reported in the 1931–1934 *Diary,* that he could not understand what Nin was doing in this innovative work:

> Henry was mystified by my pages. Was it more than brocade, he asked, more than beautiful language? I was upset that he did not understand. I began to explain. Then he said, "Well you should give a clue; we are thrown into strangeness unexpectedly. This must be read a hundred times."
>
> Henry was writing about June so realistically, so directly, I felt she could not be penetrated that way. I wrote surrealistically. I took her dreams, the myth of June, her fantasies. But certainly myths are not mysterious, undecipherable. (*Diary* 130)

Nin defines their techniques in terms of opposition: Miller writes "realistically"; she writes "surrealistically." As a woman Nin is able to write about June in an intuitive way, illuminating the subject through a representation of women's dreams and myths, which Miller as a male cannot understand, much less emulate. By using the verb "penetrate," Nin slyly undermines the phallocentricity of her mentor's understanding: as a man he may penetrate the body of woman but not the totality of June because the feminine consciousness is impervious to the masculine.

The gendered artistic conflict over *House of Incest* emerges as a major point of contention in the *Diary* and inaugurates a shift in Nin's and Miller's previously assumed roles as protégée and mentor. After Nin explains her objectives to him, Miller becomes wildly enthusiastic about her prose poem. However, his subsequent efforts to rewrite it for her, which he describes as both "presumptuous" and "a sacrilege" (Nin, *Passion* 117, 146), as well as his parody "Into the Night Life," disclose his inability to appreciate it. Nin is distressed by the parody and realizes Miller's limitations as mentor: "Does he satirize what he does not understand? Was it a way of conquering what eludes him?" she asks rhetorically (*Diary* 131).

The first sequence of *House of Incest,* a prose poem divided into seven major narrative parts, is prefaced by a sort of mythical flashback, an account of the daughter's metaphorical "first birth," her encounter with the presymbolic regained through the medium of the dream:

> All round me a sulphurous transparency and my bones move as if made of rubber. I sway and float, stand on boneless toes listening for distant sounds, sounds beyond the reach of human ears, see things beyond the reach of human eyes. Born full of memories of the bells of the Atlantide. Always listening for lost sounds and searching for lost colors, standing forever on the threshold like one troubled with memories. (*Incest* 15)

It is significant that Nin presents this encounter in the "preface" retrospectively: though written in present tense, she uses analepsis, "the evocation after the fact of an event that took place earlier" (Genette

40). The prose poem also goes on to characterize the powerful but am-biguously sexed mother figure described by Kristeva as the "phallic mother" (*Revolution* 47, 65), a retrospective formulation.

This passage in *House of Incest* is much more explicit than the *Diary* in depicting a connection with the presymbolic through the encounter with a mother figure. Nin's woman's "myth" returns to the wholeness of the dyad, the pre-mirror-stage mother-child fusion. Fluid feminine images suggest Kristeva's semiotic *chora:* the *House of Incest* sequence places the narrator, an "uncompleted self" (*Incest* 15), in the maternal "giant bosom" of the sea. Her state of mind is pre-analytic, in direct physical contact with the mother: "There were no currents of thoughts, only the caress of flow and desire mingling, touching, travelling, with-drawing, wandering" (17). The passage ends with the narrator's sym-bolic birth, "I awoke at dawn, thrown up on a rock" (17). Thus, it dra-matizes both the mother-daughter bond and the formative stage of acquiring separate identity, "moving into the body of another" (17).

The dramatization in *House of Incest* contains less of the mysterious femme fatale than the *Diary* portrait, and more emphasis on mother-daughter bonding. On one hand Sabina is the destructive warrior woman, a powerful role model for the daughter: "The steel necklace on her throat flashed like summer lightning and the sound of the steel was like the clashing of swords . . . . Her necklace thrown around the world's neck, unmeltable" (*Incest* 21). At the same time Sabina em-bodies nurturing, maternal qualities: "there is no mockery between women. One lies down at peace as on one's own breast" (24). As in the 1931–1934 *Diary,* the narrator recognizes a feminine self she had not previously acknowledged: "From all men I was different, and my-self, but I see in you that part of me which is you. I feel you in me; I feel my own voice becoming heavier" (*Incest* 26). The images are those of doubles, of mirroring, because as a woman the narrator is acquiring both a sense of self and a sense of self-as-other. And both are femi-nine: "Deep into each other we turned our harlot eyes" (22). The Sabina sequence allegorically represents the daughter's discovery of her gendered identity and potential subjectivity.

Sharon Spencer has described Nin's prose as an *écriture féminine* using Nin's own descriptor—a language of the "womb"—to describe a "flow-ing" language centered on women's (often tabooed) experiences (165). In different ways both the diaries and *House of Incest* correspond to re-cent definitions of *écriture féminine*. Christiane Makward succinctly de-fines the stylistic features of this discourse as "open, nonlinear, unfin-ished, fluid, exploded, fragmented, polysemic, attempting to 'speak the body,' i.e. the unconscious, involving silence, incorporating the simul-taneity of life as opposed to or clearly different from logical, nonam-biguous, so-called 'transparent' or functional language" (96). Nin's diary and prose poem exemplify this definition, but as she distills the portrait of June in *House of Incest,* Nin intensifies many features of this presymbolic, feminine discourse. The preface announces the writer's intent to write her body as she disgorges, simultaneously, her book and her heart. The fragmentation of the diary is exacerbated in the prose poem; the unconscious is not merely given expression (as in the diaries) but also visually represented in the highly symbolic "house of incest." Moreover, the texts are, in different senses, "unfinished": Nin continued to write her diary until the end of her life (but requested that the final volumes, detailing her fight with cancer, remain unpublished). The prose poem is eternally "unfinished" through its ambiguous final passages.

At the same time, the prose poem modifies the prose account of June from the *Diary,* and even the "symbolic shape" she describes in the *Diary* (128) is a blend, a prose poem, at once novella and poem, combining genres associated with the female (novelistic) and male (poetic) traditions. Although Nin's self-proclaimed purpose is to write as a woman, *House of Incest* was in one sense also written for men—in an effort to placate Miller and Rank, who complained that the diary was diffusing her energy as a writer.[16] Within *House of Incest* the narrator claims to be writing Sabina for men· "The soft secret yielding of woman I carved into men's brains with copper words; her image I tattooed in their eyes. They were consumed by the fever of their entrails" (*Incest* 22). In a major difference from the literalistic diary presentation, Nin attempts to communicate with men by delivering the portrait of a woman in symbolic language to which they can respond and by writing in a more exalted literary genre.

In the prose poem Nin echoes the associations established in her diary portrait, but she modifies the previous account of June by substituting more figurative, poetic language. Nin embellishes on the diary portrait by imbuing the portrait with surreal qualities: Sabina's "face was *suspended* in the darkness of the garden" (*Incest* 18; my emphasis). Sabina represents the primordial woman—god and mother—with her "ancient stare, heavy luxuriant centuries flickering in deep processions" (18). The surreal images do not say what Sabina is like, using simile, but render the essence defined by the unconscious and the dream. Much of the linguistic tension in *House of Incest* results from Nin's attempt, simultaneously, to depict June as a feminine archetype discovered through an encounter with the presymbolic and to bridge the gap of gendered discourse by representing her in the figurative language of the symbolic.

A MEDIATOR FOR PATRIARCHY

Both in the 1931–1934 *Diary* and in *House of Incest,* Nin presents the encounter with June as a metaphoric flirtation with lesbianism, which she finally rejects as incestuous, a narcissistic love of the self in the

Other. The woman-to-woman identification is presented as more literally lesbian and thus exclusively female in an erotic scene as it is constructed in *Henry and June*. Both the 1931–1934 *Diary* and *Henry and June* recount Nin's visit to a brothel at 32 rue Blondel for an "exhibition" of two female prostitutes making love. In the *Diary* account (as in the earlier scene introducing June to Anaïs), it is Henry who suggests the entertainment and who accompanies her. In *Henry and June*, however, it is Nin who takes the more active role: she suggests the visit to her husband, Hugo; she chooses the prostitutes herself; and she requests "lesbian poses."[17] The framing of the scene in the *Diary* provides another significant variation. Because the *Diary* lacks transitions between entries, their juxtaposition often creates a complex context. In the passage directly preceding the visit, Nin tells Miller his "relentless analysis of June leaves something out" and wonders if he'll ever "see the world as I do" (*Diary* 58). The brothel incident reveals what his patriarchal view cannot perceive: the woman-to-woman bond.

What is the function of the male voyeur who accompanies the female voyeur in this scene, compelled to gaze upon lesbian lovemaking? In the *Diary* passages that directly follow the 32 rue Blondel sequence, Nin proclaims: "I feel I have taken [Henry] into a new world" (*Diary* 60); it would seem that his instruction is a major objective. The two versions of the diary depict quite differently the male voyeur's responses. In the 1931–1934 diary, Henry's reaction is not rendered at all after he chooses the women. It would appear that the "new world" teaches—and silences—him. In contrast, Hugo's response is represented in *Henry and June*. The husband and wife are much more androgynous, reversing traditional gendered roles in their reactions. This more flexible heterosexual relationship permits Nin and her husband to experiment with more fluid gender roles. Toward the end of the scene, Nin exclaims:

> I am no longer woman; I am man. I am touching the core of June's being.
>
> I become aware of Hugo's feelings and say, "Do you want the woman? Take her. I swear to you I won't mind, darling."
>
> "I could come with anybody just now," he answers.
>
> The little woman is lying still. Then they are up and joking and the moment passes. Do I want . . . ? They unfasten my jacket; I say no, I don't want anything. (*Henry and June* 72)

The account in *Henry and June* places Nin in the more active, traditionally "masculine" role: imagining herself June's lover, offering prostitutes to her husband, being solicited by the women. Furthermore, in *Henry and June* (the less-censored version), Nin initiates the incident; it is her artistic creation, her fantasy.

The various versions of the episode refashion the June/Anaïs, mother/daughter dyad through an erotic fantasy in which the male role, even as gazer, is diminished. The participants and observers enter a vaginal, womblike room: "like a velvet-lined jewel casket. The walls are covered with red velvet." According to Nin the prostitutes are "like mother and daughter." The contrasting appearance of the two prostitutes— one "vivid, fat, coarse" and the other "small, feminine, almost timid" (*Diary* 59)—exaggerates and parodies the antithetical features of June and Anaïs, a contrast accentuated in Philip Kaufman's cinematic depiction of the scene, in which the "vivid" prostitute is a near-double of the actress who plays June and whom Nin seeks out alone, unsuccessfully, in a later scene. Although the lesbian sex scene with a male voyeur is a set piece in male-directed pornography, the traditional function of the male role is that of subject, suggesting that love between women exists for his titillation. In the episode represented in *Henry and June,* however, Nin breaks out of the convention to the extent that she adds a new figure, the female voyeur, whose primacy contests his role: she insists it is "*my* evening"; the *patronne* reassures them that, although there will be no man in the exhibition, they will "see *everything*" (71; emphasis added). But both versions make clear, in different ways, that although they perhaps do not see "everything," they do see something new, and see differently. The visit is an initiation into an exclusively female sexuality, one from which men are excluded.[18]

Thus, the two accounts of the scene emphasize rejection of the "third term" of the family triangle, the patriarchal obstacle to the mother-daughter relation. When the big woman ties on a rubber penis, the exhibition's love poses teach "nothing new" to Nin (*Henry and June* 71). The phallus is "a rosy thing, a caricature," but when it is discarded, the "little woman loves [the caresses], loves it better than the man's approach" (71). From the encounter Nin learns "a source of a new joy, which I had sometimes sensed but never definitely—that small core at the opening of the woman's lips, *just what the man passes by*" (72; emphasis added). This scene, in which the gazer gazes upon herself (the "little woman") in a figurative union with the presymbolic mother, also functions to reverse the usual psychoanalytical (Freudian) conception of the daughter's discovery of her mother's "castration." According to Nancy Chodorow, the daughter's "common genital arrangement with her mother does not work to her advantage in forming a bond with her mother . . . . her mother *prefers* people like her father . . . who have penises. She comes to want a penis, then, in order to win her mother's love" (125). In her revision, Chodorow softens the Freudian interpretation, reinterpreting the value of the penis as an instrument to gain the mother's affection. Nin's revision of the Freudian family triangle goes even further: the penis is now extraneous. Freed from the penis/phallus, the woman-woman gaze produces not castration fear (as for the male gazer) but the acquisition first of gender identity, then of libido.

The revision of Freud (and to a lesser extent Lacan) is accomplished in the 32 rue Blondel sequence—as well as the deprivileging of the male—in a scene included in *Henry and June* but excluded from the diary published in 1966. It is significant that the expurgated experience takes the form of a dream:

> I begged [June] to undress. Piece by piece I discovered her body, with cries of admiration, but in the nightmare I saw the defects of it, strange deformations. Still, she seemed altogether desirable. I begged her to let me see between her legs. She opened them and raised them, and there I saw flesh thickly covered with hard black hair, like a man's, but then the very tip of her flesh was snow-white. What horrified me was that she was moving frenziedly, and that the lips were opening and closing quickly like the mouth of the goldfish in the pool when he eats. I just watched her, fascinated and repulsed, and then I threw myself on her and said, "Let me put my tongue there," and she let me but she did not seem satisfied while I flicked at her. She seemed cold and restless. Suddenly she sat up, threw me down, and leaned over me, and as she lay over me I felt a penis touching me. I questioned her and she answered triumphantly, "Yes, I have a little one; aren't you glad?" (*Henry and June* 91)

This encounter suggests the daughter's discovery of her mother's Lacanian "lack," accompanied by the traditional threat of castration, but as the dream progresses Nin rewrites the Freudian/Lacanian scenario of the daughter's supposed horror at finding her mother has no penis/phallus. According to Freud this discovery—and the daughter's return to the mother, a movement toward identification—would be accompanied by the daughter's desire to have a baby as compensation for the absent penis. Anticipating Chodorow's revision of Freud, however, in the dream Nin enacts the daughter's wish to satisfy the mother's desire, as well as the impulse to be the object of the mother's desire. She is unsuccessful in these efforts, though she does participate in a failed contest for erotic dominance ("she . . . threw me down") with the mother. Ultimately, Nin discovers that the mother has a clitoris, "a little one," of her own. In *Henry and June* this encounter reveals to Nin a female sexuality symbolized as presence, not absence; she does not discover lack but the potentiality of her own genitalia, asserting the presence of the clitoris, foreshadowed in the discovery at 32 rue Blondel. Nin toys with lesbianism in this dream sequence and revises Freud to some degree. Yet ultimately she compromises: formulating women's erotic potential as powerful but still essentially phallic (a "little one"), conceived within terms of patriarchal domination.

The first published version of the June story ("Djuna") excluded the brothel episode; but in the story Johanna claims she used "a Lesbian act" to revenge herself on Djuna ("Djuna" 106). Here the two women terminate a lesbian flirtation with charges that combine a mutual rejection of each other with collaboration with the male. Djuna comes to see Johanna as a "whore" and assumes a male stance: "I walked away unsteadily, like a man returning from a heavy debauch" (88). She betrays Johanna, oblivious to the needs of her "child-like face" (88), letting her "depart with her deep distress, like a whore one has finished kissing, instead of withholding her and making her the gift of my love" (89). For her part, Johanna retaliates by calling Djuna a "spider," who will "devour" Hans; "he's got a Lesbian on his hands" (107)—an accusation Hans made previously in the story against Johanna. Thus, in the earliest published version, the woman-woman relationship was ultimately subordinated. Nevertheless, this triangular sequence ends on an ironic note. Convinced that Hans is eavesdropping outside the door, they open it only to discover him asleep, snoring, both external to and oblivious of their conflict: "Even when his eyes were closed they seemed to be laughing" (108). Nin's revisions vacillate between an ironic suggestion about the male's extraneousness and an assertion of it. Likewise, the diminishing of the male role—to a mere onlooker in the rue Blondel sequence and to a reduced phallic presence (mirrored in the woman's "little one") in the erotic dream in *Henry and June*—suggests the inevitable isolation of men and women, resulting from gender difference and the asymmetry of the family triangle. The child can never identify with both parents in the same way; there are concomitantly certain gendered and linguistic experiences that men and women never can share. Nin privileges the woman-woman bond, but she also exhibits it, problematically, for a male gazer.

The June scenes ultimately reveal the equivocal nature of Nin's role as aesthetic mediator between the sexes. This role makes some feminist critics uncomfortable. To Judith Roof, for example, the rue Blondel episode demonstrates how "attempts to depict lesbian sexuality expose the governing binary logic of heterosexuality" (2). Roof is correct in that Nin never completely transcends or writes beyond patriarchy; but she does rewrite it with an emphasis on the female. Not content to write an exclusionary lesbian fantasy, Nin enacts subject status through communicating it to Henry/Hugo/a male (as well as female) audience. Only in the dream (the feminine subconscious or presymbolic) is man excluded. Her insistence on including the male reveals Nin's refusal either to abandon men or to cede them subject status. Her aesthetic commitment to both sexes is articulated in a typical statement about the feminist movement:

> There is far too much imitation of man in the Women's Movement. That is merely a displacement of power. Woman's definition of power should be different. It should be based on relation to others. The

women who truly identify with their oppressor as the cliché phrase
goes, are the women who are acting like men, masculinizing themselves, not those who seek to convert or transform man. ("Notes on
Feminism" 28)

Politically and aesthetically, Nin tries to accomplish seemingly contradictory objectives, emphasizing both the difference of the sexes and
the mediating role of the woman.

. . .

In the diary published in 1966, as earlier in "Djuna," Nin denies
any "lesbian" impulse; she vows to "collaborate" with Miller in "understanding June" (*Diary* 41–42). This decision functions as an explanation for the stylistic and generic changes she makes when she re-
creates June in *House of Incest*. For Nin, a denial of "lesbian" impulses
represents a recognition that to write in feminine language, to write
for women only, is to relinquish the opportunity to help man understand woman and to abandon woman to the male gaze. Nin's an-
nounced objective of collaboration differs from the contemporary,
egalitarian use of the term *collaboration:* it is an act of mastery and a
declaration of subjectivity. Nin will write as a woman and act as mediator to articulate woman for man. In the *Diary* Nin dramatizes the
conflicting impulses of the woman writer: she views literalistic, prose
language and the feminine genre of the diary as her best vehicles, yet
to write in an exclusively feminine language and genre would be to
place herself outside of communication—incommunicado as it were—
with the literary community at large, leaving it to men to write
women for themselves and retaining the status quo, the patriarchal
literary tradition. Similarly, to identify fully with June, the presymbolic mother, is to remain inarticulately within the *chora*.

Nin attempts in *House of Incest* both to articulate her intuitive, feminine understanding of June and to communicate it to Everyman (or
Henry Miller), the representative of the symbolic discourse community. *House of Incest* is a double-discourse, revealing the daughter's
ability to speak two languages. Nin's prose poem reveals that her
dilemma is that of the woman writer in patriarchy. Her effort to serve
up a creation that will please men, articulated by means of a feminine
aesthetic, represents a major contradiction in her work.[19] Her complicity with male desire and language leads her to create for herself an ultrafeminine persona, which has been detrimental to her reception by
contemporary feminists. Yet Nin's accounts do not exclude or marginalize the female through the male gaze, in contrast to male-authored
accounts. Rather, her accounts establish a bond between subject and
object through woman-to-woman identification.

Nin's contribution has often been denigrated for perpetuating the feminine mystique or an essential femininity. It is true that she is more successful in her efforts to write against rather than beyond patriarchy. The June portraits suggest, however, the inevitable complexity of the woman writer's acquisition of subjectivity within a gendered discourse community. Nin's experiments with language and genre in the June portraits reveal the woman writer's uncomfortable stance: a Colossus of gendered discourse, she straddles the gap between masculine and feminine language. The irony of Nin's individual plight is that, in assuming the identity of a feminine writer, she may have excluded her writing from both the established literary canon and the revisionist canon of women's writing. Ultimately, by the time the romantic liaison with Miller evolved into a nonromantic professional friendship, Nin had moved on to define a professional writer's identity that yielded a financially remunerative and personally gratifying cult status in the 1970s, but a marginalized place in any canon by the century's end.

Rebecca West with novelist G. B. Stern and H. G. Wells.
Photograph courtesy of McFarlin Library,
Special Collections, University of Tulsa.

CHAPTER TWO

Revenge and Parodic Appropriation in Rebecca West's *Sunflower*

> If autobiography is not merely the drive to be other but the drive to exist in another medium, something may be done to reconcile the varied and apparently mutually exclusive drives that writers have displayed. The move to write oneself down as a text combines the impulse to confirm the self as it is (the same) and the impulse to become or to make it strange, ideal, or permanent (the other).
>
> —Fleishman, *Figures of Autobiography*

Rebecca West's unfinished novel *Sunflower*, written in the late 1920s and published posthumously in 1986, fictionalizes the final phase of her relationship with H. G. Wells through the characters Sybil Fassendyll ("Sunflower") and Lord Essington. The novel also fictionalizes her infatuation with Lord Beaverbrook, presented as Francis Pitt. Wells was notorious for his unconventional arrangement with his wife, Amy Catherine, whereby he was allowed "passades," or extramarital affairs to which she gave tacit consent.[1] Rebecca West and H. G. Wells met on September 27, 1912, and they became lovers in November or December of 1913 (Ray 13, 32). The affair lasted until 1923, and during that time Rebecca bore an illegitimate child. Although one critic wrote in 1986 that West "never exploited the fictional possibilities of the affair" (Orel 13), one might interrogate his use of the word "exploited."[2] Since *Sunflower* remained unpublished during her lifetime (probably because of its potentially libelous depiction of Beaverbrook), West never profited financially from her novelistic treatment of the relationship. Her motives were more intimate; her "exploitation" took the form of seemingly therapeutic—and retributive—texts.

She appropriated autobiographical material, a mutual possession, to exploit fictionalized versions of her liasons in *Sunflower* for nonpecuniary motives. West asked, "When I die how much will those

who come after me be able to discover about my most intimate relationships?" (Hammond 236). Her means of dealing with the "intimate relationships" was to write her own auto/biographical interpretation to counter both the experience itself and the various
versions presented in the novels and prose of her illegitimate son,
Anthony West, and her lover (his father) H. G. Wells.[3] Couples often
implicate a third party in their conflicts (as June became the focal
point for Nin and Miller), and in the West-Wells liaison, their son
became an active participant in the lovers' postromantic struggle
through his own literary production. The unconventional nature of
the liaison produced a transposition of family roles in both their
lives and their texts. Wells referred to Rebecca as a sister as well as a
lover. Anthony called his mother "Aunt" and his father "Wellsie."
Within this family, both mother and son were called "Panther"
(Anthony was even given Panther as his middle name). In her fiction
West textualizes Wells as an uncle and a baby. Using displacement
and substitution, often through the devices of acting and role-playing,
Rebecca's fictionalized auto/biography both reproduces and obscures
the rivalry and strange Oedipal permutations of her unconventional
family triangle.

In *Sunflower* the fictional lovers are both writers, rivals in the same
field: she is an actress; he, a Cabinet member. Though Sunflower and
Essington are not literally writers, the couple's major project is to
define (to figuratively name or write) Sunflower; their struggle—and
conflict—centers on her subject status. In real life West named herself, dropping her birth name, Cicely Fairfield, to adopt Ibsen's
Rebecca West when she began to write for the *Freewoman*.[4] But in
Sunflower she critiques the process through which "the Lacanian
subject . . . . inherits its language and its desires from the Other" (Silverman, *Semiotics* 199). Sunflower's vocation—acting—is a crucial
substitution through which West explores the construction of the self
(the actor) and various roles in relation to the Other (the
audience/the gaze).

The mutable roles that characterized West's liaison and its aftermath suggest alternatives to the unitary subject of conventional autobiography. Early in their relationship, West and Wells played the
roles of siblings, engaging in potentially egalitarian collaboration, as
they worked on literary criticism in which their common subject,
Henry James, plays the role of a father and a third party, giving their
partnership a triangular configuration.[5] In *Sunflower* and selected
prose works, West reassessed and rewrote her relationships with her
lovers, with her son, and with patriarchy more generally. These projects critique the values and seductions of patriarchy, particularly the
difficulty it presents for women's subjectivity. The flexible roles established in her liaison with Wells materialize in West's fictionalized

KING ALFRED'S COLLEGE
LIBRARY

auto/biography through her experiments with a plural, more varied sense of the self.

PUBLIC WRITING AS COURTSHIP AND INTIMATE EXPOSURE

As is typical in literary liaisons, where private and public worlds overlap, West and Wells used published writing as a form of personal communication, courtship, lovemaking, and revenge. Victoria Glendinning, the official biographer of Rebecca's early life, notes that "Wells and West conversed through their work, always, as well as in person"; for example, Wells used the depiction of Amanda in *The Research Magnificent* to send Rebecca "warnings" about behavior he found alienating (*West* 66, 65). It was his reaction to her taunting review of his novel *Marriage* that first brought the two together. In the review, published in the feminist journal *Freewoman* on September 19, 1912, West called Wells an "old maid among novelists," who indulged himself in "the sex obsession that lay clotted on *Ann Veronica* and *The New Machiavelli* like cold white sauce," and who exhibited "old maids' mania, the reaction towards the flesh of a mind too long absorbed in airships and colloids" ("Marriage" 64). Bonnie Kime Scott notes that these "culinary and spinsterly metaphors" attacked "Wells's virility" but did not alienate him, serving rather to initiate their ten-year affair (*Refiguring Modernism* 1:25). Scott tellingly uses a metaphor that eroticizes writing—West's review functioned as "foreplay," she claims (170), a metaphor significant for its combination of writing and sex, inextricably yoked in literary liaisons.

In the posthumously published autobiography of his love life, Wells reveals that West's writing attracted him even before he met her. Her byline stimulated and curiously materialized her existence for him: "She appeared first as the signature to a number of very witty and boldly written critical articles" (*Wells in Love* 94). In 1913 he described one of her articles in the *Clarion* as "the most beautiful love letter" (Scott, *Refiguring Modernism* 1:27). Before their affair began, he also tells of making love with Elizabeth von Arnim as an act of defiance, literally on top of an article in which the prudish Mrs. Humphrey Ward attacked Rebecca's reviews (Scott, *Refiguring Modernism* 1:25). Wells was attracted both by Rebecca's vigorous writing style and by the sexual-literary nature of her provocation; the challenging, ambivalent nature of their relationship was evident from the beginning.

In *Sunflower* West draws imagery and experiences from her own love affair to expose a shared private fantasy. In their intimate talk and letters, West and Wells depicted themselves as two strong felines: Wells was Jaguar, West was Panther; Wells illustrated his love letters with cats representing the lovers. In *Sunflower* West describes

Essington sitting "like some great cat with delicate bones, a puma or a cheetah" (48). Throughout the novel he looks like "a great big lovely cat" (58) who purrs, whose moustache is viewed as whiskers or "silver feelers" (54). By attributing feline qualities to Essington, not only does West identify him as Wells, publicizing the personal, but she also violates one of the cardinal rules of any sexual relationship: not to reveal the intimacies of the bedroom. The highly personal nature of this imagery is confirmed by Gordon Ray, who argues that Wells used the cat metaphors to avoid "mere grossness" in his love letters to West (38). We can only imagine what Wells intended when he wrote West to prepare for "thorough lickings" (Ray 75) upon his arrival. According to Ray, "Panther and Jaguar were far more than mere affectionate nicknames. They stood for the whole attitude toward life evolved by Rebecca and Wells, who continued to use these names as long as their love lasted. They emphasized the ruthless withdrawal from society that the relationship entailed, the fact that Rebecca and Wells were not part of the pack and did not acknowledge its law" (36). Wells himself attributes the invention to West: "She filled our intimate world with fantasies and nicknames" (*Wells in Love* 108). Wells also revealed this intimate metaphor in his fiction, using the names Leopard and Cheetah in his novel *The Research Magnificent* (1915); indeed, his posthumously published auto/biographical "postscript," *H. G. Wells in Love* (1984), discloses intimate details about all of his affairs. In his response to West's treatment of him in her essay "Uncle Bennett," Wells wrote as a parting shot: "There my dear Pussy is some more stuff for your little behind. You sit down on it and think" (Glendinning, *West* 125). His tone hovers between intimacy and the condescension with which an adult might treat a child. Here the intimate cat name is both familiarized and colloquialized: Panther is demoted to "Pussy," a nickname for an everyday pet—and for a part of the female anatomy.

West's auto/biographical exposure, however, reveals much more than bedroom talk and personal intimacies: the feline imagery uncovers a dream, an idealized fantasy, of an egalitarian relationship. Panther and Jaguar are matched as powerful hunters, but their equality is difficult to sustain. West's revelation of intimacies has asymmetrical gendered implications that make it different from Wells's revelations. West not only appropriates the content of the relationship, but as a woman transforming intimate biography into print, she also appropriates the "public" space, a masculine realm under patriarchy: she displaces the private into that realm. It was Lord Beaverbrook rather than Wells, however, who thwarted this autobiographical transgression. After he heard gossip about the roman à clef she was writing, he sent out warnings that prevented her from publishing, and perhaps even from completing, *Sunflower*. In a letter of spring

1928, West describes him as "half mad, bitterly vindictive, and . . . unscrupulous" (*Selected Letters* 102). A letter from her friend, novelist G. B. Stern, commends West's "decision about *Sunflower*" and confesses: "I've been terrified for years over what might fall on you, when you published it. . . . If you have the courage to finish it, as you say, and then keep it back until our loved one has left us for a better land, and it's safe to do so, then I'll take my hat off to you" (undated letter; Tulsa).[6]

LITERARY SIBLINGS, MUTUAL INFLUENCE, PARALLEL PLAY

Because of Wells's age, masculine privilege, and more developed literary reputation, the young Rebecca West was "referred to in print as H. G.'s protégée" (Rollyson, *Life* 95), a subordinate characterization slighting the significant mutual influence of the partners. Although there is little evidence of full authorial collaboration (what Laird de fines as collaboration "at every stage of composition, playing all these roles of verbal companion and author, writer and editor, with each other" [7]), West and Wells did serve as informal editors, reading and commenting on each other's work. Rollyson describes how Wells turned to Rebecca when he was stalled in his work on *Britling* in 1915, quoting from a letter Wells wrote her: "It does no end of good to get you into my work. I was frightfully *tired* of the old book and now it's alive and fresh again. All because old Panther has read it" (*Life* 60).

Some critics, moreover, find evidence of mutual influence in their work. J. R. Hammond, for example, argues that Wells's influence on West, though "difficult to quantify" is "readily identifiable and traceable" (247); he finds the imagery in *Sunflower* indebted to Wells's short stories (245). There are parallels between Wells's impressionist style in *The Research Magnificent* (1915), a novel that fictionalizes their liaison, and West's *Harriet Hume* (1929), a stream-of-consciousness Jungian fantasy that Wells, in contrast to his habitual criticism of her fiction, found "too little appreciated" (*Wells in Love* 99). Hammond also claims that Rebecca had an influence on Wells's fiction, and that six of his major characters are based on her (243). William Scheick finds that the liaison informed Wells's *The Passionate Friends* (1913), *The Wife of Sir Isaac Harmon* (1914), as well as *The Research Magnificent* (1915; Hammond 8). When an author creates a fictional character based on autobiography, however, does this constitute a literary influence? In fictionalized auto/biography where a literary liaison is the subject, the border between literary and personal influence is more blurred than in other fiction or autobiography.

Wells was interested in being a mentor to West and tried to foster her writing career and her economic independence. He used his influence, for example, contacting Walter Lippmann about making her a contributing editor to *The New Republic* (Rollyson, *Life* 58). He gave her unsolicited advice about her writing, particularly suggesting that she follow an outline or plan. Glendinning describes Wells's criticism of West's wandering from her original plot in *The Judge* (*West* 84). But Margaret Diane Stetz views *Sunflower* as "the main site of her battle with Wells over her independence as a woman writer" (53); and Ann Norton finds that it "presents most of West's ideas about the problems of long-term sexual relationships" (113).

West dismissed Wells's criticism and caricatured him as a "nagging schoolmaster" (Hammond 124). When asked about male influence in an interview, West replied: "The men near you always hinder you" (Stetz 44). Stetz argues that Rebecca resisted Wells's desire to influence her fiction; she "continued to follow her own aesthetic instincts and to forge a style that was not compressed, but generous," and she sought literary mothers in the Brontës and literary fathers in the visual arts and music (52, 49). Moreover, Stetz claims that West specifically chose nonliterary areas to emulate because Wells "could not follow her" there and because "she enjoyed a superiority that even he acknowledged" (49). Henry James, D. H. Lawrence, Ford Madox Ford, and Marcel Proust are frequently cited as the male writers who most influenced West (Hammond 247; Winegarten 227). But Scott finds female writer Dora Marsden, editor of the feminist journal *Freewoman*, to be someone who "helped shape West's style" (*Refiguring Modernism* 1:42).

Early in West's relationship with Wells, he offered to employ her as a secretary, asking for her editorial help with the work that eventually became *Boon*, a parody of contemporary writers, Henry James foremost among them (Ray 30). Rather than subordinate her interest in James to Wells's, or collaborate with him on a joint study, West wrote her own slim book on James. These parallel books, published within a year of each other (Wells's in 1915, just before James's death, West's, just after his death, in 1916) are potentially rival projects that take the form of parallel play. Like young children playing side by side, each with an individual rather than a shared purpose yet aware of the presence of a companion, West and Wells adopted James as a common subject, while each developed an agenda in relation to his work. As literary children, West and Wells are competing not for the individual attention of a father but for the opportunity to reject his influence.

At this point in the liaison, however, the rivalry between them is generally latent. Despite a generation's difference in their ages, Wells wrote West quasi-incestuously: "You are my sister" (Rollyson, *Life* 55). His use of the term "sister" reveals the egalitarian, nonhierarchical potential of the relationship that attracted West to Wells. Ironically,

West and Wells may have been closest to egalitarian roles early in their liaison, when their status as professional writers was publicly most unequal. Kram's finding that the cultivation stage of a mentorship is the least conflicted may explain their assumption of sibling roles. The parallel projects they chose may have also facilitated this greater equality, relative to their later roles and conflicts.

The gendered permutation of the traditional Oedipal father-son rivalry in the couple's parallel James projects establishes the Victorian novelist as a third party in the pattern of triangulated desire and conflict that recurs in various forms throughout West's life and career. West was writing her study of James during the winter of 1914–1915 during the last two trimesters of her pregnancy—simultaneously working on two creations, one might say, that were in some sense parallel, and (in the case of her child, Anthony, at least) collaborative with Wells. Wells wrote his study first and asked for her help with *Boon*, and he reciprocated, subsequently reading her study. Anthony West views the James projects as essentially competitive, at least on Rebecca's part: "Had my mother wished to drive a wedge between them, she could hardly have hit on a better way of doing it than by publishing this particular book at that particular moment" (*Aspects* 50). Rebecca and Anthony West are notoriously malicious in ascribing motives to each other, but he is correct that the project contained emotional subtexts—for both West and Wells. However, the third party in this triangle, James, played a pivotal role that Anthony West misses. Hammond views the essential conflict of the triangular project as between two male writers; Wells "regarded James as a man who, over a period of many years, had pretended to give him encouragement and praise whilst secretly despising his work (James had made his real attitude all too clear in 'The Younger Generation')" (96). Wells is thus using the James project to throw off a burdensome male mentor. Perhaps because of her difference from James as a woman, West's rejection is less personal and more political. Although she finds much to admire and to reject in James, her project exhibits signs of neither unqualified admiration nor a personal vendetta against him, but rather a generational literary ambivalence about a Victorian predecessor. At the same time, West's undertaking of this project reveals the naivety of her presumption that she can assume a place, without contestation, in the symbolic order represented by a revered male writer such as James.

Both West and Wells use the project to debate gender issues in that they both express dissatisfaction with James's women characters, but for different reasons. As a feminist West attacks the superficial, one-dimensional nature of his depictions: James "refused to dramatize in his imagination anything concerning women save their failures and successes as sexual beings; which is like judging a cutlet not by its flavour, but by the condition of its pink-paper frill" (*James* 85). It is interesting that this criticism of James echoes her initial criticism of Wells's preoccupation with women and sex in the review that precipitated their meeting. In contrast, Wells's criticism takes a different angle, more aesthetic than ideological. The Jamesian female character, he claims, lacks realism: she is too abstract, "a woman, yet not so much a woman as a disembodied intelligence in a feminine costume with one of those impalpable relationships . . . that people have with one another in the world of Henry James, an association of shadows, an atmospheric liaison" (*Boon* 122–23). West praises James's subtlety and "his capacity to imagine characters solidly and completely" (*James* 29), whereas Wells ridicules James's method of introducing characters, "going round with the lantern [as] when one is treacling for moths" (*Boon* 126). Wells is exasperated by his indirection: "You are never told the thing exactly. It is by indefinable suggestions, by exquisite approaches and startings back, by circumlocution the most delicate" (129–30). The major difference in the two studies is that West makes some pretense at an objective, balanced study, at defining James's value and appeal as a writer. Wells on the other hand finds a way to render ridiculous even those qualities that seem to be assets— the "exquisite approaches," for example.

Taking James as a common subject, the writers enact different, gendered roles in their rejections of him. Wells plays the rebellious, Bloomian literary son to settle a personal debt with James; West projects the youthful, defiant, passionate New Woman persona that initially attracted Wells. She grants James the status of "Master" ("Marriage" 104) and "genius" (117), yet she develops her criticism of him as a negative exemplar, defining what she does not want to be as a writer. Her metaphors are chosen to emphasize the infirmity, impotence, and age of her predecessor. In addition to his "invalid" sentences, he exhibits "an old man's lapses into tiresomeness, when he split hairs until there were no longer any hairs to split and his mental gesture became merely the making of agitated passes over a complete baldness" (*James* 116). West finds a certain enervation, a lack of intensity, in James's fiction: "The profound truth that an artist should feel passion for his subject was naturally distasteful to one who wanted to live wholly without violence even of the emotions; a preference for passionless detachment was at that date the mode in French literature, which was the only literature that he studied with any attention" (52).

Through their parallel projects on James, West and Wells try to define their individual aesthetics and settle a score, but the battles are neither reciprocal nor symmetrical. Both are trying to break away from the literary traditions of the past, but Wells avenges himself on James, the male predecessor, whereas West speaks through James to her male contemporary—and cannot resist revealing her disappointment in Wells's choice of a marriage of convenience (as she saw it) over one of passion. In a subtext emanating from her liaison she incorporates, in her reproach of James's protagonist Isabel Archer, a barb directed implicitly at Wells's continuing, largely asexual marriage to Amy Catherine Wells: "for there could be nothing less delicate than to marry a person for any reason but the consciousness of passion" (*James* 70).

During the early phase of their relationship, the rivalry between West and Wells remained diffused, even submerged, in keeping with the enthusiasm of a new mentorship. The parallel James projects might have developed into the earliest stages of collaboration, which Laird defines as a "conversation [through which] a creative work is contextualized and conceptually generated as well as inaugurated" (8). Their early focus, however, was on developing and articulating their individual aesthetics in relation to their literary predecessors as well as to each other. When the relationship began to deteriorate in the 1920s—at the time of West's publication of *The Judge* (1922), and certainly by the publication of *The Strange Necessity* (1928)—and their passion evolved into a conflicted, postromantic friendship, literary production became a site of rivalry and a focal point for articulating their general dissatisfaction with each other.

DISPLACEMENT, PARODIC REPRESENTATION, AND SATIRE IN *SUNFLOWER*

Over the years West reassessed her relationship with Wells and described it variously. In 1944 she wrote in her diary "that he treated me with the sharpest cruelty imaginable for those horrible years, that he humiliated me . . . that he overworked me and refused to allow me to rest when I was ill, that he has cheated me of all but one child, that his perpetual irascibility ruined my nerves, that he isolated me and drove away all my friends" (Ray 120). In 1949, during her marriage to Henry Andrews, West could not see her relationship with Wells as "anything but an utter failure and a waste of my youth" (Glendinning, *West* 210). But in 1973 she claimed, "Wells was a delightful person to be with, his company was on a level with seeing Nureyev dance or hearing Tito Gobbi sing" (Hammond 142). A letter she wrote shortly after his death in August 1946 to the daughter-in-law who also worked as his secretary encompasses both poles of her ambivalence:

> I loved him all my life and always will, and I bitterly reproach myself for not having stayed with him, because I think I was fairly good for him. But you know the reverse of the medal, the tyranny that was the incorrigible part of him. I could not have submitted to it all my life—nor do I

think that he could have loved me or that I could have loved him if I had been the kind of person that could. And indeed he got on pretty well without me. (Ray 193)

In another letter from the same time, West wrote a friend: "Dear H. G., he was a devil, he ruined my life, he starved me, he was an inexhaustible source of love and friendship to me for thirty five years, we should never have met, I was the one person he cared to see to the end, I feel desolate because he is gone" (Scott, "Refiguring" 27; West's punctuation).[7] Although her ambivalence about their liaison was never resolved, in *Sunflower* it is explored and worked through, in a retrospective process similar to psychoanalysis, by being recast in fiction. Whereas psychoanalysis is a process, fictionalized auto/biography results in a product, written for the writer and for posterity—written, as Fleishman comments, not only to record what was but to make it "strange, ideal, or . . . 'other'" (33).

Fictionalized relationships often recast the original experience using parody as a kind of literary revenge. The parody, imitation for comic effect, is often achieved through displacement, substituting an ironic fictional context for the biographical original. "Defamiliarization through quotation in an incongruous context is of course the defining characteristic of parody," according to Rita Felski (101). West adapts this technique as her lover's actual words appear recontextualized: the fictionalized "quotation" is taken from the biographical rather than from a literary context. Rather than reflecting Wells's texts in parodic imitation, West's parody often takes the form of personal caricature, a ludicrous exaggeration of Wells's own character. In *Sunflower* she creates a series of deflationary metaphors to describe his fictional counterpart, challenging and deauthenticating reality by casting it mockingly in a different mode. As she moves from the caricature of a particular man to a critique of masculinist values, however, West's parody enlarges into satire. Hutcheon explains that, although parody and satire often work together and are often confused, satire "is extramural (social, moral) in its ameliorative aim to hold up to ridicule the vices and follies of mankind, with an eye to their correction" (43). The nearly 270 pages of the *Sunflower* manuscript (Tulsa) that West completed, of a projected ninety thousand words, describe a romantic triangle between Lord Essington, Sunflower, and Francis Pitt, a triangle that anatomizes the abuses of patriarchal power, using parodic depictions of Wells to develop a larger, satiric feminist critique.

Early in the novel Essington is repeatedly and unerotically described as an infant, viewed tolerantly but maternally by Sunflower. He "rub[s] his face against her warm flesh like a baby or a puppy" (*Sunflower* 16). Her bedroom is not the site of erotic play but rather a place where Essington indulges in "childlike gusts of angry weeping in her bed" (26). West's juxtaposition uses the infant metaphor to undermine the reality of the relationship as Essington and Sunflower each defines it. For example, the limited first-person stream-of-consciousness narrative shows that Sunflower believes she understands something only after Essington has provided an explanation. Yet within the same sentence his authority is undercut, and it is revealed that his perception is defectively egocentric: he "cr[ies] out for her with closed eyes, utterly dependent and quite uninterested in how she might be, like a very young baby with its mother" (5). Although the fictional version is exaggerated, the child-mother dynamic was indeed part of West's relationship with Wells, "who wanted sex but also mothering, whose letters to Rebecca were childlike and needy" (Rollyson, *Life* 71).[8]

West's auto/biographical depictions parodically recontextualize material from her real-life relationships, often using displacement and reversal as major appropriative techniques. For instance, words uttered by one partner in life are attributed to the other in fiction. As their relationship was ending, Wells wrote her in June 1924: "You are the woman of my life and I've got a great desire to liquidate what is left of our old bankruptcy and get back to terms again" (Ray 158). In the novel, however, it is Sunflower who invokes the bankruptcy metaphor and in an entirely different context. Thinking of "the central falsity of her life," the seemingly inarticulate Sunflower creates metaphors to describe it: "She saw a vast desert. The words bankruptcy, starvation, crashed through her mind. The trapped rat feeling that came to her often in the night came on now in spite of the sunshine" (*Sunflower* 18). For Sunflower "bankruptcy" defines not capital to be reinvested but the poverty of the relationship, which leads inevitably to its end. Another kind of displacement enables the writer to criticize her partner through the words of an outsider, a fictional character without any biographical counterpart, the protagonist's friend Maxine, who articulates a criticism of Essington that applies also to the West-Wells liaison. Maxine calls Essington a hypocrite because he disdains alcohol and yet he makes "just as much a pig of himself swilling down your youth as other men do when they swill down champagne" (217–18).

West's fictional appropriation of the relationship goes beyond parody and personal writing-as-revenge. Through a sustained social critique it satirizes the patriarchal values Wells had come to represent for her. A major parodic strategy of this novel is to exaggerate the stereotypical gender binaries through the characters of Essington and Sunflower, showing each to be both victim and agent of socially constructed gender opposition, the target of her social satire. Scott argues that West has a particular "engagement with this structure," and that she specifically "'re-figured' binary reasoning in . . . *The Judge* and *Harriet Hume*" ("Refiguring the Binary" 169, 172). Such revisions of gender binaries work through hyperbole in *Sunflower*. Whereas Essington is all intellect, an enemy of instinct, Sunflower is maternal (though childless) and intuitive, an interesting contrast to the young West, who saw herself as unmaternal. Essington epitomizes Wells's ultralogical (phallologocentric) intellect: "It was his faith that nothing could be evil save the passionate instinctive gesture: thought was the means by which mankind was saved from its vile propensity to instinct. Because the means he took to batten his egotism on life was cool and intellectual he felt they must be saved and should be pushed to the extremest lengths" (*Sunflower* 154). Essington's intellect is characterized as a sterile, clinical weapon: his speech is "a scalpel," a "surgical instrument; kept in the locked cabinet of silence when it was not required for real work" (53). He is devoid of interest in people and nature, the sensual and the aesthetic: "Nowadays it seemed as if hardly anything concerning personality could hold his attention; he cared only for thick books; for interminable talks about ideas that would go on being true if the human body had no flesh on its bones, if trees were not green in summer, if there were no such thing in the world as sound" (6).[9] Although the portrait of Wells as Lord Essington pays tribute to his wit, his verbal proficiency, and his intelligence, the novel shows that these traits have been extensively developed at the expense of his emotional side (a frequent feminist complaint about the deficiencies of patriarchy).[10] When Pitt's friend Hurrell is dying of tuberculosis, Essington identifies with him and tries to show compassion. Yet when Hurrell begins to cough blood, neither Pitt nor Essington can bear the physical manifestation of the illness, and ultimately the crisis is left for Sunflower and the nurse.

West parodies her own class conflicts with her lover through a displacement creating alternative social class backgrounds for the fictional lovers in *Sunflower*. Essington is a lord whereas Wells's parents were actually of the trade and servant class; Essington is a gentleman, compared to his romantic but vulgar rival, Francis Pitt. There are, nevertheless, hints of Wells's own struggle for upward mobility in Essington's resentment concerning the depletion of family finances by his parents' numerous children, the reason Essington had to teach to pay for his college education. Essington inherited wealth, not from his own family but from a widowed politician whom he served (*Sunflower* 46). West, whose own family was impoverished but of a more genteel background, is given more humble fictional antecedents: Sunflower is a former shopgirl, berated in the novel for her cockney accent (78). Elevating Wells fictionally to the status of lord might seem a technique to reveal his essential gentility or a tribute to his upward social mobility; on the other hand it makes Essington's denigration of the lower-class Sunflower all the more ungentlemanly. Anthony West argues that social class parody was one of Rebecca West's weapons, that she used her status as critic "to finish my father off as quickly as possible" (*Aspects* 369). According to Anthony's interpretation of his mother's motivation in *The Strange Necessity,* she assigned the lower-class name Queenie to Wells's typical woman character in order to suggest that "he had a cockney imagination, and that he had never been able to rise above its limitations" (*Aspects* 369, 370).

In West's notes for the projected ending of *Sunflower,* social class played a major role in the plot; Sunflower was to run away to America, seek love with a poor man (the antithesis of Essington), and make her living as a waitress. Her experiences in America were to place her in contact with men of diverse social classes: she "surrenders herself to George Mayhew, the head of a great packing house," but she also experiences African American culture, "negroes," in a sequence where she goes to church in Harlem and "falls at the negro preacher's feet." Finally, she would get a job as a hotel waitress in a small Illinois town (Notes for novel; Tulsa). Evidently West thought that social class disparity was an obstacle for her fictional character. The fictional couple is used satirically to critique a social system wherein males hold the financial advantage and it is socially acceptable for them to look to the lower class to satisfy their physical needs. This detail suggests (as so many others that significantly rewrite her relationship with Wells) that West is using parody to exaggerate autobiographical material or to create alternatives that move toward satire as she explores larger problems of gender and class hierarchy within society. In her notes for the novel, West identified two thematic premises: first that women "have remained close to the primitive type because doing the same job—wife and motherhood. Men have departed from the primitive type because they are doing different jobs"; and second that the "type of civilization men have produced demands great men—greatness that presses too hardly on the men. They are bound to buckle under the strain" (Notes for novel, Tulsa; see also Glendinning, "Afterword" 276). Hegemony, thus, is a problem for both those who wield power and those who struggle against it.

West relied upon parodic displacement again in an essay entitled "Uncle Bennett," forming part of her collection of republished articles, *The Strange Necessity* (1928). In this piece Wells is one of four literary "uncles" (along with Shaw, Galsworthy, and Bennett) who influenced writers of West's generation. Wells is cast as an uncle, but her description equally suggests a lover visiting his mistress: "Uncle Wells arrived always a little out of breath, with his arms full of parcels, sometimes rather carelessly tied, but always bursting with all manner of attractive gifts" ("Uncle" 199). The gifts he brings are his books, a metaphor for the characteristic "gifts" of the literary liaison. Both the uncle and the lover are dominant figures in relation to the subject—in contrast to the more egalitarian feline representations characterizing the earlier phase of the relationship. The uncle, according to Scott, is a figure for West's desire: "Powerful men on the model of the Edwardian uncle attracted, courted, and enervated West throughout her life. The most compelling example of them was Lord Beaverbrook—William Maxwell Aitken, whom she had met socially with Wells and wanted as his successor" (*Refiguring Modernism* 1:30).

The uncle in West's essay, however, is more parodic than powerful. Echoing her ambivalent treatment of him in the review that initiated their relationship, West attacks Wells personally in sexual and gendered terms. His seductions are feminized; he extinguishes "all the lights except the lamp with the pink silk shade . . . warbling in too fruity a tenor." In contrast to the firm, tight (tumescent) writing generally held up as a "masculine" model, Wells's "prose suddenly loses its firmness and begins to shake like blanc-mange" ("Uncle" 199–200). In a later passage he is presented metaphorically as a pregnant mother. The infant he gives birth to, however, is a cheap, lewd, imaginative creation that reflects, Pygmalion-style, his own lust, sending "into the world a large blond novelette with a heaving bosom called *The Passionate Friends*" (204). West's emasculating/feminizing metaphors criticize his aesthetic taste and sexuality. Written by his former mistress, the essay contains a coded, intimate attack on his potency as both writer and lover.

In contrast to his bemused reaction to the critical review that brought them together, Wells responded angrily to this attack (Hammond 165), revealing the previously latent, competitive underside that has now emerged in the postromantic-posterotic phase of the liaison. He uses a rebuttal to initiate criticism of her fiction: "*The Strange Necessity* only does for your critical side what *The Judge* did for your pretensions as a novelist. You have a most elaborate, intricate and elusive style which is admirably suited for a personal humorous novel" (which she had *not* written in either case). Wells continues by claiming of *The Judge* that as "a whole it is a sham. . . . It is a beautiful voice and a keen and sensitive mind doing 'Big thinks' to the utmost of its ability—which is nil" (Rollyson, *Life* 126). Wells moves adroitly from her criticism of his fiction to an attack on her fiction. The compliment on her sensitive "mind" is undercut by an attack on her ability to deal with great thoughts and the novel of ideas—obviously his domain.

Had *Sunflower* been completed and published in the 1920s it would probably have been viewed by Wells—and by Beaverbrook—as a brutal disclosure of personal affairs and individual eccentricities. It is ironic that Beaverbrook nevertheless wanted to serialize, in the newspapers he owned, Anthony West's novel *Heritage*, which contained a cruel portrait of his mother as the actress Naomi Savage. Beaverbrook was forestalled only by the combined forces of Rebecca West and Wells's legitimate sons, Gip and Frank Wells (Glendinning, *West* 217). Rebecca West is clearly aware of the implications of an intimate exposé, as shown by her self-referential treatment of Sunflower's public exposure. Essington fumes when his private nickname for his mistress becomes public. It is exposed in the caption to a photograph in the *Daily Show:* "Miss Sybil Fassendyll, the famous actress, who is England's favourite representative of the type of blonde beauty. Tall and slim and golden-haired and sunny in face and disposition, she is known to her friends as 'Sunflower'" (*Sunflower* 20). Sunflower is not only named by her lover but also defined by the press, which views her as a national type, walking propaganda for the fair, amiable British. In naming her Sunflower (just as Wells changed his wife's name from Amy Catherine to Jane), Essington bestows a signifier on her. In Lacanian terms, a "given signifier (a pronoun, a personal name) grants the subject access to the symbolic order, but alienates it not only from its own needs but from its drives" (Silverman, *Semiotics* 200). Through this act, then, Sunflower enters the symbolic, the domain of the father, of patriarchy; but she is inscribed in his terms. Defined by Essington and by society, Sunflower clearly needs her own subjectivity. Despite Essington's anger, Sunflower believes, "it was as likely as not that her secret name had leaked into print through his indiscretion, for he was careless in talking to her on the telephone in front of the servants and secretaries" (*Sunflower* 20).

Since everyone in the novel except strangers calls her Sunflower rather than Sybil, and the novel's very title exposes her private name, this incident dramatizes the consequences of illicit relationships for women during the first decades of the twentieth century. Sunflower is named—defined—in society by her affair with a public figure, an act that relegates a professional actress to the narrow and demeaning role of mistress. In the novel, the personal consequences of this naming are dramatized as strangers whisper about her; they think of her immediately in sexual terms because the affair is public knowledge. As a writer West may not have been quite as exposed as Sunflower is as an actress, yet she suffered similarly. When she lectured in America, for example, there was talk of banning her from Boston because of the perceived immorality of her personal life (Glendinning, *West* 86). Anthony was expelled from private school after Wells visited him there. Rebecca West was even subjected to attempted blackmail by a servant—apparently not apprised of Wells's marital arrangement—who threatened to inform Wells's wife of the affair (Ray 64).

It is not merely as an agent of patriarchy whose prerogative is naming that Essington becomes Sunflower's means of self-definition. As a result of his criticism she internalizes his labeling of her as "stupid" until her mind circles in self-defeating tautologies: "Since she was stupid, there was no good her thinking" (26). He becomes her internal Other; as a Lacanian critic describes the process: "One takes that causal alterity upon oneself, subjectifying that which had previously been experienced as an external, extraneous cause" (Fink xii). Early in the narrative Sunflower reacts to a passing idea by observing, "That had been Essington's thought; it was now hers. Though she rebelled against him, she was part of him. How could she leave him? How can one leave oneself?" (*Sunflower* 24). As Sunflower and Essington end their relationship, she fears that if "nobody was fond of you, you wouldn't quite exist" (239). Although initially she feels "she was already beginning to exist less definitely," she comes to realize that her earlier fears were delusional and "she felt more real than she had ever done before" (239).

Intimate exposure functions as auto/biographical indictment when West uses parodic exaggeration to present Essington as verbally abusive. Essington not only berates Sunflower for her stupidity, for her bad acting, for eating too much, for behaving inappropriately, but characteristically, he also blames the abuse on his victim: "Why do you let me do such awful things to you, why do you let me say these dreadful things! You don't look after me, Sunflower" (*Sunflower* 88). When he strikes her, near the end of the novel, he asks her to think "what you must have done to me to get me to the point of striking you!" (234). Essington's continued verbal abuse demeans her and prevents her from achieving subject status. West makes the character violent and obtuse, exaggerating through Essington Wells's abusive tendencies as a lover. West herself described incidents that suggest he may at times have mistreated her. She claimed that, during a vacation in 1922, "he forced [her] to play out painful public dramas as 'the ill-treated mistress' of a man twice her age" (Ray 117). His mistreatment was so evident, she claims, that a hotel proprietor and an English chaplain offered to assist her to escape (Ray 117). By creating in Sunflower a protagonist who appears to be of limited intelligence (compared to herself), her characterization emphasizes Essington's cruelty. Unlike Panther and Jaguar, Sunflower and Essington are not equally matched mentally or linguistically for verbal battle.

There is no suggestion by any of their biographers that Wells ever physically abused West, but the fictional relationship ends when Essington finally strikes Sunflower, something she has foreseen—and feared—for years.[11] In this scene, the climax of the novel, Essington's cruelty and cowardice are exposed at the same time as his real power and domination over Sunflower are undermined. Sunflower realizes, as the moment she has dreaded finally arrives, that he "was not as strong as she was" and "he had always been afraid of her and . . . all

his contempt had only been a disguise for fear" (*Sunflower* 233–34).[12]
It is the revelation of the spurious basis for hegemony within the relationship that brings it to an end: "I can't stay after this," Essington
comments (234). Since the relationship is premised on his supremacy—on an agreement concerning Sunflower's deficiency, her
"lack"—there is no longer a basis for it to continue. West designs the
scene in such a way that the blow itself is never actually dramatized, a
technique that undermines patriarchal violence by refusing it representation. The scene moves from Sunflower waiting "until his fist
came down on her breast" (233), to her realization that "he was going
to strike her again" (234), to her efforts to help him save face: "She
tried to help him in putting it all right by lurching backwards under
his blow" (234). Although, as is typical of their relationship, her efforts to bolster his masculine ego provoke feelings of her own failure—"she knew that he had seen what she had been trying to do and
seen too why she had failed" (234)—by not dramatizing the blow itself, West nevertheless refuses complicity with patriarchal violence at
the same time as she reveals its impact.[13] The scene epitomizes West's
technique of fictional auto/biographical exposure, which is both a
personal retaliation and a public exposé. West's appropriation seizes
the shared autobiographical relationship, characterized by incompati-
bility and possible verbal or physical abuse, in order to reproduce and
recast it—in the form of social critique.

ANOTHER RIVAL:
THE ROMANTIC SEDUCTIONS OF PATRIARCHY

Another of West's triangulated relationships is scripted in *Sunflower*
through the characters of Sunflower, Essington, and Pitt. As the long-
term affair with Essington comes to an unhappy end, Sunflower becomes increasingly attracted to Pitt and initially finds a measure of
freedom and independence in contemplating the new relationship.
The fictional triangulation does little, however, to establish the traditional comedic and dramatic conflict of a love triangle: Francis Pitt is
not so much a better, more correct love object as he is a vehicle for
the presentation of women's complicity with conventional romance.
The character facilitates ironic depiction of Sunflower, revealing that
her experiences with the abusive Essington have left her vulnerable to
fantasies of masculine protection. West uses Pitt not only as a foil to
Essington but also as a device, a catalyst, to reveal the complexity of
gender binaries and the seductions of patriarchy. Superficially Sunflower seems to vacillate between two men, but the actual third term
in the triangle is her own subjectivity.

Glendinning argues that Sunflower represents her creator's desire
for a more passive life—enacted through West's marriage to Henry

Andrews—but Sunflower may also be viewed as an example of what West feared for women. The notes for the unfinished portion of the novel present Sunflower as a floundering but courageous female Everywoman, setting out for America in search of faith and love. The search was, however, intended to be unsuccessful. West wrote that the "main theme [is] to show Sunflower giving herself away all the time" (Notes to novel; Tulsa). Sunflower's desire for subject status is repeatedly undermined by her quest for love. Norton points out that her nickname both "evokes the myth of Clytie, a nymph who was so obsessed by her love for Apollo that she did nothing but stare at the sun all day until she turned into a sunflower," and also characterizes her passivity under "Essington's domination" (29). Sunflower's attraction to Pitt depicts the emotional appeal of a more romantic patriarchy than that embodied by the tyrannical, intellectual, ultimately violent Essington.

Pitt seems at first to offer not only a conventional relationship but also a chance for Sunflower to achieve or acquire more active subject status; he is the manifestation, and the mediator, of her desire for this elusive and abstract acquisition. Sunflower wants to *acquire* Pitt's strength, not just submit to it. She believes that she will acquire Pitt's strength vicariously: "the force that rode her after him, as a huntsman rides a horse to hounds after the fox, dug its spurs into her and said, 'You fool, he has something that you need.' That was true. His strength, his power, she must have that" (*Sunflower* 204). Unlike Essington, who silences Sunflower when her speech is not as witty or original as his own, Pitt is a man to whom she "could tell . . . anything" (140). With him she feels a sexual desire that now appears to originate in herself, rather than merely as a response to masculine desire: "Suddenly and keenly she wanted him to be immediately her lover. For the first time she knew desire not as a golden cloud but as a darting line of light. But of course it could not happen, not anyhow, since she was with Essington" (193). The suggestive discourse echoes—and reverses—Freud's privileging of the amorphous vaginal response over the sharper, more focused clitoral stimulation and reflects West's own notoriously frank avowals of her own desire for sexual gratification.

Sunflower's sharply defined desire for Pitt seems in conflict with her fantasies of passivity. Sentences such as "[f]or some reason she felt as if her thirst for passivity were about to be quenched" (199) imply that the relation she seeks with Pitt is indeed that of the conventional, passive woman. Sue Thomas claims that *Sunflower* incorporates the "popular primitivistic romance of the 1920s, a genre which also ambiguously enthralled D. H. Lawrence in the same period" ("Questioning" 101) and that West developed a basically essentialist view of women's passivity ("Second Thoughts" 90ff). At the same time Thomas finds this view essentialist, she also finds that "West was arguing counter to the idea that female sexuality is innately passive by demonstrating that passivity is conditioned in woman by a sick culture" ("Second Thoughts" 94). Thomas's thesis explains the occasional seemingly antifeminist tone of *Sunflower* and the contradictory desires of its heroine. Norton views West's use of these conventional roles as evidence of her pervasive "paradoxical feminism." Sunflower's relationships with both Essington and Pitt "show the difficulty men have in accepting a successful, and sexual, woman's desires, and how their failure to achieve proper 'masculinity' results in women's failure to be properly 'feminine'" (Norton 29).

West gives the name "passivity," however, to a concept that differs significantly from woman's traditional role, defined in opposition to male activity. Although some of the fantasies Pitt inspires in Sunflower are of a passive nature, in her actual interactions with him she often assumes the active—albeit maternal—role. When he emerges blood-splattered from Hurrell's bedroom, for instance, she takes charge and cares for him as if he were "a drowsy baby" while he lies on the bed immobilized in horror and disgust. The metaphors with which she pictures herself in the relationship are not only those of conventional romance but of power and strength as well, of someone "called to some tremendous battle" (*Sunflower* 176) and with "her own inexorable intentions" (178). In a complex, seemingly contradictory passage, West uses Sunflower's stream of consciousness to reveal that what she calls passivity is also a receptiveness to her own desire. West creates a fluctuating, unstable play of gender roles appropriated from conventions of romantic courtship:

> Yet in a queer way it had been nice when she had been kneeling and he had been standing. She would have liked not to have got up but to kneel in front of him and take his hands and kiss them. Then perhaps he might have bent down and kissed her on the lips. It came to her like a thunderclap that there was nothing that a man can do to a woman in the way of love which she did not wish him to do to her. She was in love with Francis Pitt. Pleasure swept over her, pricking the palms of her hands; and she seemed to have been promised the kind of peace she had always longed for, an end to the fretfulness of using the will, passivity. She felt as if she had become as stable, as immovable as one of the chestnut trees. But this passivity would be more passionate than any activity, for like a tree she had a root, force was driving down through her body into the earth. It would work there in the darkness, it would tear violently up through the soil again and victoriously come into the light. She thought of that moment at her mother's

funeral when the four dark figures stood beside the hole in the ground
where there lay a black box holding the body which had caused them
all. The ground, the ground, she had at last become part of the process
that gets life out of the ground. (143)

As Sunflower vacillates between passive, conventionally feminine desire (what "a man can do to a woman") and a reversal of traditionally
gendered courtly love imagery (a woman here kneels to the man),
West deconstructs traditional binaries by associating Sunflower with
both masculine forces of insemination (the penetrating root) and feminine forces of gestation and growth (pushing up through the soil).
Sunflower wants to cultivate her intuitive, physical, maternal being—
including her reproductive potential—in ways the intellectual Essington denied her.

Binary gender opposition is also manifested through West's depiction of Sunflower's stereotypically feminine weakness for conventional romance clichés. Sunflower has fantasies of romantic thralldom
with Pitt, imagining herself "running across the flagstones to him in
the dress of some other age" (*Sunflower* 135) and as a "girl with a high
white coif on her head riding on a led palfrey through the forest into
a clearing . . . where she would find him between two tall guards, his
hands tied behind him" (175). The latter passage, however, varies the
convention notably by placing Pitt in the traditionally female position of bondage, confinement, and passivity. Inflating gendered
clichés and creating variations upon them, West emphasizes both the
mass appeal and the delusion of such impulses as she explores the
process of "gender socialization": "the process through which women
come to identify themselves as sexual beings, as beings that exist for
men. It is that process through which women internalize (make their
own) a male image of their sexuality *as* their identity as women"
(MacKinnon 531). According to Thomas, "West's ambivalently subversive and conservative interrogations of the narrative conventions of
romance . . . are central to an understanding of her shifting feminism" ("Second Thoughts" 95).

Sunflower naively believes that Pitt will rescue her from her desul-
tory relationship with Essington, but the "object" she is actually pursuing is neither man, but rather her own subject status. She credits
Pitt for having "a complete conception of her" (*Sunflower* 241), for
thinking "her completely into existence" (240), and "saving her"
(258). The use of a nonanalytical protagonist facilitates dramatic
irony, for it is clear, after the scene in which Essington strikes her, that
Sunflower is stronger than both men, characterized metaphorically as
infants. Through her protagonist's exaggerated romantic notions,
West dramatizes the obstacle that women's socialization poses to their
acquisition of subject status. Thomas argues that "West urged that the

subjectivities and bodies of women of all classes were rendered artificially passive, were deformed by corrupt and corrupting material practices contingent on patriarchal discourses of femininity and by understandings of femininity produced within those discourses" ("Second Thoughts" 92). One reviewer noted when the novel was first published that "it is the poignant contradiction between the vivid inner life of Sunflower's mind and fantasy, and her desire to be at rest in submission to a man, that is the real 'unfinished' centre of the novel, and which overrides the fact that West herself did not consider the book complete. In a sense the book is as complete as it ever could have been; Sunflower's desires are irresolvable" (Wandor 27). Such analysis ignores the pragmatic reasons the novel was not finished and published in West's lifetime, but it is true that her notes for the novel's unfinished portion do not solve—or even resolve—the protagonist's conflicts with patriarchy.

Thirty years old and ten years a man's mistress, Sunflower's discovery of her own desire is facilitated by her attraction to Pitt, but it is actually achieved only after she can conceive of herself as separate from Essington. In an autoerotic scene after she breaks with Essington Sunflower discovers her own body: "She passed her hands over her face and under her bedclothes down her body, over her round breasts, down the strong hoops of her ribs, down her flanks, admitting their beauty as honestly as if they were in marble" (*Sunflower* 240).[14] Sunflower's self-conscious recognition of her desire suggests a post-mirror-stage development of subjectivity: "Desire has its origins not only in the alienation of the subject from its being, but in the subject's perception of its distinctness from the objects with which it earlier identified" (Silverman, *Semiotics* 176). Still, the scene of self-discovery is introduced by an announcement that Sunflower's increased self-awareness is facilitated by Pitt, by the perception of an appreciative Other: "Because she knew he set a high value upon her, she felt infinitely precious" (*Sunflower* 240). Pitt is important to her perception of distinctness not in and of himself as a kinder successor to Essington but, rather, as he functions as a sensual man, and as an unattainable fetish to Sunflower's own desire and her growing perception of it.

Her attraction to Pitt—whom she characterizes in animal imagery, associating him with a fox and with dogs—allows her to recognize her desire, however unlikely it is that she would realize it in a relationship with him. Thomas notes, "the fantasy wild beasts Pitt subdues are her doubles" ("Questioning" 103). Glendinning further states that the novel is "about the unsatisfied physical desire of a woman for a man" ("Afterword" 268). When Pitt speaks to Sunflower of saving her strength, she realizes that sometimes "her body tingled from head to foot with undischarged force" (*Sunflower* 183). The adjective "undischarged," suggesting an as yet repressed ejaculation, attributes to Sunflower—as in the phallic images in the passage above—desires and power that are traditionally granted to men. At the same moment as Sunflower desires "passivity," she simultaneously associates herself with active phallic forces, which "driv[e] down," "work," and "tear." Thomas reads this passage as indicative of the "vital, earthing passivity" advocated by West during this period of her career and argues that in context "the trees [are] not phallic symbols" ("Second Thoughts" 94, 105n. 35). However, if one considers it "phallic" in Lacanian terms, signifying power and the traditional privilege that defines the masculine, as opposed to more literal male sexuality (the penis), the reference is indeed phallic, and it is significant that Sunflower appropriates this force for herself.

Her physical response to this new man is often active and assertive, yet Sunflower is mistaken about what Pitt actually offers, for he praises her silence: "Dear Sunflower, who hasn't a word to say for herself for ever so long after she comes into a room. Just sits mum. But who all the time is the best company in the world" (*Sunflower* 181). If their relationship were to develop, Pitt's valorization of Sunflower's nurturing qualities and her difference from the active male principle would relegate her to traditional feminine virtues. The projected ending of the novel—in which an enduring relationship with Pitt remains unrealized (as West's was with Beaverbrook)—emphasizes how deluded she was to fantasize subjectivity within such a relationship and how pervasive are the social conventions that hinder such acquisition.[15] In *Sunflower*, West exposes the complexities and difficulty of a female subjectivity conceived within patriarchal society.

ACTING THE SUBJECT

The fictional transposition of West's vocation as writer into Sunflower's vocation as actress has been viewed as an obvious extension of West's early training in the theater. West is fictionalized as an actress not only in *Sunflower* but also in H. G. Wells's *The World of William Clissold* (1926) and in Anthony West's autobiographical novel, *Heritage* (1955). By making Sunflower an actress rather than a writer, West publicly obscures the literary rivalry between Wells and herself. More important than this distinction for a Lacanian reading, however, is the essential parallel in the two professions: an actor, as a writer, creates characters—representations of the self. The acting profession is a vehicle to explore the creation of the self and the issue of subjectivity. The early pages of the novel demonstrate Sunflower's need to establish subject status, and her difficulty in distinguishing between life and art, between feeling and acting.

Non-analytic and nonverbal, Sunflower has difficulty in pinpointing her problem, but clearly she is no longer content merely to act, to create characters on stage and in films for the gaze of the Other. Sunflower "became absorbed in contemplation of this mystery which nowadays was constantly vexing her, as to what the art of living could possibly be. One went on to the stage properly dressed and made up as the character and said the words as they would be said in real life. How could there be anything more to it?" (*Sunflower* 3). The rhetorical question has an obvious answer. She wants to participate in "a process that nobody talked about, that could hardly be seen," but cannot do so because "she did not understand what it was" (34). The context of this passage associates the mysterious "process" with Sunflower's mother, with Alice Hester (the mother of eleven children), with reproduction, with the earth, and with materiality. It reveals the irony that despite—and because of—woman's archetypal association with creation and representation through giving birth, subjectivity is an especially vexed and complex acquisition for women under patriarchy

The central role of acting in the novel reveals that West, like Nin, is concerned with woman as perceived by the gaze. Whereas Nin explores the implications of a woman-woman gaze, however, West uses the more conventional male gaze to represent that of society. Thomas finds West's sense of "cultural crisis in heterosexual relationships" at this time to be grounded in "the masculine gaze" ("Questioning" 116). West does not necessarily assume that all spectators are male; there is a scene, for example, where Sunflower becomes the object of gossip for a mixed-sex crowd of people, who have recognized her because of her profession. Nonetheless, for West, the trope of the actress perceived by her audience is analogous to the woman subject and her difficulty in achieving subject status in patriarchal society. West's objective is social criticism; thus she assumes a male audience in order to critique the perception of women by the patriarchal status quo. Essington explains to Sunflower that her success results from the public's associating her with "two of the great legendary figures that man has invented everywhere and in all times: Venus and Cinderella" (*Sunflower* 7). Essington suggests that through her representation of these prototypes, man can imagine the perfect beauty of the goddess and upward social mobility. However, Sunflower's own image of her self—fragmented, immobilized, vulnerable, "a vast naked torso . . . fallen helpless on its side in some public place" (13)—emphasizes the consequences of constructing the self in relation to the needs of the Other. For Essington, Venus and Cinderella fed "desires that must be fed if man is not to lose heart and die" (7). As an actress, publicly displayed for the gaze of an audience, Sunflower cannot escape its construction of her self. She sees a movie poster of herself and she reflects: "What's the good of a person going to a film theatre to forget themself if all there is for them to see is themself?" (22).

West foregrounds the consequence of the gaze and public display, but she also suggests the potential of acting. Sunflower's method of assuming a character evokes the process of acquiring subjectivity:

> she had found out that if she imitated the facial expression and bodily motions of a really good actor she began to experience feelings that were evidently what he was feeling since they were not her own and made her understand his conception of the part. Often she had stood in the darkness of a stage-box and mimicked someone great, and found it work; though she had never gone on with it very long, for she found that the feelings that were roused in her were such as she wanted to use not on the stage but in real life. (*Sunflower* 30)

Sunflower discovers that through imitating subjectivity she can achieve it—as well as the troubling desire to retain it. Yet West also reveals the problematic role of the Other in the process; the subjectivity Sunflower experiments with is not only mediated through another, the "feeling" and "conception" of another, but through another actor (an Other enacting a self).

The process of subjectivization—"of making 'one's own' something that was formerly alien" (Fink xii)—is best shown in Sunflower's momentary assumption of the role of Alice Hester. In the long courtroom vignette early in the novel, Sunflower observes the lower-class woman who is charged with bigamy, a legal status she accepted in order to satisfy the common-law husband with whom she lived for forty years after he rescued her from her abusive legal husband. Alice Hester's situation ironically reflects Essington and Sunflower's. More literally than Essington's act of adultery, Hester enacts an illicit "ceremony of marriage" with one partner (*Sunflower* 30) while still married to another, knowingly becoming a bigamist. Hester's plight is an ironic echo of Essington's, however, because she is punished by a social system that privileges legal marriage over emotional commitment, whereas Essington, the adulterous husband, goes unpunished. Hester's motivation is to gratify her loved one; Essington's motive is self-gratification. For her part, Sunflower studies Alice Hester as a harbinger of her own fantasy of a woman rescued by love. As she watches Alice, she imitates her; Sunflower "assumed the pose" and "a sense of its rightness flowed like water through her body" (*Sunflower* 30). As she knows this "was a marvellously good woman" (30), Sunflower becomes this woman, but only temporarily, for her fantasy of Pitt's rescuing her aborts because the novel is unfinished. Moreover, West's projected ending refuses such romantic salvation.

The Alice Hester sequence also embodies a kind of Lacanian mirror-stage recognition. Early in the novel Sunflower is at the beginning of her acquisition of subject status, and she seeks in Alice Hester the model for a simple, unified self. This model, like Lacan's mirror image, however, is characterized by an "apparent smoothness and totality [that] is a myth. The image in which we first recognize ourselves is a *misrecognition*" (Rose, "Introduction II" 30). It is significant, therefore, that the sequence is placed at the start of the novel, and that Alice's maternal nature is emphasized, suggesting the centrality of the mother in the process of identity.

West, more optimistic than Lacan, argues that a woman can—and must—create her subject status herself. In 1913 she wrote in the retitled and reestablished *New Freewoman:* "the woman who is acting the principal part in her own ambitious play is unlikely to weep because she is not playing the principal part in some man's no more ambitious play" (Glendinning, *West* 51). West uses the acting profession in *Sun flower* to suggest woman's various possible roles, and the multiplicity of potential selves. The recurrence of fictionalized depictions of West as an actress—by herself, by Wells, and by her son—are significant not only autobiographically but also symbolically. Despite his brutal attacks on his mother's failings, Anthony West seems ultimately to grasp this point about the constructed self. His cruel fictionalized portrait of his mother as the actress Naomi Savage nevertheless ends with an insight about role-playing and the self.[16] The fictional son, Richard Savage Town,[17] muses on his mother's sudden flight from her dull husband, Colonel Arthur:

> I saw her as she had played to Max, the New Woman proud of herself and her freedom going to choose herself an equal as a partner; I saw her again as she had created herself for me, as the innocent victim of a Byron-like seducer; I saw her again in those middle years as a woman of the theatre existing only in her roles, a woman whose personal life was a mere diversion; and then I saw her once more as the natural aristocrat who, trapped by necessity into the humiliations of the life of the theatre, had been rescued and had returned to her true level as the Lady of Marshwood House. (*Heritage* 306)

She is, Town decides, "like the pieces of a jigsaw puzzle" (306). He reveals that Naomi is ultimately not a hypocrite but that these roles are a normal response to various people's expectations, and that he similarly had acted the varied roles of Colonel's Heir, Wronged Child, Unrecognized Genius, and so forth (308). This passage reveals that Rebecca West and Richard Town (and probably Anthony West) realize not only the multiplicity but also the perils of the constantly split nature of the subject, and the role of the Other in perceiving and establishing the subject. The subject can never escape the Other, because "the fate of the subject is necessarily bound up with the existence of the Other. The Other is the essential condition of self-consciousness" (Grosz, *Subversions* 6).

The complex, problematic nature of representation and subjectivity is further explored through West's interpolation in the novel of a two-page extract from a book on acting.[18] The book of drama theory by A. B. Walkley that Sunflower reads chastises academic Shakespeare critics for conceiving of the stage character as "an actual person" (*Sunflower* 86). The inclusion of Walkley's meditation on acting and the self functions as a metacommentary on the role of the self in the process of subjectivization. According to his reader-response perspective, a character is partially "determinate": only the "text, the stage directions, and *nothing else*" are fixed (Walkley's emphasis); the rest of the character is comprised of the perceiver's "surmise." West's inclusion of this extract and her own treatment of Sunflower as an actress reveal her skepticism about the nature of the subject as well as auto-biographical representation: there is no absolute, *complete* self apart from that created by a text, be it a play, a performance, or a fictional auto/biography. The self represented will be perceived variously since "no two imaginations coincide" (*Sunflower* 86).

The interpolated extract also comments on an earlier scene in the chapter, where Sunflower tells the story of Alice Hester to guests at an informal dinner, and various characters "interpret" her performance. Essington's interpretation is intellectual and logocentric: he wants to know whether Alice was able to tell "a coherent story" (*Sunflower* 63); his question contains implicit criticism of Sunflower's storytelling ability. Pitt's reaction discloses that he sees Alice's situation as analogous to Sunflower's: he asks, "Did she show any embarrassment at getting up in court . . . and owning to having lived with this man?" (63). Sunflower's interpretation, as Essington points out to her during their argument after dinner, gives away "the most intimate details" of their relationship, particularly her desire to have a child (78). In juxtaposing this scene and the extract on acting, West explores a reception theory of acting and the presentation of the self to the Other.

The placement of the interpolated passage on acting, at the beginning of the novel, illuminates Sunflower's prior inadequacy both as an actress and as a person seeking subject status. Walkley tells the actor that "your reality . . . while it prevents you from fully and satisfactorily representing *x*—that is to say, coinciding with the spectator's mental image of your part—will give you the great advantage over that pale image of definiteness and substance" (Walkley, quoted in *Sunflower* 87). West's use of dramatic irony to present Sunflower's professional ability ambiguously has vexed critics. Norton accepts the denigration of Sunflower's acting by some of the characters, because, she argues, Sunflower's "bad" acting indicates "how poorly she is suited to the actress role" (31). Rollyson argues (in my opinion correctly) that we can believe "she is maturing as an actress" (*Legacy* 49). As Sunflower begins to develop subject status—a "reality"—in the sec ond half of the novel, partly as a result of the receptiveness to her own desire that her experience with Pitt has elicited, her acting improves and she receives "several marvellous notices" (*Sunflower* 167).

In other words, until she acquires subject status Sunflower can be only "the spectator's mental image of [her] part" (Walkley, quoted in *Sunflower* 87). Although West finds that there is no complete, uncontested subject, subjectivity is, however, a prerequisite for a satisfying performance of the self: "You are able to offer him a real man for an imaginary one" (87). Walkley argues that the "real person and temperament of the actor" will inform the interpretation and subse quent representation of a character: "For it is, of course, flagrantly untrue, though often spoken of as true, that an actor can divest himself of his own personality and put on the personality of someone else. Just as an author is always really identical with his work . . . so the actor's histrionic is always part and parcel of his real everyday self" (87). Paradoxically, acting represents both subjectivity (or the process of subjectivization) and the obstacle to a fixed establishment of subject status.

West nevertheless evades one part of Walkley's argument—that the "author is always really identical with his work." She creates an "alternative self" through the character of Sunflower (Glendinning, "Afterword" 268), an alter ego, in many ways not just different from but the exact opposite of the dark, witty, articulate, independent West. Blond and maternal (though childless), Sunflower longs for a pram, whereas West gave birth at twenty-one and felt she was not "good with cubs" (Glendinning, *West* 114). West would appear to have been sexually vibrant. She felt men's treatment of women was a conspiracy to deny women sexual satisfaction: "men's extravagant sexuality is an affectation. Men have nearly all such extramarital relationships out of hostility to their wives, not that they have any personal hostility to them, but they dislike women in general, and a wife is one woman who has got the law on her side, and they punish her by denying her sexual satisfaction" (*Family Memories* 203). While she was writing *Sunflower* West was also undergoing psychoanalysis and she wrote notes on her treatment in some of the manuscript notebooks in which she drafted the novel (Notes on novel; Tulsa). She went into analysis to try to understand why her intelligence seemed to render her male lovers impotent (ironically, she described it as "her" problem). Sunflower, in contrast, does not seem to enjoy sex, at least not with Essington, but compares it to "giving a man a queer kind of medicine" (*Sunflower* 16), though she is evidently attracted to Pitt. The substantial differences between Sunflower and West as women subvert Lejeune's autobiographic conflation of author, narrator, and character—a variation that is an essential part of West's parodic auto/biography.

. . .

West's creation of an alterbiography in *Sunflower* and her emphasis on multiplicity—in the form of various kinds of triangular configurations of characters and parodic displacements of auto/biographical material as well as her treatment of acting and role-playing—demonstrate her awareness of the additional complications posed by woman's subjectivity in the patriarchal role of man's Other. An actress playing many different roles, Sunflower dramatizes—quite literally—that women's roles are social constructions. Acting is a metaphor for a fluid concept of the subject and illustrates the potentiality of a constantly decentered subject. This surprisingly postmodern view of the self is West's answer to the hegemony of the self/Other dyad. The more flexible, variable self vexes and contests the subjugation of the Other. In her own life West played—serially and alternatively—the parts of radical feminist, journalist, novelist, mistress, mother, and wife. West fictionalizes the mistress role, not to idealize her relationship with Wells, but to exaggerate the power imbalance and thus to enlarge her experience into a feminist statement about the problem of women's acquisition of subject status within patriarchy. Her depiction of Sunflower shows she does not agree with Walkley that "an author is always really identical with his work," though her writing of auto/biography concedes a semblance of identification or equivalence. By creating a protagonist who is more vulnerable, more typical of her era and its society, than herself, West foregrounds the dilemma of women in patriarchy. *Sunflower* explores alternative possibilities and societal dilemmas through parodic re-creation of West's own life in fiction.

West's need to appropriate the liaison fictionally for posterity is, in part, an inevitable impulse arising from her doubts about the possibility of truthful, honest communication between individuals or between writers and their readers: "my skepticism long ago led me to the belief that writers write for themselves and not for their readers, and that art has nothing to do with communication between person and person, only with communication between different parts of a person's mind. A writer composes a book in order to put down what the warring elements in him think on some subject which interests them all, and to arbitrate between them" ("Art of Skepticism" 168).

Accordingly, West fictionalizes internalized conflicts that characterized her relations with Wells, as well as with Beaverbrook and her son.
Her evocation of "warring elements" within the self echoes the Lacanian post-mirror-stage loss of unity. Her fictional auto/biography suggests that the desire to rewrite her life and to "exist in another
medium" (Fleishman 33) did not produce a coherent story or an
"ideal biography." Instead, the "warring elements" in *Sunflower* are often expressed as a battle for her protagonist's subjectivity, which is
not only an external societal struggle but also a private struggle with
the internalized Other.

Zelda and F. Scott Fitzgerald, 1921. Photograph reprinted by permission of Harold Ober Associates Incorporated on behalf of the Fitzgerald Trustees.
Courtesy of Princeton University Library.

CHAPTER THREE

Zelda Fitzgerald's
Save Me the Waltz
Household Plagiarism and
Other Crimes of the Heart

Estranged from language, women are visionaries, dancers who suffer as they speak.

—**Kristeva, "Interview"**

Zelda Fitzgerald has attracted the interest of feminists as a real-life exemplar of the story told in Charlotte Perkins Gilman's "The Yellow Wallpaper," a woman incarcerated after being driven mad by her husband's prohibition of her writing.[1] Although such interpretations are extreme, Zelda is the only writer in this study to issue public charges of plagiarism—albeit partly in jest—for her husband's theft of her work. Scott Fitzgerald is the only writer to insist—with considerable seriousness—that his partner stop writing altogether.[2] Dale Spender argues that among "examples of the appropriation of women's words by men, the case of Zelda Fitzgerald must rank as one of the most definitive and damning" (175). As with the other couples in this study, conflict was waged over shared autobiographical material, the role of writer, and subject status. This struggle had its origin in Scott's prior appropriation of Zelda, which remained largely uncontested until she reached her late twenties. Andrew Turnbull claims it was around 1927 that Zelda was "no longer satisfied to be simply the wife of Scott Fitzgerald. He had written her into his books and made her a legend, but she didn't want to be an artist's model—she wanted to be an artist herself. For a long time Zelda, the artist, had been obstructed by an indolent Zelda" (*Scott Fitzgerald* 177).

Zelda's biographer Nancy Milford counts six novels that to some degree fictionalize their marriage (234): Zelda's *Save Me the Waltz* (1932) and her unfinished *Caesar's Things;* Scott's *This Side of Paradise* (1920), *The Beautiful and the Damned* (1922), *The Great Gatsby* (1925), and *Tender Is the Night* (1934). This proliferation of novels demonstrates the central role of autobiography in both writers' fiction. One biographer of the couple, James Mellow, claims they "used these stories as a form of private communication. . . . Fiction became a method of discourse about their marriage, allowing them to air their grievances and dissatisfactions, fix the blame, indulge in bouts of self-justification—even, it seemed, to play roles they had not managed to play in the reality of their marriage" (*Lives* xvii). *Save Me the Waltz* is the most extreme example of such an airing. The novel not only dramatizes their marriage but became itself the focus of an unprecedented marital and literary dispute. Their conflict, in the relationship and its fictionalization, centers on a struggle for exclusive possession of shared material, for the role of writer, and for a unified self.

Through *Save Me the Waltz* Zelda attempts to reclaim her own autobiographical material, her self, as her own text. Zelda's version of her story in this novel not only universalizes her upbringing but also critiques it as a woman's initiation within patriarchy. Essential to Zelda's critique are two fictionalized sequences based on her experience as a ballet dancer. The parallel episodes challenge patriarchal gender roles by creating, alternatively, an idealized and a nightmare depiction of a female community. The first exclusively female community, led by the ballet instructor "Madame" in Paris, presents an alternative to the patriarchal family structure previously experienced by the main protagonist, Alabama. Her entrance into the female ballet world reiterates the conflicts of her family and marriage but seems to offer a solution to her problems of identity and vocation through initiation by Madame, a powerful mother figure. Although Alabama is ultimately thwarted as a dancer, and the fantasy community is exposed as an impossible dream by the second, parodic, nightmare sequence set in Naples, Alabama nevertheless comes to sense the need for her own subjectivity, defined in relation to patriarchy, as well as to achieve a sophisticated skepticism concerning the position of women in the symbolic order.

PRIVATE LIVES AND PUBLIC EXPOSURE

Zelda publicly communicated her private reservations about her husband's plagiarism through a book review. Her review was neither the taunting aphrodisiac written by West about—and to—H. G. Wells, nor the generous encomium written by Nin to advance publication of Henry Miller's *Tropic of Cancer*. Because of the glamorous-couple mystique of the Fitzgeralds, publishers and editors encouraged Zelda to write pert wifely reviews to promote her husband's writing, a task she subverted while ostensibly complying. In a review of *The Beautiful and the Damned*, solicited as a fluff promotional, she undermines her husband's originality by revealing that "on one page I recognized a portion of an old diary of mine which mysteriously disappeared shortly after my marriage, and also scraps of letters which, though considerably edited, sound to me vaguely familiar. In fact, Mr. Fitzgerald—I believe that is how he spells his name—seems to believe that plagiarism begins at home" ("Husband's" 388). She compares his learning to her own schoolgirl term papers for its "literary references and the attempt to convey a profound air of erudition. It reminds me in its more soggy moments of the essays I used to get up in school at the last minute by looking up strange names in the *Encyclopaedia Britannica*" (389). Nevertheless, the tone of the review is ambivalent rather than hostile, and as Spender points out, her "husband's habits were perceived as *playful* plagiarism at this stage" (177). Zelda was to develop full-fledged resentment only sometime later.

In addition to this curious review, another unusual artifact of the Fitzgerald marital-literary conflict is a 114-page report of the mediated dispute over Zelda's *Save Me the Waltz*, recorded while she was at the Henry Phipps Psychiatric Clinic of Johns Hopkins. Zelda and Scott's war over the novel's publication was refereed by Dr. Thomas Rennie at the clinic during May 1933 and was transcribed by a stenographer. Scott was angry because he had not been consulted before Zelda sent her manuscript to Scribner's editor Max Perkins (Mellow, *Lives* 396), although Zelda had informed him that she was at work on a novel. She had written him in March 1932, "I am proud of my novel, but I can hardly restrain myself enough to get it written. You will like it—It is distinctly École Fitzgerald, though more ecstatic than yours—Perhaps to [sic] much so" (F. Scott Fitzgerald, *Correspondence* 286).

Scott later claimed exclusive rights to the shared autobiographical material from their experiences on the Riviera in the early 1920s for his novel *Tender Is the Night,* published two years after *Save Me the Waltz.* At the time that Zelda was writing industriously, Scott was writing with difficulty and doubting his future as a novelist. According to Matthew Bruccoli, he "struggled with [the novel] for nearly a decade" (*Composition* xiv). Zelda was able to finish her novel in less than three months, though she was allowed to write only for two hours a day while institutionalized (Bruccoli, *Epic* 324). Ultimately, Scott attributed his own inability to publish a novel for several years to the distractions caused by Zelda's mental illness and his need to pay for her treatment (*Epic* 325).

Behaving privately as literary contestants, the Fitzgeralds were presented publicly as collaborators by the magazine *College Humor.* Contributing to the glitzy couple image, the editors touted "Southern Girl" as a story "the Fitzgeralds have done for this issue" (Milford 152). The statement is suspect as a promotion, but it does seem that the Fitzgeralds had some potential to work as collaborators—or at least as constructive critics of each others' work.[3] They did collaborate to some extent on one story, "Our Own Movie Queen," and Bruccoli argues that, although they "did not work successfully as collaborators" and "rarely collaborated," their work nevertheless suggests an "emotional collaboration" ("Preface" 12, 8). Scott was also capable of a kind of appropriative collaboration, mining Zelda for information to use in his fiction. According to his secretary, when writing *Tender Is the Night,* "he would go up to [Zelda's] room and ask advice about things they had done together, conversations they had. . . . He couldn't write about anything he didn't know" (quoted in Milford 267).

A potentially rich coupling of talent, the partners at times served as facilitators of each other's work; Zelda was not only a source for but also a critic of Scott's work. Scott's biographer Turnbull claims that Zelda "criticized with tangible results" *The Beautiful and the Damned* at proof stage, and Perkins was in agreement with Zelda's suggestion that Scott delete the moralistic ending he had written for the novel (Turnbull 129). On at least one occasion, Zelda asked Scott to "teach [her] to write" (Milford 205). He revised her writing and pushed her to complete her own revisions and corrections, even proposing to send her the manuscript of one of her previously written stories for her to revise while she was a patient at Prangins, a Swiss sanitarium, so he could get it published (Milford 163). At the same time, however, their ambivalence about joint authorship is revealed by Zelda's comments in an interview: "I like to write. Do you know, I thought my husband should write a perfectly good ending to one of the tales, and he wouldn't! He called them 'lop-sided,' too! Said they began at the end" ("Flapper" 112). Even the title of the interview, "What a 'Flapper Novelist' Thinks of His Wife," reflects the rampant misappropriation that surrounds the Fitzgeralds: during most of the interview Zelda is speaking about herself and the subtitle states that Scott Fitzgerald "Interviews His Own Bride" ("Flapper" 112); yet the title suggests that his opinions are the ones that predominate.

Contests over image and authorship characterize their marriage. For example, when Scott objected to the cover illustration of *The Beautiful and the Damned* for its depiction of "a sort of debauched edition of me," Zelda responded not with a more dignified illustration of Scott or of them as a couple, but with an illustration that evoked her own controversial public image, that of a slim nude blond with a bob haircut in a champagne glass (Milford 87).[4] Financial considerations motivated Scott's decisions to publicly ascribe his own or joint authorship to Zelda's work, but these decisions ultimately created friction between them.[5] A short story that Zelda may have primarily authored, "Our Own Movie Queen," was credited exclusively to Scott when it was published in 1925.[6] It received two stars in an annual short story collection. Milford explains that "Zelda was not, however, given credit for having written it. . . . He was paid $1,000 for it, which they split" (102). Although she appeared to accept the financial advantage of ceding the bylines to Scott, Zelda's subsequent anger and resentment over his appropriation of her authorship is graphically transcribed for posterity on extant magazine covers where she crossed out Scott's name and their joint byline and substituted "Zelda."[7] The result was the loss of her posthumous literary reputation: "That the image of Zelda as foolish and frivolous has been fostered is hardly surprising given that so much of her serious literary work appeared under her husband's name" (Spender 179). On the occasions that Zelda and Scott worked together, each struggled to achieve individual power, authority, and ultimately subjectivity.

MARITAL APPROPRIATION: ZELDA AS TEXT

The autobiographical material underpinning *Save Me the Waltz* raises issues about the role of gender in purported ownership of source material.[8] Elizabeth Aldrich argues that the Fitzgeralds' struggle for ownership of autobiographical material converged in the use of "Zelda as *text*, Scott's incorporation into his fiction of "her diaries and letters, essays and short fiction, even medical records relating to her" (131–32). Michelle Payne notes, "it has only been during the last twenty years that feminist critics have begun to question the gender politics involved in such appropriation" (39). According to Mary E. Wood, *Save Me the Waltz* contests Scott's "representations" of Zelda's life and "refuses to tell an explicit tale of mental illness." Wood views the novel as moving "into the foreground the cultural construction of women as the material of male art, whether in dance or psychiatry" and "wider issues of women's relationship to psychiatric authority, the institution of marriage, and the right to authorship" (253). Spender notes that this novel was a "battleground in the struggle to establish whether it was the husband or the wife who *owned* Zelda's life experience, and writing" (184). Judith Fetterley makes a similar argument about Scott's novel, contending that "*Tender Is the Night* has buried at its heart Scott's awareness that his sanity and his career were purchased at the price of Zelda's and purchased by his manipulation of the power accorded men over women" (127).

When Zelda had an opportunity to publish her diaries, Scott refused them to George Jean Nathan, coeditor of *The Smart Set* and Scott's first publisher, because he planned to incorporate some of the material into his own work (Milford 71). Indeed, Scott periodically transcribed Zelda's conversation and letters into his fiction. Lawton Campbell, one of Scott's Princeton friends who also knew Zelda from Montgomery, "was struck by Fitzgerald's habit of scribbling down Zelda's chance remarks on scraps of paper and the backs of envelopes" (Mellow, *Lives* 118). Words from one of Zelda's letters turned up in Rosalind's dialogue in *This Side of Paradise* (Milford 44). Zelda's confused utterance upon coming out of anesthesia after the birth of their daughter was placed in the mouth of Daisy in *The Great Gatsby* (Milford 84). Zelda clearly is the source for Nicole Diver, the mentally ill protagonist of *Tender Is the Night*. Scott did not hesitate to appropriate and make public her most painful experiences: "that she might object to it, be wounded by it, did not seem to have disturbed him. He saw it only from a writer's point of view" (Milford 219). Sarah Beebe Fryer provides an extensive comparison of Nicole Diver and Alabama Beggs Knight, and she argues that the

> most significant differences between Scott Fitzgerald's fictional female characters and Zelda's stem from the authors' own differences in attitudes towards women's roles. Zelda's protagonist, Alabama Beggs, is a new kind of woman, willing to take responsibility for herself and her own happiness by dedicating herself to something outside her marriage; but Scott's principal female character, Nicole Diver, is for the most part confined unhappily to traditional standards of feminine behavior in the midst of an era of change. (59)

Wood, moreover, notes the way Zelda's own novel "challenges the version of [Zelda's] life that later would be set forth by her husband in the character of Nicole Diver" (249).

The partners also had asymmetrical conceptions of ownership of shared autobiography. Zelda, unlike Scott, does not argue for exclusive rights to auto/biographical material; she maintains, in a letter she wrote him in 1934, that the raw material of all art is "common property": "I wonder if anybody has ever got nearer the truth than Aristotle: he said that all emotions and all experiences were common property—that the transposition of these into form was individual and art" (*Writings* 475). Her phrasing, however, reflects key legal terms dealing with marital property, "tenants in common" and "communal property," arguing for mutual rights to shared experiences, suggesting that such source material for art is not individually owned. Neither Zelda nor Scott apparently considered the possibility that appropriation of the other's autobiographical experiences might be construed as libel (and the question of libel for married partners is particularly vexed).

In the Phipps transcript cited by Milford, Scott made clear that, as the "professional" writer (the one with public recognition and monetary remuneration), he believed he owned exclusive rights to this shared autobiogrphical material: "I am the professional novelist, and I am supporting you. That is all my material. None of it is your material" (273). It was this claim of exclusivity that fed the dispute over Zelda's novel. In the battle over appropriation occasioned by her composition and publication of *Save Me the Waltz*, Scott charged that "literally one whole section of her novel is an imitation of [the fifty-thousand-word manuscript of his that she had heard], of its rhythm, materials" and that she had used two episodes *"upon which whole sections of my book turn"* and which he wanted her to cut (Milford 216). The Phipps transcript demonstrates that Scott actually spelled out for Zelda detailed restrictions on the content of her writing: "If you write a play, it cannot be a play about psychiatry, and it cannot be a play laid on the Riviera, and it cannot be a play laid in

Switzerland, and whatever the idea is, it will have to be submitted to me" (Bruccoli, *Epic* 353).

Zelda fought back during the session transcribed and did not accept his restrictions complacently, at one time pointing out that he was "making a rather violent attack on a third rate talent" (Milford 273). She reacted to Scott's intervention with her publisher and her psychologists by stating, "I have always done whatever I wanted to do, whenever I could possibly manage it. My book is none of my husband's Goddamned business" (253). Milford reveals that the "psychiatrists at Phipps were surprised by the vehemence of Scott's reaction and could only apologize for having allowed Zelda to mail the novel . . . without first gaining Fitzgerald's release" (217). Milford does not comment on their apology, but the account suggests that the psychiatrists were complicit with Scott's belief that the writer who was remunerated (and who paid their fees) was exclusively entitled to the shared material. Clearly, Scott and her doctors also believed that, as a mental patient, Zelda had given up her right to make decisions concerning her own work and her own texts.

The Fitzgerald correspondence provides evidence that there were substantial revisions to *Save Me the Waltz* as a result of the dispute; Zelda worked on them for one month, but not much is available to specify their exact nature (Milford 224; Bruccoli, *Epic* 324). It is unfortunate that the original manuscript and the changes Zelda made on it have been lost (Milford 224), because they might have revealed the extent and the kind of revisions required by Scott. It is curious that Zelda had originally given her male protagonist the name Amory Blane, the name of the protagonist of Scott's *This Side of Paradise*. This act could be merely an exploitation of shared property, or evidence of a lack of imagination on Zelda's part, or an impulse to imitate her husband's writing, or some kind of revenge. It seems that Scott saw it as revenge; he criticized Zelda for using "the name of a character I invented to put intimate facts in the hands of the friends and enemies we have accumulated *en route*" (Bruccoli, *Epic* 325). Bruccoli notes that the proof copy of the novel contains two "heavily revised" sets of galleys in which Zelda totally rewrote the opening section of the second chapter. He also comments that the "revised galleys are drastically worked over, but almost all the marks are in Zelda Fitzgerald's hand. F. Scott Fitzgerald did not systematically work on the surviving proofs: only eight of the words written on them are clearly in his hand" (Bruccoli, "Note on the Text," *Waltz* 241). Both Scott's *Tender Is the Night* and Zelda's *Save Me the Waltz* clearly draw on the same prototypes for their protagonists and both set a significant portion of the novel on the Riviera, but the final versions of their novels contain only minor overlap. Zelda's novel possesses no discernible echoes of Scott's "rhythms." Extant evidence suggests that *Save Me the Waltz* was the site of considerable marital animosity for the couple (perhaps too personal in implications for outsiders to understand fully), but that Zelda was indeed its legitimate author.

The partners' quarrel was not just about ownership of source material but also about entitlement to the role of writer. Scott disparaged *Save Me the Waltz* in particular, as well as Zelda's ability to write in general. He admitted she could write "sketches," but he argued to Zelda's psychiatrists that "she has nothing essentially to say" (Bruccoli, *Epic* 349). He wrote Scribner's in terms that place him in the role of protecting Zelda—and her literary reputation—from herself: Zelda's novel would "seriously compromise what literary future she may have and cause inconceivable harm in its present form" (Milford 217). After revisions were made, he wrote Perkins and asked him not to react to the novel with too much enthusiasm, but to keep *"on the staid side"* any positive reactions (Milford 225). Either because her revisions satisfied him or because he saw the financial advantage of having the novel's sales applied to his debt to Scribner's, Scott subsequently changed his evaluation of the novel and wrote Perkins, "Zelda's novel is now good, improved in every way" (Bruccoli, *Epic* 327). Scott did, with some ambivalence, finally remove his prohibition on Zelda's writing in a letter to Dr. William Elgin in 1934.

In this letter he concedes that Zelda had a right to use those experiences *in which he did not share,* and he claims he will offer "impersonal and professional" criticism of her "own material" (Milford 216). He writes to Dr. Elgin, "I must tell you that while I have been very convinced and even dogmatic about the idea that she should not write serious fiction at present still I am not unamenable to change in that regard. For it there is to be said that she grew better in the three months at Hopkins where it was allowed and she grew apathetic in the two months at Craig House where she was continually dissuaded. Also, it provides a direction and might lessen the sense that I am frustrating her" (*Correspondence* 363). His ambivalence is revealed not only by his vacillation and his double negative ("not unamenable") but also by his ultimate abdication of responsibility to the psychiatrist: "The things against it, such as reawakening betes noires, my inability to keep her writing within reasonable bounds at home, her inability to take disappointments healthily, etc. I went over with you Friday but would appreciate it if you would weigh these factors, one set against the other, because there you can control automatically the time she works at it and because even in the broader aspect of the matter my initial position may be absolutely wrong" (*Correspondence* 363–64).

Scott's reaction to Zelda's (re)appropriation of common material also reveals confusion about the boundaries and integrity of his own self. He wrote that she had constructed "this dubitable career of hers with morsels of living matter chipped out of my mind, my belly, my nervous system and my loins" (Milford 222). His corporeal imagery alludes to the biblical creation of Eve out of Adam's body—implying, however, not the gain of a companion but the loss of a part of Adam's self. The fragmented imagery reveals the nature of his own fear: the "loss of numerous 'parts' of itself" that accompanies a subject's entrance to the symbolic order (Silverman, *Acoustic Mirror* 6) and the resultant anxiety Lacan describes regarding the *corps morcelé*, the body-in-pieces, the fragmented post-mirror-stage body that is not a totalized whole. Scott also expresses confusion about the reality of Zelda's material existence: "Sometimes I don't know whether Zelda isn't a character that I created myself" (Milford 283). Tellingly, he views himself as her creator, confusing his fictional creation with the real-life Zelda. In a 1921 magazine interview he stated narcissistically: "Indeed, I married the heroine of my stories. I would not be interested in any other sort of woman" (Frederick Smith, "Flappers" 79). A Galatea who picks up the pen, Zelda threatens her Pygmalion's identity by revealing her independent material existence, her agency, her rivalry for the role of writer, and her competition for material he thinks he authored.

Scott's confusion may have been abetted by Zelda's prior complicity. During their courtship and the early years of her marriage, Zelda had accepted, even advocated, woman's conventional role as facilitator for the man's identity. While Scott was in New York trying to establish himself both financially and as a writer, she wrote him, "I don't want to live—I want to love first, and live incidentally—"; without Scott she would "have no purpose in life—just a pretty—decoration. . . . I feel like you had me ordered—and I was delivered to you—to be worn—I want you to wear me, like a watch—charm or a button hole boquet [*sic*]—to the world" (Milford 41). In a 1924 article Zelda depicted herself as oblivious to vocation: "I think a woman gets more happiness out of being gay, light-hearted, unconventional, mistress of her own fate, than out of a career that calls for hard work, intellectual pessimism and loneliness" (Milford 125). By the time of the publication battle over *Save Me the Waltz*, however, Zelda had developed a critique of the decorative, subordinate role of women. Her letters express a desire to placate her husband over *Save Me the Waltz*, but the novel itself contains evidence not only of Zelda's understanding of the problems of women's subjectivity within patriarchy, but also of retaliation for her long-standing resentment about the appropriation of her life and her self for Scott's fiction.

RECLAIMING HERSELF AS TEXT

Zelda's autobiographical novel at first appears to sidestep the conflict over shared material and the role of writer by giving each spouse a different vocation: David is a painter, Alabama is a dancer; neither is a writer. This solution, used by West and Hall as well, is anticipated in an early interview when Zelda listed her ideal vocations as ballet, acting, and writing ("Flapper" 113), subordinating to third place the profession that placed her in a rivalry with Scott. She thus displaces or minimizes a central conflict that emerged in her marriage. Critics have also noted her desire to write a story other than that of her own madness (a story Scott wrote in her stead). Wood views *Save Me the Waltz* as a story of substitution: "a narrative about Alabama's bodily experience is substituted for a suppressed story of mental illness"; it "exposes those representations and the psychiatric discourse surrounding them as dependent upon an appropriation and objectification of female bodies" (247). Payne, in a Foucauldian analysis, reads the novel as a tale of the "discipline of 'femininity'" that uses anorexia nervosa as an alternative to the more biographically accurate story of madness (40).[9] The dance sequences in the third and fourth sections of the novel replace and rewrite other auto/biographical narratives as well.

As a female Bildungsroman, *Save Me the Waltz* provides an almost allegorical account of a woman's formation and maturation, her upbringing and marriage, as well as a critique of that formation. The novel traces, in impressionistic style, Alabama Beggs Knight's growing awareness of herself in a family with a strongly patriarchal father (Judge Austin Beggs), a nurturing but unassertive mother (Millie Beggs), and two older sisters (Joan and Dixie). After a brief initiation as an iconoclastic Southern belle, Alabama marries David Knight, a painter, and gives birth to a daughter, Bonnie. The rest of the novel fictionalizes the Fitzgeralds' experiences on the Riviera, culminating in a detailed dramatization of Zelda's experiences as a dancer.

Alabama's early acquisition of identity is hindered by her ineffectual mother, Millie. When she wants to go to New York to "be my own boss," Millie's response is fraught with irony in relation to her own powerless position in her home: "Being boss isn't a question of places. Why can't you be boss at home?" (*Waltz* 16). Alabama's efforts to find identity through her mother are futile because Millie herself has no volition, no subjectivity: "'Tell me about myself when I was little,' the youngest girl insists. She presses against her mother in an effort to realize some proper relationship" (5). When asked how she came to marry Austin Beggs, Millie answers that he "wanted to marry me" (202). As Linda W. Wagner notes, "Alabama's search for identity underscores her mother's relinquishment of her own being" (*"Waltz"* 202). In Alabama's family, the female household—consisting of Millie, "the good mother" (*Waltz* 200), and her daughters, Joan, Dixie, and Alabama—is subordinated to the powerful patriarch, Judge Beggs.

Beggs's desire has created and named his family. As is characteristic of the Lacanian *nom de père,* Judge Beggs demands that his daughters "respect [his] name. It is all they will have in the world" (*Waltz* 14).[10] By virtue of both his profession and his personality, the judge dominates the people and the natural forces within his domain: "The deep balance of the father's voice subjugates the darkness to the final diminuendo of the Beggs's bedtime" (6). Wife and daughters function as a collective object for the judge's subjectivity: "Alone his preference in women had created Millie and the girls" (24). Alabama credits her father exclusively with her creation, noting at the time of his death: "Without his desire, I should never have lived" (200). Although the first line of the novel begins with bravado, "'Those girls,' people say, 'think they can do anything and get away with it'" (3) because of their father's power, the novel reveals how little the daughters actually can do, how little they can really get away with, and how false is their supposed privilege. As a result of Alabama's early formation, she naively views her family as a collective, genderless unit. Lacking individual identity, "'Things happen to us' she thinks. 'What an interesting thing to be a family'" (7). She "swell[s] virtuously submissive to the way of the clan" (7). The tumescent phallic metaphor, combined with the girl's limited understanding and submission, reveals how Alabama mistakenly assumes that as a female member of the family she can partake in the judge's potency.

The entire house of Beggs women, however, is arrested in development, naively waiting for agency and subjectivity to be bestowed upon them by the symbolic. Joan, the second daughter, lacks substance, like "a ghost of her finest points awaiting inhabitation" (*Waltz* 24), whereas Alabama, the youngest, is a girl

> filled with no interpretation of herself, having been born so late in the life of her parents that humanity had already disassociated itself from their intimate consciousness and childhood become more of a concept than the child. She wants to be told what she is like, being too young to know that she is like nothing at all and will fill out her skeleton with what she gives off, as a general might reconstruct a battle following the advances and recessions of his forces with bright-colored pins. She does not know that what effort she makes will become herself. It was much later that the child, Alabama, came to realize that the bones of her father could indicate only her limitations. (5–6)

Alabama anticipates a passively achieved entrance into the symbolic ("to be told what she is like"), not realizing that it is contradictory to expect such initiation from the patriarch—whose inherent constitution or "bones" can contribute only to a negative definition based on her lack or "limitations" in comparison with his own. Within her family Alabama hopes to compensate for lack and to find identity through seizing the experience of others; she "appropriates her sister's love affair" before having her own (8). Since Alabama's sisters are as much defined by lack as she, such appropriation is not propitious. This appropriation nevertheless anticipates the auto/biographical tactics of the novel's ending, in which Zelda reclaims herself as text through her fictional persona.

Pre-mirror-stage, Alabama is an unformed, inarticulate vessel who "never could place what woke her mornings as she lay staring about, conscious of the absence of expression smothering her face like a wet bath-mat. She mobilized herself. Live eyes of a soft wild animal in a trap peered out in skeptic invitation from the taut net of her features" (*Waltz* 8). When David Knight arrives as suitor, he is able to rescue Alabama only to the extent that he names and reifies her alterity, carving her identity into a post as "Miss Alabama *Nobody*" (37; my italics). This episode fictionalizes an incident from Zelda's own courtship and clarifies one source of resentment: "Scott carved their names in the doorpost of the country club to commemorate their first meeting, and it irritated her a little when he told her again and again how famous he would be, for he neglected to include Zelda in his enthusiastic prevision" (Milford 33). Defined by multiple negatives, Alabama's marital status is the unmarried "Miss." Her name designates not an individual but the region, the state, that produced her (one of her sisters is named Dixie). Just as Alabama is passed from father to husband as a possession through her marriage, so her function as Other, her role in relation to male subjectivity, now belongs to David, the artist, who "exhibited her to his friends as if she were one of his pictures" (*Waltz* 147).

In a parallel to Scott, who named himself to fame during their courtship, David is able to name himself on the post because of the cultural advantage bestowed on him through male privilege, which facilitates his passage through the mirror stage and his acquisition of subjectivity. In contrast to Alabama's unarticulated formlessness, he "verified himself in the mirror . . . as if he had taken an inventory of himself before leaving and was pleased to find himself complete" (*Waltz* 38). To be courted by David does not aid Alabama's developing identity but attenuates it further: "She felt the essence of herself pulled finer and smaller like those streams of spun glass that pull and stretch till there remains but a glimmering illusion. Neither falling nor breaking, the stream spins finer. She felt herself very small and ecstatic" (38). The etymology of ecstasy (ex-stasis) suggests that she is pulled outside herself, alienated from her already fragile sense of self. This self-alienation ordinarily is part of the Lacanian process, but Alabama seems too frail to survive the transition. David's wholeness is a culturally fostered illusion, however. He enters the text in conjunction with Alabama's wartime collection of insignias. While the box filled with icons of men's identities provides Alabama with a false sense of security (by autumn "she had a glove-box full"), David is introduced as incomplete, a "blond lieutenant with one missing insignia" (35).

The problems of women's acquisition of subjectivity in a patriarchal society are explored through Alabama's search for vocation. Her lack of subjectivity impedes her ability to focus on a single vocation. Raised in the insular Southern culture, Alabama is a throwback to the Victorian era. Her desire for identity and vocation echoes those of nineteenth-century predecessors such as Dinah Craik Mulock, who stated: "it appears to me that the chief canker at the root of women's lives is the want of something to do" (64). Alabama cries repeatedly, "What can I do with myself?" Her phrasing defines a malleable self and establishes activity as prerequisite to identity and vocation (*Waltz* 90).[11] The question of Zelda's vocation was apparently a recurrent one in the Fitzgerald household, as a diary entry by the couple's friend McKaig suggests. After a visit early in their marriage, he wrote: "Went to Fitzgerald's. Usual problem there. What shall Zelda do?" His glib solution to the problem, "I think she might do a little housework," suggests his conventional expectations for women's work (Mellow, *Lives* 117). Scott forbade Zelda to use the material of their lives to make herself a writer, yet he had earlier disparaged her lack of vocation in 1930 to Dr. Oscar Forel, one of her psychiatrists in Switzerland, describing her as "my wife—who had never tried to use her talents and intelligence" (*Correspondence* 242).

It would seem that Zelda was a gifted woman, with several competing but underdeveloped interests and talents. During their courtship she wrote Scott, "It's so *much* nicer to be damned sure I *could* do it better than other people—and I might not could [sic] if I tried—that, of course, would break my heart" (Turnbull 177). Turnbull argues that she turned to painting and dancing because "Scott had pre-empted the field of letters" (177). According to the Canadian writer Morley Callaghan, who visited the Fitzgeralds in Paris, "Zelda suddenly began to talk about her own writing; she was at pains to insist that she too wrote, and wrote well. He was taken aback by her assertion, not so much because he thought she did not write well, but because of her intense insistence" (Milford 149). Also an artist, Zelda exhibited her paintings five times (Mellow, *Lives* 426).[12] Rather than emphasize the potential of these multiple interests, Scott berated her for not excelling in any: "You are a third rate writer and a third rate ballet dancer" (Milford 273). In a similar way David, the Scott character in her fiction, plays an inhibitory rather than a facilitative role in Alabama's search for vocation. He tells her "he would help her to be a fine dancer, but he did not believe that she could become one" (*Waltz* 153).

Even Alabama's daughter's nanny, a working woman herself, is sympathetic to Alabama's desire for vocation: "We must all have something to do," she commiserates as Alabama begins her rigorous ballet training (*Waltz* 147). Zelda herself was finally able, in her late twenties and thirties, to articulate the desires for self-expression and independence that she had sensed only as vague dissatisfaction and restlessness in her early twenties: "I determined to find an impersonal escape, a world in which I could express myself and walk without the help of somebody who was always far from me" (Milford 175). Zelda wrote in order to pay for dancing lessons, because she "wanted her dancing to be her exclusive possession" (Milford 152). Yet when she had the chance to dance a solo in *Aïda* with the San Carlo Opera Company in Naples (Milford 156), in contrast to her more adventurous fictional self, Alabama, she did not take the opportunity.[13]

Alabama muses on the inequality of the sexes in their personal quests for vocation: "Men, she thought, never seem to become the things they do, like women, but belong to their own philosophic interpretations of their actions" (*Waltz* 117). Inhabiting the symbolic, men transcend their literal being. In contrast to women—defined by Lacanian lack, lack of activity, and thus lacking literal being (nobody)—men have a surplus of subjectivity that allows them to supersede their actions with a transcendent sense of self. David's transcription of their names on the post during their courtship reveals that his identity is overdetermined whereas Alabama's is negated: "'David,' the legend read, 'David, David, Knight, Knight, Knight, and Miss Alabama Nobody'" (*Waltz* 37). Zelda's use of the word "legend" in 1932 is fraught with suggestions about the true identities of the real-life prototypes, the real people behind the legendary literary couple.

As a fictionalization of Scott, David is neither idealized nor villainized but, rather, humanized—and minimized. Aldrich argues that Scott's anger over *Save Me the Waltz* is not limited to rivalry over "competing shares of a limited market." She analyzes a telling comment he made to Zelda's psychiatrists:

> "My God", he wrote, "my books made her a legend and her single intention in this somewhat thin portrait is to make me a non-entity." Whether or not Fitzgerald considered the portrait thin and Zelda a "third rate writer" is irrelevant to his distress. This last term should, I think, be given its full, literal weight of non-being; it seems that the portrait, once made, takes a kind of ontological precedence over the model, drains it of its own being. Art does not simply copy the life of its subject, it draws *on* that life, or draws it *out* and into its own. (139)

It is ironic, however, that Scott complained of being a "non-entity" in *Save Me the Waltz* after he himself insisted on revisions to excise undesirable traits from—and thus minimize—his fictional character.

Zelda's fictionalization nevertheless grants Scott's character a vocation. David's artwork is respected and significant; the "steely concision" of his style influences contemporary "interior decoration" (*Waltz* 99)—unless, of course, the latter is considered a slight because it associates his power with the domestic sphere. Given Zelda's own egocentric interest in her husband's female protagonists, however, and particularly "the ones that are like me" ("Flapper" 112), it is not surprising to hear of Scott's disappointment at finding himself a "nonentity" in Zelda's novel. There is, perhaps, some element of retaliation in Zelda's erasure of Scott's real profession and her attribution of one of her own central interests (painting) to his fictional persona. In making him a painter rather than a writer, she places him in a non-verbal alternative to the linguistic realm inhabited by Scott as a writer. Scott objected to the early version of his character, complaining of "turning up in a novel signed by my wife as a somewhat anemic por trait painter" (Bruccoli, *Epic* 325). It is not clear whether Scott is over-reacting to the final characterization of David Knight or whether the earlier version of this character was less appealing than the final one.

The Fitzgeralds' distress over each other's fictional renditions of their individual selves reveals the fundamental conflict between the egocentric self and the potentially egalitarian couple. The conflicting interests of self and Other in a relationship are explored during Alabama's stifling summer in Paris:

> [Alabama] half hated the unrest of David, hating that of herself that she found in him. Their mutual experiences had formed them mutually into an unhappy compromise. That was the trouble: they hadn't thought they would have to make any adjustments as their comprehensions broadened their horizons, so they accepted those necessary reluctantly, as compromise instead of as change. They had thought they were perfect and opened their hearts to inflation but not alteration. (*Waltz* 129)

As individuals within a marriage, Alabama and David are capable only of "inflation," distention without improvement or amelioration, rather than personal growth or development. The couple is a site for incessant struggle for dominance, not productive interaction and maturation. Further, the structure of *Save Me the Waltz* emphasizes Alabama's individuality "rather than the story of the Knights as a pair" (Wagner, "*Waltz*" 204). In contrast, Scott frequently featured the couple as a protagonist in his novels. In *Tender Is the Night,* for example, Rosemary falls in love with "The Divers" before she zeroes in on Dick. Although David answers the phone for "both the Knights" (*Waltz* 100), throughout most of Zelda's novel the couple is subordinated to the woman's story.

The early phase of Alabama's relationship with David suggests the narcissism of the early-mirror-stage reflection of the self in the Other: "So much she loved the man, so close and closer she felt herself that he became distorted in her vision, like pressing her nose upon a mirror and gazing into her own eyes" (*Waltz* 38). However, during her career as a dancer, she begins to realize that individual vocation can be antithetical to relationship:

> A growing feeling of alarm in Alabama for their relationship had tight-ened itself to a set determination to get on with her work. Pulling the skeleton of herself over a loom of attitude and arabesque she tried to

weave the strength of her father and the young beauty of her first love
with David, the happy oblivion of her teens and her warm protected
childhood into a magic cloak. She was much alone. (129)

The "skeleton" metaphor echoes the bone imagery persistently associated with Judge Beggs and the patriarchal heritage bequeathed to the
daughter. The curt final line reveals how impossible it is to include others in an individual vocation. The realization is illuminated when Alabama describes her motivation for dancing as "not trying to get anything—at least, I don't think I am—but to get rid of some of myself"
(141). What Alabama is trying to exorcise is her internalized Other, the
self she has constructed in relation to David. Her contradictory solution
to fragmentation is a counterproductive attempt to reduce the size of the
self through self-destructive behavior—frenetic activity, for example. The
fragmentation of the postsymbolic is suggested by the nervous habit of
picking at her face, a self-mutilating, compulsive habit. She picks at herself, she explains, because of an absence of alternatives, "If there'd been
anything else to do, I wouldn't have done the damage" (58).

Alabama begins to hope, as she matures, that there might be an
identity outside of the Other's construction of the self. During her parents' visit early in the marriage, she thinks "that no individual can
force other people forever to sustain their own versions of that individual's character—that sooner or later they will stumble across the person's own conception of themselves" (*Waltz* 55). Her desire is that
someday her parents will see her as she constructs her self, outside of
"their own versions" of her. Yet after her disapproving parents leave, Alabama redefines the process as a constant contestation of the Other's
conception: "Our rôle will always be discounting the character they
think we are from now on'" (56). If the Other's construction cannot be
changed, she concludes, one can either accept it or destroy parts of that
self. David's adultery leads Alabama, in a gesture reminiscent of her face
picking, metaphorically to pare away part of her self as if removing a
diseased organ or assigning parts of her self to a filing cabinet:

> "I don't care," she repeated convincingly to herself: as neat an incision
> into the tissue of life as the most dexterous surgeon could hope to pro-
> duce over a poisoned appendix. Filing away her impressions like a person
> making a will, she bequeathed each passing sensation to that momen-
> tary accumulation of her self, the present, that filled and emptied with
> the overflow. (117)

It is ironic that reduction, or self-destruction, is presented as Alabama's strategy for self-preservation.

Alabama's decision to become a dancer coincides with David's infidelity with the actress Gabrielle Gibbs (who successfully plays roles—
Others—created by men) and with David's pitying comment on

Alabama's life: "It must be awful just waiting around eternally" (118).[14] Although her husband's friend Hastings tells her "You're a man's woman and need to be bossed" (115), Alabama understands her own need for agency: "'It's very flattering,' she said, propelling herself to the bathroom, 'to be sought after, but more provident I suppose, to seek'" (101). She must play a role in her own self-construction. She tells the Englishman during their crossing to Europe, "I am only really myself when I'm somebody else whom I have endowed with these wonderful qualities from my imagination." Yet, in the same conversation that she tells him "I am a book. Pure fiction" (70), she defines herself by negation, telling him, "I am not a writer" (71). The inconclusiveness of this presentation—the variety of alternatives presented without the emergence of a solution—reveals the numerous obstacles confronted by women seeking artistic identity and, ultimately, the nonexistence of the wholeness Alabama seeks.

THE POWERFUL MOTHER MENTOR

The mother's potential to serve as a mentor facilitating identity and vocation—a process left incomplete within her family of origin—is suggested by Alabama's encounter with the virtuoso ballerina, Madame, in the studio behind Olympia Music Hall. The career displacement that makes Alabama a dancer rather than a writer places Madame, the ballet teacher, at the center of the novel as Alabama's mentor and object of desire. The mentor function is displaced from the autobiographical partner to a fictional third party (a technique used also by Hall, who creates mentors for both partners), thus subordinating the story of her husband and marriage in this section of the novel. Zelda fictionalizes her own ballet training: in her late twenties she took lessons at the Philadelphia Opera School of Ballet with Catherine Littlefield, and she subsequently trained in Paris with Lubov Egorova, "a highly respected dance instructor" who had danced with Diaghilev (Mellow, *Lives* 317). In the fictionalized dance sequence Alabama reenacts and revises her family experience; this fantasy episode functions as an exalted encounter with the Kristevan presymbolic *chora* as a place apart from patriarchy and with the mother as an idealized, powerful, alternative mentor. The dance studio is a place where Alabama recovers "one of the permanent 'scenes' of subjectivity, not so much superseded as covered over and denied by succeeding spatial development" and where she achieves "a privileged access to the archaic mother" (Silverman, *Acoustic Mirror* 105–6). Although her training in Madame's studio is a transitory experience, it comes to occupy a permanent place in Alabama's psyche.

An archetypal Mother, nameless and generic, the fictional Egorova is always referred to as Madame. Even her husband lacks a surname and is referred to as the Prince. A master teacher, she is omnipotent in her studio. In the manner of a child imagining the private life of a teacher, the ballet student Stella tells Alabama that "the studio is [Madame's] home" (*Waltz* 149). The studio is a metaphor for the mother's body or her self, "its walls so impregnated with her work" (149). The dancers comprise an alternative family into which Alabama "wished she had been born" (162). As a surrogate daughter, Alabama finds details from Madame's childhood and her past to be "glamorous and poignant" (134). The dancers' devotion to Madame is complete; in return, Madame instills confidence in her daughters. She is exacting, and their ability is "never enough to please Madame" (132), but her pupils gain an "air of complete confidence" in their work (135). Zelda seems to have felt the same about the prototype for Madame:

> My attitude towards Egorowa [*sic*] has always been one of an intense love: I wanted to help her some way because she is a good woman who has worked hard and has nothing, or lost everything. I wanted to dance well so that she would be proud of me and have another instrument for the symbols of beauty that passed in her head that I understood, though apparently could not execute. I wanted to be first in the studio. (quoted in Milford 168)

The encounter with an exceptional female mentor thus inculcates the desire to emulate and excel, a kind of artistic ambition rooted in affinity. When a faded photograph of a ballerina is discovered in the studio, the dancers speculate upon its subject, whom they cannot identify: Is it Madame as a young woman or it is her mother?[15] The ambiguity suggests that the professional woman can indeed bequeath an image—in contrast to the usual Lacanian maternal function as a merely passive mirror reflecting the child in the process of identity acquisition. In Naples, Alabama's teacher, Madame Sirgeva, says that Alabama has come to resemble Madame; she is no longer "Miss Alabama Nobody" (*Waltz* 169). The process of identity acquisition incorporates, nevertheless, both an element of subordination (of the daughter to the powerful mother) and the possibility of succession. While Alabama's husband is a Knight, Madame's is a Prince; yet after Alabama has studied with Madame, David in Switzerland is addressed as "Prince."[16]

Within the ballet company (an alternative to her biological family), Alabama transfers her affection from the judge to Madame, from father to mother—a reversal of the Freudian schema for a daughter's development. Whereas Alabama has always been financially dependent on men, Madame and the other women dancers financially maintain their husbands, an inversion of the patriarchal economy. Alabama delivers her own daughter, Bonnie, to Madame as a pupil in a kind of matrilineage, an inversion of the patriarchal transfer of women she herself experienced. This part of the novel signals a stylistic shift, as

Henry Dan Piper notes, because "Zelda reaches the point where her life takes on purpose and meaning—in the dancing studio of Egorova" (200). The change in style reflects the presentation of a compelling alternative to the power of the patriarch presented in the first half of the novel. While she is pursuing her own career in Naples, Alabama's father is "stricken" (*Waltz* 190), and Alabama returns home to find her father, "thin and little," now "withering on the bed" (199).

The novel, in juxtaposing female with male mentors, represents the child's competing desires for mother and father. Initially torn between her two mentors, Madame and David, Alabama is also caught in the mirror-stage transition from the imaginary to the symbolic order. David, the male artist, attempts to instruct her in the supremacy of symbolic language: "Nothing exists that can't *be* expressed" (*Waltz* 128; my italics), he confidently claims. In contrast, although Madame is expressive, she is essentially nonverbal: "Madame never said much. . . . Inevitably the sense of her words was lost for Alabama, drifting off into that dark mournful harvest of the tides of the sea of Marmara, the Russian language" (148). Inhabiting the *chora,* which "precedes and underlies figuration" (Kristeva, *Revolution* 26), Madame speaks a "foreign" language. Although her communication is primarily expressive she nevertheless articulates truth. It is fitting that David's insult to Alabama—defining her as an amateur when he says, "the biggest difference in the world is between the amateur and the professional in the arts"—is answered by Madame's perceptive description of the falsity of the unified self: "I do not know how anyone can *be* anything" (*Waltz* 147, 128; my emphasis).

Madame teaches Alabama a new language of the body in which women communicate through dance:

> The classes swayed to the movements of her arms like an anchored buoy to the tides. Saying almost nothing in that ghoulish Eastern tongue, the girls were all musicians and understood that Madame was exhausted with their self-assertion when the pianist began the pathetic lullaby from the entr'acte of *Cleopatra;* that the lesson was going to be interesting and hard when she played Brahms. Madame seemed to have no life outside her work, to exist only when she was composing. (148–49)

Alabama is at first intimidated by Madame and discouraged by her own inability to achieve similar control of her own body (124–25). Because she comes to ballet in a transitional state, between the imaginary and the symbolic, her body is at odds with itself: "She said to herself, 'My Body and I' and took herself for an awful beating" (124–25). Payne reads this bodily split through the trope of anorexia in the novel; "Alabama's body becomes the 'stage' on which she acts out the (culturally inscribed) story of herself versus herself" (49). Alabama is also at war with the internalized Other, a result of her failed mentorship with David. Thus, the "foreign" Madame and her alternative culture are necessary to Alabama's developing artistic identity.

Under Madame's influence Alabama's priorities and behavior change. As she loses her own "necessity for material possessions" (*Waltz* 139), she spends her money generously on rare, extravagant flowers to be given in tribute to Madame—a Demeter figure associated with plants and flowers, whose eyes are "like the purple bronze footpaths through an autumn beech wood where the mold is drenched with mist, and clear fresh lakes spurt up about your feet from the loam" (148). The choric world of the ballet is characterized by tireless energy and exuberance, a place where the "voluminous ruffles of the skirts wouldn't fit in the closets or drawers" (145). In the studio Alabama dresses in a "less restricted medium," and her objective is primarily emotional, to express her moods (145). Symbolic language is inadequate for the expression of this exuberant primal force.

The choric exuberance and excess characteristic of the language she learns from Madame are communicated through extravagant Jacobean imagery. In one of these passages, for example, she courts Madame with the exorbitant tributes necessary to impress a Demeter:

> Yellow roses she bought with her money like Empire satin brocade, and white lilacs and pink tulips like molded confectioner's frosting, and deep-rose roses like a Villon poem, black and velvety as an insect wing, cold blue hydrangeas clean as a newly calcimined wall, the crystalline drops of lily of the valley, a bowl of nasturtiums like beaten brass, anemones pieced out of wash material, and malignant parrot tulips scratching the air with their jagged barbs, and the voluptuous scrambled convolutions of Parma violets. She bought lemon-yellow carnations perfumed with the taste of hard candy, and garden roses purple as raspberry puddings, and every kind of white flower the florist knew how to grow. She gave Madame gardenias like white kid gloves and forget-me-nots from the Madeleine stalls, threatening sprays of gladioli, and the soft, even purr of black tulips. She bought flowers like salads and flowers like fruits, jonquils and narcissus, poppies and ragged robins, and flowers with the brilliant carnivorous qualities of Van Gogh. (*Waltz* 138–39)

This passage contains a surfeit of courtship symbols; the flowers are not only archetypical romantic tributes from the natural world but are also compared metaphorically to conventional man-made gifts of courtship: poetry, candy, luxurious fabrics and accessories. The extravagance of the gifts signals Alabama's enthusiasm and accomplishment; in an imaginative coup d'état, the daughter outdoes Demeter herself, goddess of prosaic grain, by giving flowers that supersede nature's creations. Synesthetic tulips "purr," and Alabama finds unique hybrids that transcend Nature's classification—"flowers like salads and flowers like fruits."

The enthusiastic but compulsive nature of Alabama's ballet practice has led one feminist critic to view dance in the novel as "transient kinesis" and to argue that it is "impossible for us to read *Save Me the Waltz* as a text about feminine entry into the male echelons of high art" (Davis 348).[17] Alabama nevertheless appears to enter this masculine domain momentarily. As she discovers a vocation through dance, "Alabama went secretly over her body. It was rigid, like a lighthouse" (*Waltz* 114). This contemplation of phallic expression through dance is ultimately rejected, however, as Madame teaches Alabama an alternative to the symbolic, to patriarchal language: a writing of the female body.[18] This powerful, physical language is synesthetic, transcending the ordinary division and classification of the senses. Madame urges Alabama to surmount the limits of the auditory and to "convey hearing with the lines of her body"; until she gains proficiency in this language, she is "humiliated to listen with her hips" (*Waltz* 142). At the same time "she would know when she could listen with her arms and see with her feet. It was incomprehensible that her friends should feel only the necessity to hear with their ears" (143). Alabama learns from the preverbal mother this physical, synesthetic language, coming to think more comprehensively, "visually, architecturally, of music" (156). Piper somewhat ambivalently connects Zelda's synesthetic language in the novel to her desire to communicate in the visual arts and to the "schizoid personality": "The need to go beyond the borders of the senses, to express the inexpressible, was also responsible for her weird, synesthetic prose" (201–2). This language, however, represents the potential of the female body to communicate, transcending the limitations of male art.

Just as Madame functions as a more powerful mother, a surrogate to Millie Beggs, in this section of the novel the women dancers present more extreme variations on the Beggs daughters; Stella and Arienne are Alabama's surrogate sisters, rivals and doubles, in this alternative family. Stella parodies Alabama's less successful efforts—the weak, unsuccessful daughter, loyal to her mother but "the butt of the studio," "massive" and "clumsy" (*Waltz* 148). Madame's pronouncement to Stella is the verdict Alabama fears for herself: "You know you can never dance, why do you not get work to do?" (137). Arienne is Alabama's more successful self, the graceful daughter with the promise of becoming as adept as the powerful mother (rather than that characterized by Lacanian "lack"), and thus Alabama's rival. Arienne "played on her body as if it were a xylophone, and had made herself indispensable to Madame" (152). They fight over the photograph of Madame and are attracted to each other by "a desire to discover what they were mutually jealous of in each other" (152); they work together in a "state of amicable hatred" (157). The narcissistic lesson derived by Alabama from her rivalry with Arienne applies equally to Zelda's sibling rivalry with Scott: "Professional friendship would not bear close inspection—best everybody for herself, and interpret things to conform to personal desires—Alabama thought like that" (157). The conflicting interest within the self/Other relationship, this sequence suggests, is a rivalry endemic in professional friendship.

Simone Weil Davis praises the dancers' "camaraderie based on a common commitment to Madame" but finds considerable masochism in this sequence, comparing Madame's relations to her dancers to that of "the mistress" to a "slave" (356). Ultimately, she argues, the ballet community provides an inappropriate model for a female Bildungsroman because it simply rewrites the values of the male world: "Alabama reappropriates not only the field of bodily presentation but even the competition with other women and the self-abnegation that she knew in her life before" (Davis 349). But although Arienne and Alabama are indeed competitors, and the studio is rife with sibling bickering, the dancers exhibit compassion toward each other. To satisfy Stella's craving for shrimp, for example, Alabama treats her to a meal at the expensive restaurant, Prunier's. Stella tries to reciprocate the kindness by furtively removing lobster eyes from her bouillabaisse and hiding them in her napkin, thinking they are pearls she will give to her colleague-mentor. Alabama can then form her own dance troupe, Stella proposes, and she will dance for Alabama, elevating her friend to Madame's status as a master teacher (*Waltz* 140). The studio is a protosocialist community—the dancers receive lessons whether they can pay for them or not—illustrating the Marxist dictum "from each according to his abilities, to each according to his needs." Although it is not a feminist utopia, the ballet community nevertheless offers both a figurative encounter with the maternal *chora* and a woman-centered enclave within the patriarchal order through which Alabama discovers her identity as an artist in an alternate realm.

The strong current of lesbian erotics present in this sequence also suggests an exploration of the woman-woman bond as an alternative to heterosexual friendship and romance. Alabama uses a towel to "smack across Arienne's rigid buttocks"; Arienne pushes Alabama "into the group of naked girls. Somebody pushed her hurriedly back into Arienne's gyrating body," forcing her to collide "with Arienne's hot, slippery body" (*Waltz* 160). Just as Zelda displaces her writing competition with Scott onto Alabama's rivalry with Arienne, so her attraction to her female mentor is explored through a fictional alternative. Mellow claims Zelda reacted nervously to Hemingway and Scott's banter about sexuality and homosexuality, and "if Zelda had begun, as she recalled, to have anxieties about her attachment to Egorova, she would have felt threatened" (*Lives* 326). Zelda fretted over her attraction to her teacher, revealing the homophobia both Scott and she intermittently displayed.[19] In a long letter written in 1939 she revealed: "I began to like Egorowa—On the boat going back I told you I was afraid that there was something abnormal in the relationship and you laughed" (*Writings* 454).

When Zelda was institutionalized, her fear of lesbianism was considered one of her "obsessive ideas," a symptom of her disease (Bruccoli, *Epic* 293), but was not explored for other possible significance. One of her psychiatrists, Dr. H. A. Trutman, reported that "Mrs. F. put herself into a state of excitement at the thought that on one hand she was losing precious time, and on the other that the things most precious to her were being taken away: her work as a dancer and her Lesbian tendencies" (Bruccoli, *Epic* 295).[20] Zelda's less credible biographers (those with obvious personal axes to grind, such as Ernest Hemingway and Sara Mayfield) have quibbled inconclusively about Zelda's sexual preference. It is unlikely that Zelda herself had consciously worked through her feelings on this matter, but the lesbian undercurrent of the ballet sequence in *Save Me the Waltz* connects dance with lesbian impulses to explore the implications of gender likeness and a female community as alternatives to heterosexual difference.

COMPETITION AND THE PLACE OF ALTERITY: THE NAPLES SEQUENCE

The Naples sequence, occupying most of the final section of the novel, exposes the previous ballet sequence as a fantasy incompatible with the symbolic. Alabama's initiation into the idealized Paris ballet community is parodied in this revisionary episode, which contextualizes the fantasy female community by depicting the protagonist's problematic interactions with patriarchal society, scenes that suggest a microcosm of woman's relations to the dominant order. In this portion of the narrative Alabama competes with her husband, David, as a cross-gendered double. Their daughter, Bonnie, plays a pivotal allegorical role as the object of a gendered rivalry between her mother and her father, ultimately reiterating Alabama's own childhood and reinforcing her comprehension of the daughter's role in patriarchy. In this nightmare inversion of her previous, exultant experience, Alabama encounters a series of patriarchal males (a tyrannical maestro, a violent taxidriver, condescending sexist critics, fiendishly alien doctors), who undermine the gendered triumphs of her Parisian experience. The sequence culminates in a return to her father, the judge, on his deathbed. Alabama's eventual failure in the Naples sequence suggests that the solution previously offered, an escape to an exclusively female community, can only be a temporary retreat.

In the Paris sequence Alabama confronted a female rival, but in the Naples sequence her rival is a man, her husband and double. Zelda and Scott's quarrel over the auto/biographical material of *Save Me the*

Waltz and *Tender Is the Night* revealed a strong element of competition in their relationship, resulting from resemblance and shared interests, which is reflected in several of the relationships in Zelda's novel. The doubles relationship of Alabama and David has its genesis in the attraction and affinity Scott and Zelda felt for one another. Their friend and biographer Turnbull commented on their resemblance: "People remarked that they looked enough alike to be brother and sister, but how much more they resembled each other beneath the skin!" (87). Mayfield "sometimes wondered if the love between them were not essentially narcissistic" (173). Many of Scott's fictionalized couples are psychological doubles or metaphorical twins. Mellow comments that Scott took the twin metaphor in *The Beautiful and the Damned* from one of Zelda's early letters on the "subject of 'soul mates' and bisexuality, culled from Minnie Sayre's theosophical doctrines" (*Lives* 130). Mellow also suggests that the parallel maladies or illnesses they often experienced reveal that "there was something symbiotic in their dependence on one another" (*Lives* 280).

This cross-gendered doubling does not convey equality in Scott's view, however. Rather, it aggravates hierarchy as it inspires a defensive insistence on gender difference: "When I like men I want to be like them—I want to lose the outer qualities that give me my individuality and be like them. I don't want the man; I want to absorb into myself all the qualities that make him attractive and leave him out. I cling to my own innards. When I like women I want to own them, to dominate them, to have them admire me" (Scott cited in Milford 266). Scott's statement reveals a fundamentally inegalitarian impulse behind the cross-gendered double that applies equally to Alabama and to David: both subordination and absorption are strategies to preserve the self at the expense of the Other. Juliet Mitchell explains that, for the double,

> reciprocal and circular relationships manifest themselves throughout life as the expressions of the various desires that the person has to return to things past, to restore the status quo, to retreat to a position of non-difference, in other words, to achieve the annihilation of the other person in whose presence one had first to establish one's own subjecthood. (388–89)

Doubling, created out of likeness, ironically produces a desire for the destruction of the Other. Without mutual trust and a concomitant willingness to cede subject status to the Other, at least temporarily, the narcissistic likeness that underpins competition is, then, inevitably detrimental, and antithetical to an egalitarian relationship.

In the Naples episode, such competition is waged by the Fitzgeralds' fictional counterparts, Alabama and David, over Bonnie, the fictionalized Scottie Fitzgerald. The parents vie with each other, trying to impress her by giving children's parties. Alabama's party is consistent with her tawdry but self-sufficient poverty in Naples: her teacher helps her by producing two children for the party, "one with a sore under its nose, and one who had had to have its head recently shaved. The children arrived in corduroy pants worn over the seat like a convict's head. The table was loaded with rock cakes and honey and warm pink lemonade" (*Waltz* 178). In contrast, the guests at the party David arranges for Bonnie in Switzerland are clean, "decorative" children (183). The Neapolitan children are dark, swarthy—obviously marginalized—whereas those in Switzerland are blond members of the privileged society. The Swiss scenery is paradisiacal: "The green hills stretched away like a canvas sea to faint recesses of legend. Pleasantly loitering mountain vegetation dangled over the hotel" (183). After the party—where Alabama's female competitor, Arienne, dances triumphantly—the children are transported home in "the bright armor of Bonnie's father's car. . . . Safe in the glittering car they rode: the car-at-your-disposal, the mystery-car, the Rajah's-car, the death-car, the first-prize, puffing the power of money out on the summer air like a seigneur distributing largesse" (187). Although Alabama is, significantly, absent in this sequence (the sole instance in the novel), the resentment of all those who are marginalized is communicated by the narrator's metaphors of capitalism, feudal privilege, and death. Clearly, the parent who is sanctioned by patriarchy and its wealth will win Bonnie's approval. Bonnie claims, "it is too 'sérieuse' to be the way Mummy is. She was nicer before" (147). As a result of the Naples party, Bonnie becomes ill, foreshadowing Alabama's own fate after she relinquishes the comforts of marriage for independence.

In the highly allegorical Naples sequence, Alabama dances the starring role, a solo in *Faust,* a story reflecting the negative consequences of ambition and the underworld nature of the Italian experience. Regarding the choice of ballet Grace Stewart notes the "pattern of descent and subsequent inability to surface victoriously," as well as Alabama's choice "between personal relationships and art; she must turn her back on the former if she is to dance in the *Faust* ballet" (31–32). The entire sequence suggests a descent into nightmare, a sinister parody of her Parisian experience. Madame Sirgeva is the Parisian Madame's dark double; in her studio community the dancers' suffering, poverty, and marginalization within patriarchy are more evident than in the Parisian company. In Naples Alabama lives in a tawdry pink boarding-house (*Waltz* 176), where feminine poverty resides. Her dispirited relationship with Madame Sirgeva parodies her previous romance with Madame. Alabama is able to purchase a starring role in the troupe with only a basket of calla lilies (a recycled gift from David), a flower associated with death, and a diminished version of the extravagant flowers she showered on Madame. Although Alabama's new teacher presents herself as having been Madame's mentor, she is a degraded version of

Madame, parading her ghost through the "chasms" of her studio, so large and empty that "the piano sounded very ineffectual" (168). In contrast to Madame, beautified by her suffering, Sirgeva is "as pale and dyed and shrivelled and warped by poverty as a skin that has been soaked under acid" (168). The Italian dancers are all like the unattractive Stella, grotesque imitations of the Russians.

Alabama arrives in Naples to find that the instruction she had in Madame's studio will not translate fully into this culture. "It's going to be difficult not being able to communicate," she thinks as she arrives in the city (*Waltz* 167). The male maestro, a parodic version of the rigorous Diaghilev in Paris, plays so rapidly that Alabama nearly kills herself trying to keep up with his music. Alabama dances in major productions, not only *Faust* but also *Le Lac des Cygnes*. Yet after her successful performance, as she symbolically positions herself in relation to idealized female images such as the statues of Venus de Milo and Pallas Athene (171), it becomes painfully clear that Alabama has won praise via the same process of patriarchal construction that created those images. She receives the approbation of the critics, presumably male. The reviews "agreed that the ballet was a success, and that the new addition to Madame Sirgeva's corps was a competent dancer. She had promise and should be given a bigger rôle, the papers said. Italians like blondes; they said Alabama was as ethereal as a Fra Angelico angel because she was thinner than the others" (172). But the progression of details reveals that the critics praise Alabama because of her "angelic" beauty rather than her "competent" dancing. In Paris Alabama was instructed in the presymbolic and learned an exuberant language of the female body whereas the Naples experience exposes the harsh reality: the cost of Alabama's entrance into the symbolic is a marginalized position within that order. The celebration of the powerful, if fantasized, mother in the Parisian sequence is countered with the presentation of her "castrated" counterpart in the symbolic, and the realization that, as Kristeva notes, "the mother occupies the place of alterity" (*Revolution* 47).

In Italy Alabama recalls with nostalgia her former experience with her mentor; the scent of an evening bag Madame has given Bonnie evokes her presence, and loss, through a series of sense impressions: "Handling the little silver envelope, an unexpected lump rose to Alabama's throat. A faint scent of eau de Cologne brought back the glitter on the crystal beads of Madame" (*Waltz* 175). The intoxicating physical images recall to Alabama her prior immersion in the presymbolic. Sirgeva, the mother viewed as "castrated" by the symbolic community, has replaced Madame, the powerful maternal mentor, signaling the loss that results from entrance to the symbolic: "The discovery of castration, however, detaches the subject from his dependence on the mother, and the perception of this lack [*manque*] makes the phallic function a symbolic function—*the* symbolic function" (Kristeva, *Revolution* 47). While Kristeva here assumes a male subject and a successful entrance into the symbolic, Zelda's account—in substituting Madame Sirgeva for Madame and revealing the daughter's discovery that the mother is powerless, or castrated—emphasizes woman's inferior positioning within the symbolic, a signifying system that Alabama is now learning to read.

Alabama is forced to understand the poverty of women within patriarchy. The Naples sequence opens with Alabama and David traveling second-class so that she can pay for the train herself (*Waltz* 164). Zelda appropriates for her protagonist one of her husband's experiences, translating it as the experience of a woman in a foreign land. To Alabama is attributed Scott's real-life quarrel in 1924 with an Italian taxidriver, who he believed was exploiting him as a foreigner by asking an exorbitant fare. In Scott's experience, and his subsequent fictionalization of it in *Tender Is the Night*, the confrontation with the driver results in a beating; both Dick Diver and Scott end up in jail. In *Save Me the Waltz* the incident is minimalized—perhaps this is one of the revisions Scott required so he could preserve it for his own book. And like West in *Sunflower*, Zelda refuses to represent male violence. In her novel the incident functions to show Alabama the falsity of the information she had received about Naples and her possibility of independence; she cannot live on thirty liras a week if the cab fare alone is twenty liras. Unlike her violent male counterparts, however, Alabama adjusts rather than confronts the system: she merely pays the fare.

Throughout the Naples sequence Alabama's daughter, Bonnie, articulates for her mother the reality of the daughter's position within patriarchal culture. Initially, Alabama attempts to teach Bonnie the lessons she learned herself as she became independent. The advice she gives Bonnie is "Not to be a back-seat driver about life" (*Waltz* 190). Observing Alabama's suffering in Naples, Bonnie is reluctant to emulate her mother or to accept her advice, however. She reiterates her mother's youthful experience with Judge Beggs, echoing Alabama's previous belief that the father will bestow an exalted subjectivity. She assumes that, because her father, David, is taken for a Prince, "that would make me a princess" (188). In a passage recalling Alabama's finding "that the bones of her father could indicate only her limitations" (5–6), Alabama notes, upon Bonnie's arrival, that the "bones had begun to come up in her nose. . . . She was very like her father" (174). The resemblance masks gendered difference and the underlying heritage of patriarchal limitations on women.

Seduced by the material wealth of patriarchy, Bonnie observes repeatedly that the life provided by her father is more secure and comfortable than her mother's: "It's safer to be near you," she tells her father when they are reunited in Switzerland. "It is better here than with Mummy's success in Italy" (*Waltz* 182). The dark comedy of this episode pessimistically suggests that

> Men alone can occupy the (unstable) position of speaking subject within and transgressive of the symbolic; he is the speaker/painter/musician who subjects the symbolic to its own excesses and possibilities of subversion. Only men occupy this position because only men can acquire a guaranteed unified and stable position within the symbolic order—a consequence of the decisive repression of their oedipal desires. It is only from a position *within* the symbolic that it can be ruptured or transgressed. It is only those who actually occupy the position of speaking/representing subject who can undermine or subvert the limits of representation. If women are not positioned as speaking subjects (but as spoken-for-objects), it is not surprising that they are not in any position to transgress the limits of such an order. (Grosz, *Lacan* 164)

Such a harsh generalization presumes a patriarchal society, the order represented by the Neapolitan experience. The corrective, even punitive, lesson of the Naples sequence is Alabama's punishment for attempting to transgress her subordinate position. She sees David succeed in his vocation, achieving "a guaranteed unified and stable position," while she fails to achieve her potential as a dancer. Her daughter's deliberate and well-articulated defection emphasizes that women such as the youthful Alabama, and Zelda herself, are complicit with patriarchy because of the security and comfort it offers. Painfully realistic in comparison with the previous, idealized Paris sequence, the trip to Naples dramatizes through Alabama's plight the limitations upon the woman speaking in the symbolic order. The subversive potential of the Kristeva *chora* and the archaic mother is therefore subordinated in the final sequences of the novel.

In the Naples episode Zelda projects what might have happened if she herself had taken the opportunity to dance in the San Carlo Ballet Company. Bruccoli notes, "It was the best ballet offer she ever received, and there is no explanation for her decision to decline it" (*Epic* 284). Informed by her own experiences in the predominately female ballet communities (and possibly by her experiences in the institution where she was writing the novel), Zelda envisions the penalties that women experience as a consequence of their desire for independence and vocation. Zelda herself appeared to become more woman-centered for a period; *Save Me the Waltz* was dedicated to her psychiatrist Dr. Mildred Squires, for example (Clemens 208). However, in the 1930s, shortly after her father's death and Scott's move to Hollywood to work as a scriptwriter, Zelda would seem to have again found her identity dependent on men: "I am losing my identity here without men," she complained (Milford 206). Despite their efforts to achieve subject status, both Alabama and Zelda enact a carefully considered compromise with the dominant order in the interests of self-preservation.

...

   The ending of *Save Me the Waltz* for the most part has either been ignored or read as the finale to the story of an artist manquée because Alabama "will never be able to dance again" (*Waltz* 195), much less become a successful dancer, after she develops blood poisoning from a blister on her foot. Jacqueline Courbin-Tavernier views the resultant cutting of Alabama's tendon as a "psychological amputation," for example (37). She concludes that the doctors "are, in fact, depriving Alabama of her life, her identity, and are returning her to a world dominated by men" (38). The severing also might be read as a castration, especially if we keep in mind the previous passage about her "rigid," "lighthouse" body. Given the elegiac tone of the ending and Alabama's return to the Beggs home upon the death of her father, it is inevitable that her search for vocation be viewed as a failure. Readings that emphasize Alabama's artistic failure neglect to point out, however, the knowledge she has gained. She returns to her father's home as the Ancient Mariner's Wedding Guest, "sadder and wiser," no longer willing to play the role of Southern belle and consumer wife. Alabama discovers that "joy is not in the achievement itself but in the achieving, in the work" (Courbin-Tavernier 37). The lament at the end is not only for the judge but also for the lost realm of the *chora,* represented through Alabama's career as dancer—her loss of the powerful mother-mentor and the newly acquired language of the body. Alabama is left "feeling that our estate has been unexploited to its fullest" (*Waltz* 210). Her realization is one of maturity: "we've parted with segments of ourselves more easily than other people—granted that we were ever intact" (210). She now recognizes that the unified subject is illusory, an insight that David seemingly has not acquired.
   Before the realization solidifies, Alabama's return to her father's house is marked by one last, albeit regressive and devitalized, questioning of her role within the symbolic order. The judge perceives her desire for an answer to her quest: "Did you say you wanted to ask me something?" he queries. She wonders if he has "prepared some last communication," left for her in his office (*Waltz* 202). But when she asks him a question, "The old man lay silent" and tells her, "Ask me something easy" (199). He has no answer for her. "'He must have forgot,' Alabama said, 'to leave the message'" (203). In his role as patriarch he spells out the impossible conditions of her success: "If you want to choose, you must be a goddess" (204). Alabama finally concludes, "My father bequeathed me many doubts" (204). His death offers her neither freedom nor the answers she seeks, only the heritage of patriarchy. The

daughter's inheritance from the father is her role as Other, as a surface necessary for the reflection of male subjectivity. His daughters "close the shutters on Austen's house on the light and all of himself left there" (205), but Alabama lives in a world where his heritage continues: the Name-of-the-Father is perpetuated as Alabama is now referred to as one of the "David Knights" (195).

The final sequences of the novel present her realizations about the causes of her defeat. Several critics have suggested that Alabama's hallucinations, caused by blood poisoning, represent Zelda's madness. These visions also transcribe, however, the hope and frustrations Alabama (as Zelda) experienced in trying to achieve a vocation in the symbolic. Alabama's intensely visual hallucinations are one last attempt to envision an alternative to the restrictions of the patriarchy. In this "delirious place," men and women live in an egalitarian state: "Phallic poplars and bursts of pink geranium" coexist in "a forest of white-trunked trees whose foliage flowed out of the sky." But this utopian vision terminates in the nightmare of "Alabama gouging at her eyeballs" (*Waltz* 194), in a grim imitation of Oedipus, whose story inscribes the ultimate retribution for trespassing the father's *"non."*

Before her father's death, Alabama's foray into independence ends when her foot becomes infected and she is hospitalized for blood poisoning; she cannot communicate with the doctors: "Why did the doctor inhabit another world from hers? Why couldn't he hear what she was saying, and not stand talking about ice-packs?" (*Waltz* 192). Her question—"Why did the doctor inhabit another world from hers?"—is answered in hallucinatory images that suggest an external rather than an internal defeat: she feels "beaten with heavy beams"; the walls "press her between their pages like a bud from a wedding bouquet"; "Something broke [her] neck" (192–93). Her ultimate discovery in this sequence is that she can neither live totally independent of the patriarchal order nor communicate with the dominant order through the exuberant feminine language she acquired from Madame in Paris. The agent of Alabama's defeat is revealed to her by a doctor, whom she thinks she hears "triumphantly" explaining: "the girl was raped by a calla lily . . . or, no, I believe it was the spray of a shower bath that did the trick" (193). The story of Zeus's rape of Danaë, collapsed in the hallucination with David's gift of calla lilies, epitomizes Alabama's experience in the symbolic: she faces a seemingly omnipotent opponent imbued with all the power of culture's primary patriarchal myths.

The novel's ending, however, suggests some compensation for loss and failure through the daughter's knowledge and rebellion. Although Alabama is denied full participation as a speaking subject, she has acquired an understanding of the symbolic order. Moreover, she has implicitly formulated a critique of it: "She supposed she'd spend the rest of her life composing like that: fitting one thing into another and everything into the rules" (*Waltz* 208). Resigned to this limited and limiting language, Alabama will accommodate herself to this order but refuse to let it destroy her. The novel comments self-consciously on the consequences of patriarchal appropriations of woman-as-text such as Zelda had herself experienced. The ending exposes the implications of appropriation in a final scene in which the discussion of David's current exhibition reveals that, in a parallel to Scott's appropriation of Zelda, he has incorporated Alabama's experience as a dancer into a series of paintings representing the ballet.

David's own analysis of his aesthetic intent reveals that he has appropriated more than just the subject matter: "I thought," said David, "that rhythm, being a purely physical exercise of the eyeball, that the waltz picture would actually give you, by leading the eye in pictorial choreography, the same sensation as following the measure with your feet" (209). His contradictory comment reveals his attempt to appropriate into the language of the symbolic Alabama's experiences of synesthesia, rendering the tactile sensations of dance through a visual medium. The transcendence of discrete sense impressions—acquired through her bond with Madame, the dance, and an *écriture féminine* — is first imitated, then analyzed, and returned to proper classification by David. His comprehension is limited, however; he reductively argues that rhythm is "a purely physical exercise," not fully grasping that synesthesia transcends a single sense—that rhythm may be visually suggested but it is perceived through the auditory sense as well as through the tactile (as for the deaf). The group's appreciative response to David parodies the public response Scott received for his appropriations of Zelda as text: "'Oh, Mr. Knight,' said the women, 'what a wonderful idea!'" (209).

The waltz that the novel's title asks be saved (implicitly for Alabama) is denied her, and the entire novel is an exposé of that denial. Zelda transcribes the implications of such an appropriation of her experience and thus reappropriates it for herself. The paintings she describes in the novel ultimately became her own. In the 1940s Zelda painted a variety of ballet-inspired works, and even her paintings with biblical and fairy-tale subjects depict the characters in dancing poses.[21] In writing this novel Zelda appropriates the vocations of painter and writer simultaneously, conceptualizing paintings she went on to execute, and writing an alternative to the life she lived, informed by her understanding of the consequences she experienced. *Save Me the Waltz* narrates, insistently, the effort to "transgress the limits" imposed on women. The Fitzgerald war over common property fictionalized in *Save Me the Waltz* undermines the myth of Scott's "poor lost Zelda,"[22] through a scathing and tragic exposé of the extensive obstacles to a woman's artistic identity.

Radclyffe Hall and Una Troubridge, 1927. Photograph reprinted with the permission of the estate of Radclyffe Hall and the estate of Una Troubridge. All rights reserved. Hulton Archive/Getty Images.

CHAPTER FOUR

Accommodation in Radclyffe Hall's *The Forge*

Two geniuses in one small house . . .

—Hall, *The Forge*

Lesbian modernists also produced novels depicting the writer's struggle with identity and relationship. *The Well of Loneliness,* Radclyffe Hall's controversial novel, is perhaps the most celebrated example. Hall and H.D. are unusual among lesbians in the early modernist period in that they produced fiction in which both partners are presented as writers/artists, texts centered around the interpersonal struggle over this role. The contested site in modernist novels depicting lesbian relationships is more often romantic and erotic; resentment is directed against society as the representative of patriarchy rather than against the female partner. This generalization is not intended to idealize lesbian literary liaisons, which often involve jealousy and suppressed ambition, just as in heterosexual liaisons.[1] There are several possible cultural reasons that auto/biographical liaison fiction foregrounds heterosexual partners during this particular moment in Anglo-American literary culture (see the introduction and later this chapter).[2] In this chapter I argue that parody in *The Forge,* although it cannot dramatize a solution for the parodied characters, creates a text that explores the partners' conflicted struggle for subjectivity and suggests the extratextual potential of achieving it.

In *The Forge* Hall exploits the form of the tribute, writing the other for the other, in an attempt to bridge the self/Other division as well as the unequal professional status characteristic of their relationship. As strategies to destabilize the self/Other hierarchy, Hall develops various techniques such as the cross-attribution of autobiographical traits, the articulation of the self by the other, parallel discoveries by the partners within the couple, mediation by a third party, and the parody of gendered conventions. Hall's tribute to her lover, Una Troubridge, takes the unexpectedly light form of comic social parody, a mode Hall uses to critique the limitations of the subject/Other dyad and to explore the

possibility of subject status for both partners. The novel's comic defla-
tion of Hilary, the (male) character based on Hall herself, not only critiques patriarchal privilege but also undermines the stereotyped conception of the dour and humorless lesbian.

Two other major modernist tributes, Virginia Woolf's *Orlando* (1928)
and Gertrude Stein's *Autobiography of Alice B. Toklas* (1933), gesture toward fictional literary-liaison auto/biography yet exclude themselves
from this subgroup by not depicting a writing couple, although they do
present alternatives to the heterosexual treatment of subjectivity.
Woolf's *Orlando,* her experimental fictional biography of Vita Sackville-
West, overcomes the problem of the hierarchized subject/Other by writing the book's author out of the text. This self-effacing novel is a tribute
to Woolf's lover, though it also functions indirectly to foreground her
own virtuosity as a writer in its strikingly original transhistorical experimentation with genre and gender. As Orlando finally gains fame for her
poem "The Oak Tree" (Sackville-West's *The Land*), the text fictionally
grants Sackville-West subjectivity as a writer, a gift Woolf had trouble
bestowing on her lover in real life.[3] Ultimately, however, *Orlando* can be
classified neither as a fictional auto/biography of its author nor as a liaison novel; it sidesteps the problems of writing rivalry by choosing to
write the story of the individual lover rather than the couple. Stein's
The Autobiography of Alice B. Toklas also presents an alternative to the
heterosexual roman à clef. In the inverse of Woolf's self-effacing strategy, Stein purports to surmount the inequality of the subject/Other: she
writes *herself* into text by assuming the voice of the Other. *Alice B. Toklas* may be considered a fictional autobiography in the same sense as
Nin's *Diary* (both gain classification as fiction by falsely presenting
themselves as nonfiction), but nevertheless it is not a book about a *writing* couple. The book presents Alice as a writer's assistant (and covertly,
a muse and lover); it comprises a tribute to the beloved, but through
writing for her—that is, in her place—it obscures the possibility of subjectivity for Alice as a writer herself within the text.[4]

Radclyffe Hall's *The Forge* (1924) centers on the struggle between relationship and vocation within a couple that is ostensibly heterosexual
but clearly coded as lesbian, and which draws significantly from Hall's
long-term relationship with Una Troubridge. In *The Life and Death of
Radclyffe Hall,* Troubridge compares herself and Hall explicitly to the
novel's protagonists, finding an autobiographical resemblance in their
quick decision to move to London and in the portrait of their beloved
dachshund, the fictional Sieglinde, "though some of that Lady's adventures were imaginary" (65). The device of the lesbian-coded heterosexual couple allows Hall to "write with a curious double insight—write
both men and women from a personal knowledge"—a tactic Stephen
Gordon's lesbian governess, Puddle, advocates in *The Well of Loneliness*
(*Well* 233). Puddle and Hall both anticipate de Lauretis's call for a sub-

ject that would be "at the same time inside *and* outside the ideology of gender, and conscious of being so, conscious of that twofold pull, of that division, that doubled vision" (de Lauretis, *Technologies* 10). As coded lesbian fictional auto/biography, the novel explores conflicts within a same-sex writing couple. Read as a critique of heterosexual marriage, however, the novel exposes the consequences of hierarchical gender difference for both (male) husband and (female) wife.

SUBORDINATION AND VICARIOUS CREATIVITY

The publication of Hall's critically neglected *The Forge* chronologically precedes the better-known and more experimental *Orlando* and *Autobiography of Alice B. Toklas*.[5] As a novelist, Hall is often pejoratively viewed as traditional when compared with more innovative modernist and contemporary lesbian writers, perhaps because the controversial subject matter of her best-known novel, *The Well of Loneliness* (1928), is cast in the framework of a Victorian Bildungsroman. Read as a coded lesbian novel, *The Forge* suggests that her work is indeed innovative; in some respects it is a forerunner, a prototype, of the fictional autobiographies of Woolf and Stein, texts that are also coded rather than overtly lesbian. The roles of Hilary and Susan Brent, the heterosexual protagonists in *The Forge*, may be read as a comment on patriarchy or as a butch-femme masquerade. The butch-femme masquerade mocks the Lacanian self/Other dyad. Although the masquerade appears hierarchized (with the butch assuming male/patriarchal dominance), as Sue-Ellen Case explains, "these are not split subjects" but, rather, they replace "the Lacanian slash with a lesbian bar" (56–57). What is generally viewed as the phallic privilege of the butch, and as the lack of the femme, becomes a farce because "there is no referent in sight; rather, the fictions of penis and castration become ironized and 'camped up'" (Case 64). Butch and femme are assumed roles, evading biological classification.

Hall's novel posits more flexible role-crossings than those discernible in her real-life relationship. "John" Radclyffe Hall and Una Troubridge first met in 1913, but Hall was involved with another woman ("Ladye," Mabel Veronica Batten), and they did not become attracted to each other until a second meeting in 1915. Their physical relationship began in November of that year (Ormrod 65, 71). In the early phase, mutual admiration of each other's work was important; John had purchased a statuette sculpted by Una even before meeting her (Ormrod 72). This initial artistic appreciation between the new lovers took the form of exchange: "Una and John revelled in each other's artistic gifts. Una gave John her Faun drawings; John had them framed. John read 'her two best stories' aloud to Una; Una reviewed and criticized them" (Cline 121). The relationship did not sustain this artistic equality, however. Cline concludes that Hall "was not adverse to accepting Una's offer of artistic subservience in favour of the 'greater good' of their unit" (114). In Hall and Troubridge's relationship, the role of writer remained uncontested because one partner subordinated herself to the "genius" of the other.

In fact, each of Hall's long-term lovers deferred to her talent, using her own talents to further Hall's career. Ladye (Hall's lover for eight years before her liaison with Una) sponsored Hall's writing by sending some of her short stories to publisher William Heinemann, an acquaintance (Baker 58). As a result of the contact, Heinemann encouraged Hall to write a novel rather than pursuing the short story genre (58). Ladye was Hall's "unofficial editor and publicist," according to Cline: "John's work had always been Ladye's primary concern. She corrected the spelling, did the copying, transcribed the manuscripts, orchestrated the readings. She had found composers to set the poems to music, had found a publisher to read the first fictions" (108). Cline quotes from an essay Hall wrote after Ladye's death, in which she uses a metaphor drawn from editing—"blue pencil"—as an analogy to Ladye's influence on her "character" (85). Ladye and Troubridge were rivals for Hall's love and for the role of writer's helper, but neither Ladye nor Troubridge engaged in competition with Hall for the role of writer.

Comparing herself to her predecessor (Ladye died of a stroke at fifty-nine), Troubridge wonders, "Whether she would have liked the life that (proudly and joyfully!) was mine for so many years; a life of watching, serving and subordinating everything in existence to the requirements of an overwhelming literary inspiration and industry" (39). Herself an artist and a translator, Troubridge subordinated her career to Hall's. Yet a propensity for vicarious creativity—as well as the potential for collaboration—is exhibited through the titles Troubridge invented for Hall's novels: *The Unlit Lamp, The Well of Loneliness, The Master of the House,* and *The Sixth Beatitude* were all her creations (Troubridge 69, 81). When she wrote "their" story, she nevertheless chose to write a biography of Hall rather than autobiography and claimed it was "the story of Radclyffe Hall and not of Una Troubridge" (44). Troubridge's biographer, Richard Ormrod, wonders "what she might have been without John. She had the ability to become a serious sculptor, painter or book illustrator; she possessed an intellectual, refined mind, and very considerable linguistic and musical talents" (316).

Troubridge subordinated her talents during Hall's lifetime, but she engaged in posthumous serial "collaboration" to elegize her lover, writing a biography of her partner after death had severed the relationship and subordinating personal subjectivity in her choice of subject while claiming subject status as a writer. According to Franks: "Radclyffe Hall the woman (as distinguished from the artist) is, in a sense, Una's creation, the leading character in her biography, her diaries, and, not least important, in her memories, many of which she shared with [her biographer] Dickson and which are preserved in his book" (11). Katrina Rolley's analysis of their style of dress and their gendered roles as lesbians suggests posthumous subjectivity and appropriation; she notes that, whereas Troubridge dressed more femininely while Hall was living, after her death in 1943 "Una began to wear her lover's clothes" (63). Rolley notes that this might have been a sign of mourning or it might be that "Radclyffe Hall's death freed Una from her supporting role and allowed her to take on that of 'congenital invert' in her own right, something which would have been impossible during Hall's lifetime" (64). Such speculation has implications for the notion of serial subjectivity: that partners might exchange roles and each might voluntarily assume subject status as a temporary position (obviously, and ironically, an alternative that can only be reciprocal while both are living).

Despite the inequality of the relationship, Hall did not make the mistake made by her fictional counterpart, writer Stephen Gordon in *The Well of Loneliness*, who discourages her lover, Mary Lewellyn, from helping as a secretary, leaving Mary neither a vocation nor a chance to help her lover professionally. Although Troubridge subordinated her own work to Hall's, she did write articles for various media (including the *Sunday Times*); she read for the agency that handled Hall's work; and she translated Charles Pettit's *Le Fils du Grand Eunuque* in 1924, the same year *The Forge* was published (Baker 178; Souhami 140). Franks notes that it was Una who was "solely responsible for selecting Radclyffe Hall's reading material" (7). Hall was apparently dyslexic, and Troubridge was available to help her in any capacity, including proofing her letters for spelling (Troubridge 71; Souhami 12). Ormrod characterizes Una's help as facilitative: "No longer just lover and companion, she came to see herself as an essential part of the creative process: providing and maintaining an emotionally and domestically stable and harmonious home in which John could work with a free mind" (150). Even in the difficult last nine years of their relationship, when John had developed an infatuation with Evegenia Souline and was unfaithful, Una "offered to take John's dictation in order to spare her eyes[,] . . . they achieved an 'eminently workable combination'; and Una knew 'the joy of being brought closer to her than ever before in the creative work that was an essential part of her being'" (Ormrod 260).

CODED AUTO/BIOGRAPHY AND CROSS-ATTRIBUTION

The Forge, dedicated "to Una, with love," explores in coded fashion the conflicts between love and vocation for a lesbian couple. The novel is not only autobiographically coded, as it fictionalizes experiences of its author and her long-term lover, it is also more generally coded

lesbian. Hall was insistent about establishing herself as a writer of literary merit before she broached the topic of homosexuality in her fiction,
perhaps the reason the coded *Forge* precedes the overtly lesbian *Well of
Loneliness* by four years. The first novel Hall ever wrote, *The Unlit Lamp*
(published the same year as *The Forge*), is more conventionally coded
lesbian through the device of romantic—but apparently nonsexual—
friendship. The female protagonist is prevented from leading the life of
a New Woman, and specifically from sharing a flat with a female friend,
by her all-consuming duty to her demanding mother.[6] Hall also confounds the gendering of her fictional prototype, as Hilary is described as
"such a queer mixture . . . quite unlike any other man" (*Forge* 52).[7]
Hall's use of the word *queer* anticipates current usage, and her coding of
the lesbian as "male" is congruent with her belief that true homosexuality (that is, exclusive same-sex affiliation) is genetic inversion.[8]

In *The Forge* a number of autobiographical features—Troubridge's
bobbed hair and Hall's "high-bridged nose" (67), Hall's chain-smoking
and propensity to collect oak furniture, the couple's interest in purebred dogs, their separate rooms with a "communicating door" (32),
and their proclivity to move restlessly from city house to country
house and from country to country—are represented in the purportedly heterosexual couple Hilary and Susan Brent. In self-mocking
metafictional fashion, the novel also contains a cameo appearance of a
lesbian couple who would be familiar to their contemporaries as Hall
and the monocled Lady Troubridge: "That queer woman dressed up as
a porter and the other one with the eyeglass, I should never have
known they were women; Lady—what was her name?" (133). The fictional couple is childless but establish an alternative family with their
dachshund as a child, another feature of the equivocal gender coding.
When the Brents occupy Bambury Hall, they are welcomed in the
community even though people "thought it rather a pity that Susan
bobbed her hair" (21), a coded reference to the couple's lesbianism. It
is interesting that Hall transposes and confuses their butch-femme
identities: because Hall is already fictionally identified as the "husband" (Hilary), it is Susan (the fictional Una) who is the partner coded
as "masculine" by the community. The flexibility of these categories,
and one partner's ability to assume the role of the other, provides a
hint that the self/Other hegemony is a border that can be crossed—as
long as one partner willingly assumes the role of the Other.

The cross-identification of autobiographical traits and the articulation of the self by the Other are strategies that destabilize the
self/Other hierarchy. In a technique with an effect similar to—and a
forerunner of—Stein's ventriloquizing of Toklas, Hall foregrounds her
partner's perspective. I term this *cross-attribution,* a kind of identification with the Other or an imagined crossing over from the role of self
to that of Other which breaks down barriers between subjectivities.

Troubridge's customary monocle, for example, is transposed in fiction as Hilary's eye patch. Franks quite rightly views this as a symbol of Hilary's "psychological myopia" (64). The detail also cultivates, however, the media image associated with Hall, who was often described or depicted as wearing a monocle, part of her extravagantly "masculine" costume. It is ironic that, although "not one photograph showed her with the monocle in her eye, it became her media trademark" (Cline 219).[9] Thus, in fictionalizing the couple, Hall exchanges the traits—monocle, bobbed hair, and so on—that were associated with each partner. She also obscures the boundary between the biographical reality and the media image of the two.

Unlike the heterosexual-liaison novels discussed elsewhere in this book, and although authored by the seemingly dominant partner (Hall, as Hilary Brent), *The Forge* focuses on the subordinate partner (Troubridge, as Susan Brent). Although she creates a more flattering depiction of Troubridge than of herself, Hall not only exposes the professional inequality of the partners but also compensates for it through fictionalization. She reveals the burden placed on the subordinated partner through a humorous dialogue in which Hilary complains that Susan is not keeping up with the demands of being both housekeeper and secretary to her husband. Susan protests: "I'm at your beck and call from morning to night. I never sit down to balance the books that you don't come after me to read your poems; and only last Monday when I was in the middle of ordering the food . . . you called me away to look up Hydrocephalus or Beri-Beri or something in the *Encyclopedia Britannica*" (*Forge* 43). In this sympathetic portrayal fictionalizing the contribution of the partner (Susan describes her role in helping Hilary as a "collaborator" [44]), Hall attributes a more significant professional role to her partner than the modest Troubridge ever attributed to herself.

Although the novel is written in an omniscient point of view, Susan's thoughts are more often and more sympathetically presented while Hilary is treated with a greater degree of humor and irony. For example, Hilary describes a fellow writer, Victor Lumsden, as having a "literary career [which] bore a strong resemblance to his own." Then, the parallel established, Lumsden is subsequently accused of being "a rich intelligent dilettante" (*Forge* 115–16). Hall's self-mockery is intensified as Lumsden is given "beautiful hands" (116), an attractive feature of Hall herself. During the couple's separation near the end of the novel, the narrative follows Susan's development whereas Hilary's parallel search for self is presented indirectly, and much less extensively, through his letters to Susan. The technique of cross-identification blurs the autobiographical subject position and resembles the technique several critics have associated with Stein's signature-doodle, "Gertrice/Altrude," which, according to Gilmore, indicates "Stein's ambivalence about the self as a unified figure" and the "signature on which traditional interpretations of autobiography depend" (204). Such devices have the effect of foregrounding the Other and her intermittent struggle to achieve subject status within the relationship.

The challenges facing the woman writer/artist within patriarchy are explored through Susan, a painter, displacing onto the fictional Other the conflict one might attribute to Hall. The bulk of the novel sketches a literary liaison apparently much like Hall and Troubridge's, with Susan nurturing Hilary's writing: "Why, he couldn't write a chapter without consulting her, and he had a trick of throwing all his letters at her to be opened. 'Tell me if they're interesting, Susan!' He liked to talk for hours, too, with her to listen" (*Forge* 51). Yet in the novel Hall reevaluates the partners' respective vocational status. Hilary, a poet, is much more the dilettante than Hall was—and it is revealed that Susan was "[i]n a fair way to make a name for herself as a flower painter" at the time of her marriage, a reputation Troubridge never claimed. Susan plays the role of woman artist, torn between art and relationship, who feels like a traitor and a renegade for her desire to paint and is "interrupted on some household matter" each time she sets up her materials (220). On one occasion, Susan gets angry when Hilary's demands for her assistance with his writing interrupt her work—not her painting, her work as an artist, ironically, but her socially prescribed work as housekeeper. Hilary's subsequent criticism, that Susan is both too serious and too frivolous, foregrounds his impossible expectation that Susan fulfill two roles at once: he distracts her from completing either her painting or her housework and then criticizes her resultant poor performance as both artist and wife.

Through the coded, ostensibly heterosexual union, Hall crosses gender lines by playing on the feminine metaphor frequently used to suggest women's oppression when Hilary is grieved to find a bird in a six-inch cage.[10] Although at first the caged bird would seem to be associated with the wife, the first to realize and articulate her dissatisfaction, it is subsequently revealed to be the husband, Hilary, who is the bird caged by lack of opportunity for self-cultivation. Susan tells him, "Yes, I want you to go . . . I've opened your cage door wide" (*Forge* 273). Finally, near the end of the novel, the metaphor is applied to Susan as well: "She felt that her spirit could no longer soar out and meet new adventures with rapture; it was like a bird kept too long in a cage, it could not fly far from its prison" (303). Typical of the cross-identification and mutual discovery of the couple, both are caged, not only by a relationship (as Susan's entrapment continues while separated from Hilary) or by gender in this case (since both "male" and female partners are affected) but also by profound internalized obstacles. By her coding her lesbian couple as ostensibly heterosexual, Hall explores not external social impediments to love—a characteristic theme of lesbian texts—but rather more complexly internalized obstacles, William Blake's "mind-forged manacles," to self-development.

Hall also blurs gendered distinctions and butch-femme dichotomies as both partners suffer from some allegedly "female" illness—real or imagined. Susan's response to Hilary's restlessness and depression foregrounds gendered stereotypes about mental illness: "If you were a woman, Hilary, I should say you were distinctly hysterical" (*Forge* 69). Adam Parkes, however, points to a number of critics who argue that, during the postwar period, hysteria was a sort of gendered no-man's-land; as an illness it was "an unstable, theatrical terrain where men might look like women, and where women might resemble men" (444). Susan's remark both equivocates about Hilary's gender and emphasizes the social construction that genders diseases. For his part, Hilary diagnoses Susan with stereotypically female maladies, describing her repeatedly as fatigued and exhausted when they travel. The depiction of both husband and wife as ill or hypochondriacal draws on autobiographical material (both Hall and Troubridge frequently suffered from mysterious maladies) and contributes to the lesbian coding, for both prototypes are, in fact, women.

Hall's emphasis on the drive for equality in a relationship often takes the form of mutual and/or reciprocal discovery, as in scenes where Susan and Hilary reach the same conclusion separately. Whereas in the heterosexual-liaison novels the subordinate partner becomes dissatisfied with her role in relation to her more productive or better-known spouse, *The Forge* emphasizes the self-realization of both partners. These scenes often take the form of literal cross-articulation, where one partner gives voice to a mutual revelation. The decision to give up Bambury Hall, for example, is articulated by Susan but claimed by Hilary as his own idea: "I've been longing to say the same thing to you, only I haven't dared" (*Forge* 53). A climactic scene in the novel amalgamates the contradictory desires for independence and interdependence when Susan creates a metaphor for their mutual dissatisfaction: they are "two butterflies pinned together." As she explains, each has an individual need for wholeness, "to be a complete personality again." Their dilemma is identical, but their individual needs for subjectivity must somehow be differentiated. To Hilary's expression of surprise at her articulation of his very thoughts she responds, "I'm pinned with you, so I can't help knowing can I?" (192). In a reversal, and a precursor, of Stein's technique through which the subject ventriloquizes the Other, Susan articulates Hilary's feelings to him; it is the subordinate partner who speaks the feelings of the dominant writing partner. As Susan articulates for the subject, then, there is a double irony since Hilary, after all, is the writer.

In a related scene, Hall uses a different kind of cross-articulation to expose a seeming collaboration that is actually an appropriation of the artistic production of the other. Hilary repeats Susan's conversation back to her as his own creation, appropriating her speech self-servingly for his own banal poetry: "'When the guns stopped booming in France, and the bombs stopped dropping on England,' . . . that's not a bad line for a poem," he reflects as he listens to his wife. "And I like that idea of yours about the air being so still that one could hear the echoes of one's past" (*Forge* 25). While acknowledging his debt, he still assumes sole authorship of material he has appropriated. When the novel is read as a critique of patriarchy, such scenes emphasize the unfairness of patriarchal exploitation of the woman artist. When the novel is read as the coded story of two writers, in reality both women, it suggests that texts that appear to be the work of a single creative genius may obscure a hidden collaborative origin.

Although each partner complains about interruptions and distractions caused by the other, each comes to the same discovery, that the responsibility for creation lies with the individual: "That winter, for the first time in his easy, prosperous life, Hilary felt seriously discontented with Hilary" (*Forge* 229). For her part, Susan realizes that Hilary is not the only obstacle to her career but that she creates her own distractions. Her search for a studio is presented ironically. She mentally furnishes it as she would decorate a home, and she apparently sets herself up for failure as she tells her agent she wants a studio with a "porcelain bath," "central heating," and a parquet floor "that one can dance on" and then finds just such a dream studio (226–27).

The conflict figured by the pinned butterflies, between the partners' mutual desire for both a unified self and the subjectivity of the individual artist, is further explored in Hilary's dialogue with Donna Vittoria. As Franks points out, Hilary's "capacity for self-insight is certainly more limited" than Susan's (63). Much slower than Susan to understand their conflict, Hilary insists on looking for external rivals for his wife's attention. He calls her expression of her thoughts "moral Bolshevism" (*Forge* 195). When Hilary explains that "there's no one but Susan in all the world, no one at all," Donna Vittoria counters with, "There is *Hilary*." Hilary finally grasps the mutuality and universality of their seemingly individual problem: "but there's always a ME with all of us," a subject struggling to speak (199). In a parallelism that replaces hierarchy with reciprocity, Susan recognizes she would like to return to painting, a revelation followed by Hilary's discovery that, despite his income, he needs work to satisfy other needs.

The narrative technique of the reciprocal or parallel discovery functions as a verbal equivalent of the visual "binary portrait" Terry Castle defines in her comparison of gay and lesbian circles of the 1920s, Noel Coward and Radclyffe Hall in particular. Exemplified by photographs of the era, including one of Hall and Troubridge, Castle's binary portrait is "a type of fashionable formal portrait . . . with two sitters posing as mirror opposites or as a pair of overlapping, almost identical, profiles" (25).[11] Contextualizing this portraiture as "a manifestation of '20s and '30s sexual style," Castle views it as an alternative to the "standard heterosexual marriage portrait," which visually subordinates the wife. This mode instead "often turned upon an implicitly 'homosexual' confounding of traditional sex roles . . . [to] emphasiz[e] the sameness and equality of the two individuals portrayed" (27). Hall's image of two butterflies likewise suggests "sameness and equality" within the lesbian couple.

In *The Forge* the partners each acknowledge a need for the other in the midst of a growing reciprocal respect for the other's vocation. In a comment suggesting the Lacanian need for reflection by the Other, Hilary asks, "Who's to read my work aloud to me if you're not here?" (237). In conjunction with the idea of Susan's work, he says, "You'd better potter about a bit with your painting again if you're dull; you know, just as a hobby. It wouldn't prevent your seeing to things in the house, and I think I'd feel happier if I knew that you were occupied; there's quite a good light in the drawing-room" (*Forge* 237). Although Hilary still subordinates Susan's art to his own comfort, his effort produces a rejuvenating effect on their relationship: "I feel as though I'd met you for the first time," Susan says (237). As part of Hall's critique of the inequality of heterosexual roles, the fictional account places an emphasis on mutual, parallel actions of the lovers: "she and Hilary, unknown to each other, had made a simultaneous decision. She had quite as much right to a career as he had, more, in a way, for she had been the first to start one seriously" (238).

In contrast to the heterosexual-liaison novels examined in this study, Hall's fictional auto/biography does not expose or parody her real-life partner but instead provides a vehicle for self-exploration and self-criticism. Franks argues the novel reflects Hall's "own ambivalence toward art, an ambivalence which had its origins in her psychological make-up" (66). Her exploration of hegemony within the fictional couple allows Hall to reveal the complexity of both subject and object positions. The Brents separate after Susan articulates to herself and to Hilary her dissatisfaction with her thwarted artistic career, providing the climax of the novel. "I'm not whole any more, there's a bit of me gone for ever" (*Forge* 304), she laments, suggesting the post-mirror-stage mourning for separation and loss of wholeness that is the consequence of developing the self.

The treatment of Susan and Hilary's personal conflict emphasizes that it does not result from diminished love but from a more general conflict between the interests of the couple and those of the individual self, a conflict inherent in relationships: "It was not in the least that she did not love him, but rather that she longed in spite of, or because of that love, to be a complete personality again, and not just a part of someone else" (*Forge* 192). Susan tells Hilary, "we're one, and we ought to be two." She continues, "I want to love you as my entire self, instead of just as a bit of you" (194). The construction of the self and the lover as one entity suggests Lacan's punning *"l'hommelette"* (little man–omelette), the undifferentiated, sprawling pre-mirror-stage mass that precedes the individualized self. As Hall exploits the form of the tribute, writing the other for the other, she attempts to bridge the self/Other division, an expansive view. At the same time, although the lesbian couple behind the heterosexual coding may resemble the unified mother-daughter dyad, the partners still experience the ambivalent self/Other tension between relation and autonomy. *The Forge* explores the consequences of hierarchy for the subordinated Other and advocates different solutions from those considered in the heterosexual-liaison novels.

SOCIAL COMEDY AND THE THIRD-PARTY MENTOR

The innovation of *The Forge* is its double vision—that it may be read on one hand as a coded lesbian roman à clef about Hall and Troubridge and on the other hand as a social comedy, a critique of hierarchical gender roles. As a roman à clef, the novel fictionalizes not only Hall and Troubridge as its heterosexual protagonists but also Romaine Brooks as Venetia Ford.[12] Susan's unfulfilled vocation is counterpointed with that of Venetia Ford, a successful artist, a double, and a mentor who both symbolizes and precipitates Susan's artistic aspirations.[13] Hall decenters mentorship hierarchy, the self/Other polarity, by introducing a third party and having this external mentor absorb and diffuse the tension about artistic aspiration within the couple, thus forming a triangular construction, which (further suggesting the sprawling *"hommelette"*) also expands the dyad. As a strategy for decentering the conflict over vocation and shared material, moreover, Susan is presented as a painter rather than a writer (Troubridge herself was a sculptor).

The relationship with the external mentor begins with one and one-half pages of internal monologue, conveying Susan's admiration, confusion, and distress in first meeting Ford:

> That's the real thing, that's genius, can't get very far if you don't feel that kind of urge. I felt rather a worm when she asked me what I did—no I didn't, I'm Hilary's wife—yes, I did—oh, I don't know! Awfully interesting people they were to-night. Dupont, I ought to have known about him, but I didn't. I don't seem to know about anything these days, not things that really matter. I wonder what the Duchess writes? Oh, well, I can't read French, anyhow! I wonder if they'd like my friends in London? No, I'm sure they wouldn't—bridge, poker. I can't see Venetia Ford at Ascot, somehow. I wonder what she'd find to say to Lord Lindhurst and his pigs? Perhaps he'd commission her to fresco the walls of his new

cow-sheds, it would be just like him. What a joke, I'd love to see Venetia's face! We ought to have a post card about Sieglinde; I hope she's all right. Those new boudoir caps were very cheap, only five shillings each, with the exchange. I wonder if Venetia Ford wears boudoir caps? Probably not, I don't think they'd suit her. Hilary was terribly grumpy tonight. Perhaps he's not well—he looks all right. Venetia Ford painted "The Weeping Venus" and I'm going to see the original to-morrow. I wonder what she'd have thought of my painting? Curious to think that I painted myself once. If I painted now I shouldn't have felt so out of things this evening. Those people must think "We others," as the Duchess calls us, awfully dull. Well, we are. . . . *How* I longed to dance just at the very end, I suppose it was the band got me—champagne— delayed reaction? I only had two glasses, still—Oh! No, I don't think so. What good times we had at the Slade, I was very happy there—Well, I'm very happy now, at least I suppose I am—Can't have everything in this world—I must look up Grace Hill again when we get back to London, might as well try— (*Forge* 132–34)

In its exuberance and excess, the monologue suggests that this meeting with the artist Venetia Ford is for Susan an encounter with the chaotic but potentially poetic resources of the presymbolic *chora*. At the same time, the monologue's content is banal, its effect comic. It also depicts a more superficial character than Susan's sophisticated prototype, Troubridge, who not only read but translated French. Ranging in seemingly random fashion through frivolous concerns about Ford's boudoir caps and the dachshund, the flitting of Susan's thoughts comically but ironically undermines her steadfast dedication to a vocation at the very moment she becomes obsessed with it.

In his role as philistine, Hilary is the patriarchal husband (rather than the autobiographical Hall) and plays the role of obstructive subject to the subordinated Other. He is unable to appreciate Ford's masterpiece "The Weeping Venus" as the more aesthetically sensitive Susan does; for Hilary it is "more like a corpse than a goddess" (*Forge* 147). Cline finds Hall's allusion to Brooks's "most notable" painting significant: "Romaine intended a strongly feminist theme for her painting: that women's reproductive capacities condemn them to second class citizenship, a fate from which they can only be released by death. Hall uses the title of the painting, but sanitizes and individualizes the theme so that the painting merely represents in Susan's awestruck view 'a terrible conception of love'" (190). Susan's monologue about Ford's genius may also function to comment derisively on the real-life prototype.[14] According to Franks, the purblind Susan "is so awed by Venetia's genius, so envious of her apparent self-fulfillment as an artist, that she fails to recognize the terrible strain, the life-denying and self-destructive facets of her personality" (63).

Since Hilary is a philistine who cannot appreciate any art, much less his wife's, Venetia is a more suitable, more receptive mentor for Susan. The mentorship dialogues that characterize literary liaisons occur with a fellow painter rather than with a writer and lover; it is Venetia Ford rather than Hilary who precipitates Susan's insight into her discontent by asking "What work do you do?"—to which query Susan is mortified to respond "nothing" (*Forge* 129). Susan turns to Venetia when she realizes she wants to recapture her vocation as a painter. She confesses to being the painter of the white camellias and asks Venetia, "Is it too late now for me to begin again?" (223). Susan also explores her developing aesthetic with Venetia, who purports to be satisfied with representational art: "Wouldn't it be better if you just expressed the flowers?" But Susan regards self-expression as an integral part of her art: "I want them to be part of me" (283). Susan's desire to embed her identity in her art resembles Hall's desire to use her fiction to further acceptance of lesbianism (one facet of her identity) as an integral part of her art and her writing career.

To emphasize the inextricable connection between vocation and relationship, the artistic mentor also plays the role of marital counselor when the Brents' yearlong separation is mediated by Venetia. Susan analyzes their marital problems for her: "We were too acutely conscious of each other, I think it may have been that. Hilary couldn't write because of me, he never actually said so, but I felt it; and I couldn't paint because of him, we sapped each other's vitality" (*Forge* 281). The separation does not resolve their individual problems, but it does allow Susan to explore the conflict between vocation and relationship with a more impartial guide than Hilary. She tells her mentor gloomily, "I'm not great enough, . . . I can't throw everything off. You're just Venetia; but I'm not just Susan, I'm a part of everyday things" (282).

The continuing dialogue with Venetia also provides an answer to the conflict Susan feels between the tyranny of art and the attraction of everyday life when Venetia takes her to the restaurant of the "Austrian wizard" Ries. Franks claims that "Hall never suggests the possibility of even a temporary synthesis between art and experience" (65), but this scene seems to pose at least a temporary solution. In the Bon Acceuil the chef has combined the two poles of Susan's conflict, art and the quotidian. By placing only seven tables in his downstairs room, he reveals himself to be "a man of self-restraint and an artist" (*Forge* 288). The "Fragonard of the culinary art, the pictures he produced were small but perfect" (289). However, this culinary solution—couched in the language of her own artistic vocation—apparently remains unperceived by Susan; in a manner characteristic of the comic novel, its characters are presented as less perceptive than its readers.

It is Venetia as role model who overcomes Susan's unstated fears (and Hilary's stated prejudice) that a woman cannot be an artist. Ultimately, however, the fictional treatment of Venetia is ironic. As her enthusiasm reawakens her artistic vocation, Susan naively inflates Venetia's professional dedication: "Before that art [Venetia] abased herself and prayed, and while betraying lesser things, she never betrayed her god" (*Forge* 224–25). When she sees the feminine dishabille of Venetia's bedroom, Susan fears it discredits her mentor as an artist: "there was nothing here that suggested a worker"; "I wonder if she's a fraud?" Susan says to herself (287). In the scenes where Susan cultivates Venetia's friendship it is revealed that, despite her purported artistic freedom, Venetia suffers from the same artistic block that Susan attributed to the distractions of her own relationship with Hilary. Venetia complains that she cannot paint because of her wealth; she has no privacy. Five years before Virginia Woolf calculated that five hundred pounds was the minimum a woman needs in order to be free to write, this fictional artist announces that she wishes she had *only* five hundred pounds a year (305) so that she would be freed of social obligations that hinder her art. This ironic treatment of the mentor-friend allows Susan to explore the conflict between life and art, rejecting her mentor rather than her lover when the discovery phase of artistic identity is complete—and, in this novel, aborted.

Susan reaches her vocational nadir when Hilary unknowingly comments upon a painting of hers that Venetia has purchased, "What an awfully jolly picture!" thinking it was painted by "some young thing quite unknown at the time" (*Forge* 143). Venetia recognizes the merit of the painting: "you gave it all then, all you had to give" (284). But Hilary gazes at the product of his partner's genius like "a disinterested stranger" (143). Susan cannot confess to him her vocational aspirations, and the aesthetic encounter symbolizes a personal impasse for the couple. Hilary's obtuseness concerning her talents is aggravated by Susan's inability to articulate her ambitions: she "felt herself turning a little pale, with a queer, jumbled-up emotional sensation, that comprised pride and pleasure but also shame. This was her picture of white camellias, she had painted it years ago" (143). Susan articulates a major conflict for the woman writer as she explicitly connects her marriage to her loss of vocation: "'If Venetia Ford thinks my work good, then it must have been very good indeed. I don't want to tell her I've given it all up because I married Hilary.' Then she thought: 'I'm being unjust to Hilary. Hilary found me that barn at Bambury so that I *could* paint" (144).

The novel's parodic treatment of vocation and mentorship foregrounds the inequality within a conventional heterosexual couple, developing a critique of arbitrary, socially imposed gender roles. Susan needed a mentor of the same sex because Hilary views Susan's painting as a feminine, wifely hobby: "You could paint a little, couldn't you?" he asks her condescendingly (*Forge* 253). "One can't paint a '*little*,' and my art is not an *amusement*," she responds. In contrast to socially approved "big subject pictures," he demeans her work as "flower painting" (253). Moreover, Hall parodies patriarchal blindness, its conception of women's "lack" and inability to envision, the patriarchal refusal to "see" the woman in the subject position, through Hilary's absurd failure to distinguish his wife from other material objects. The comic exaggeration of his thoughts about Susan exposes the magnitude of the problem: "Yes, that's Susan, and that's a vase of lilies over there on the table against the curtain. They're both rather lovely, but they don't seem very real; they're not unlike each other, come to think of it" (252). If Hilary cannot distinguish between the artist and the subject of her art—and is not even sure of her reality—then he is certainly not capable of ceding her subject status. His inability to see Susan as a distinct being denies her the subject's desire. Hilary only sees Susan as characterized by lack; he therefore attributes all desire to himself.

Read as a critique of heterosexual marriage, the novel exposes the intimate consequences of gender difference. As a man and a husband, Hilary is unable to comprehend Susan's dissatisfaction: "That was a curious thing for Susan to have hit upon; it went quite deep too, very deep. Now if *he* had said that he could have understood it; a man might feel that way, probably always did," he muses to himself (*Forge* 195). By depicting the fictional couple as heterosexual and cultivating the genre of social comedy, Hall provides opportunities for satire (similar to West's) that is more broadly targeted at society than at any individual lover (who derives from patriarchy his masculinist values and his authority—as well as permission for abusing such prerogatives). In contrast to male subjects in the heterosexual-liaison novel, however, Hilary the "husband" is responsive—though his reaction is presented hyperbolically—and is able to hear the "wife's" complaint. When Susan explains her discontent to him, he "listened incredulously to the tale she unfolded, scarcely able to believe his ears. Susan with ambitions, Susan longing to work, Susan also craving to be free" (273). "'So that all the time you've been feeling it too!' he said in a voice of wonder" (274). The masquerade of lesbians as a heterosexual couple—as well as Hall's technique of cross-identification of traits—interrogates the construction and possible essentialism of gender roles. Hall poses the same question Gilmore parodically attributes to Stein: "Is a woman a wife a wife a woman a husband a man a man a husband in marriage?" (Gilmore 210).

In the aftermath of her encounter with Venetia, Susan herself realizes that Hilary's concern for her art is slight; as a husband and a philistine, he is oblivious to the painting she admires. When she reveals to him that she herself painted it, his condescending response is to warn her not to "overtire" herself and to ask if she's had her tonic.

> Looking back, she realised that Hilary had never been very deeply interested in her art, although he had wanted her to paint the flowers at Bambury. She suspected, however, that this had been pure subconscious thrift on his part: having provided a barn, he wanted her to use it; hav-

ing provided the flowers, he had wanted her to paint them. Perhaps he thought that small occupations were good for women. . . . Hilary had not even suggested that she should give up painting when they married. But had he ever seriously contemplated her continuing her art as a career? . . . They had never discussed the possibility of such a thing, and in that she had been as much to blame as he; but she felt that it had always been tacitly understood that the idea would be distasteful to him. And then, in those early days, it had been enough for her to be Hilary's wife; well, now it was not, that was all. (*Forge* 222–23)

Near the end of this passage Susan's progression of ideas provides a revealing chronology: in the "early days" it was enough to have a relationship. The desire for the relationship precedes, logically and emotionally, the subsequent conflict between love and vocation. This prerequisite suggests a possible explanation for the general absence of lesbian literary-liaison fiction: when lesbians are denied the public status of couple, the struggle for social acceptance (articulated in *The Well of Loneliness*) will take precedence over the conflict between love and vocation. As feminist critics have pointed out, women are reluctant to discard "restrictive" privileges they have never acquired. "How can women, much less Lesbians, rejoice in the de(con)struction of a unified self they have never been permitted . . . to possess?" (Wolfe and Penelope 2).[15] Similarly, lesbians are reluctant to challenge or forsake relationships they have been forbidden to have.

PARODIC TREATMENT OF GENDERED CONVENTIONS

Hall uses the lesbian-coded heterosexual couple in *The Forge* to parody hierarchical gendered conventions and thus criticize the societal values they reflect and perpetuate. For example, in a conventional (often Victorian) plot, marital problems are often overcome when the wife becomes pregnant. Hall creates a comic parallel, as Susan and Hilary's discontented stay in Italy is ended by a letter from their housekeeper with the news that their beloved dachshund, described as a "person" for whom Hilary is "Father" (*Forge* 17), is pregnant. The couple rush home from abroad experiencing mock-Victorian fears that the servants will have "men in to sit in the drawing-room" (75) during their absence. This parody of conventional heterosexual gender roles is intensified as the purebred Sieglinde gives birth to "illegitimate" puppies and turns out to be a malicious mother, sitting on her puppies with "murderous intent" (215) when she becomes bored with her new role.

Hilary's "masculine" fantasies are also used to parody the conventional role of woman as muse. In his recurrent restless attraction to any locale other than where he is at present, Hilary imagines that, if he takes Susan to the mountains, isolation from society will solve the problems of their relationship:

> In the big solitudes they would find one another, and heal all their little rifts and misunderstandings. The more he thought of this the more tender he became, until at length his mind began to dwell on Susan with all the tenderness of courtship. He pictured her waiting for him at the window of some old, vine-covered inn. She was standing looking out at the distance from which he would presently come. Her eyes were bright with love and happiness; the mere fact of his approach fulfilled her. She was soft and feminine and beautifully patient, man's perfect prototype of woman. (*Forge* 206)

This idyllic pastoral fantasy, placing the receptive female Other in a romantic setting, instantaneously facilitates male creativity; immediately in the subsequent paragraph, Hilary's "enthusiasm found expression in writing poetry" (206).

Hall satirizes the notion that exalted genres and great subjects are the province of men whereas slight subjects and denigrated genres are relegated to women. Speaking as the ultimate patriarch, Hilary ridicules the notion that Susan's art can be significant, in comparison with his subject and genre, the intellectual novel of ideas: "the kind of novel that would make people *think*" (*Forge* 231). He views Susan's flower painting as "different, it's not like, well—big subject pictures, for instance" (253). The absurdity of his gendering of vocation is exposed, not only by the subsequent anticlimactic narration of his own realization, but by his inflated expression: "A man must work, and not only work, but work for posterity," he muses self-importantly (230). His gendered hierarchy of subject matter is answered by the alternative mentor, Venetia: "To paint one petal with inspiration is as great as painting 'The Weeping Venus.' It's not the subject of a picture that counts, it's the spirit of the subject that you must paint; and to find the spirit even in a blade of grass one must look with one's own entire spirit. Art is the most exacting lover in the world" (283). Art thus has the potential to displace the obtuse lover, Venetia reveals.

Hall also undermines Hilary's conventional gendering of vocation, the privileging of men's work as serious, when the narrator juxtaposes a clichéd "feminine" metaphor with his "masculine" thought: "Simple love stories were good enough for women, but a man should go deeper than that, get down to the roots of things. He determined to begin on entirely new lines, the nucleus of the plot was already in his mind. He hatched on his secret for another week, and then, unable to keep it any longer, went in search of Susan" (232). Comically and ironically, Hilary not only develops his ideas as a hen hatches her eggs but is also totally dependent on his wife for approval. Susan greets his revelation with affectionate humor: "You look so awfully funny, so, so—pompous," she tells him (232); he resembles a "city alderman . . . sticking out your stomach" (233). The contrast between the two lovers' discoveries of their necessary artistic vocation is not in the reception of the announcement by the loved one; Susan is as cool to Hilary's announcement as he was to hers. The difference, rather, is in Hilary's unreflective assurance, the prerogative of men in patriarchy: "I've always felt that I could write, that I've got real talent. Well, now I mean to write in dead earnest, Susan, I'm really going to write a novel this time" (234).

Hall's parody of gendered conventions reaches a climax in *The Forge* when Susan initially denies the stereotypical self-sacrificing role of the Victorian heroine, only to succumb in the end:

> she told herself that she had not the least intention of standing outside his study door like the angel with a flaming sword. Still, to leave him to the mercy of inspiration and the servants—no, she knew that she couldn't do it. If she did she wouldn't paint well, there would always be a hungry Hilary between her and her canvas. At this thought her resentment flared up afresh; he had purposely chosen the one job most calculated to end her ambitions. Had he known by telepathy that she meant to take a studio? (241)

Susan's assumption of this role is treated ironically, mock-heroically, but with self-perception: "She was going to be a noble and self-sacrificing woman; such a dull thing to be, she hated being noble!" (241). Whereas the Victorian novel customarily ends with resigned irony at the woman's lost potential (as with Dorothea Brooke in *Middlemarch*), *The Forge* only provisionally concludes part 3 with this resignation; after Susan's self-sacrificing resolution fails, the couple decide to separate.

Although *The Forge* ends with the typical Victorian resolution of marital conflict (the partners are, and will remain, reconciled), Hall explores the metaphor of forged chains to characterize commitment within loving relationships. Hilary claims: "The only way is to keep very close together, a slack chain doesn't hurt so much" (318). Hilary's long monologue at the novel's close reexamines the notion of chains and suggests that we should reprivilege the idea of commitment, especially for those who are idealistic or artistic: even the Crusaders are "chained to a great ideal" (316); "we're not only born with chains, the whole world's a forge, and we're always forging new ones. We actually forge them out of our pleasures and fasten them on while we're laughing" (317). The ironic variation on Shakespeare's "all the world's a stage" gives a disconcerting twist to Hilary's deconstruction of the negative associations of bondage. He claims "a slack chain doesn't hurt so much," and the partners are reconciled, choosing love over vocation. Yet the silencing of Susan, revealingly described as one of the "givers of life," following Hilary's verbose three-page monologue, undermines his rationalization. Souhami reveals that Hall's original title for the novel was *Chains* (126), and Cline claims that chains were

"Radclyffe Hall's recurring motif" (114); even in her poetry about "loving partnership" she "cannot entirely escape the notion of love as fetters. Love's bonds are chains" (Cline 85).[16]

An auto/biographical reading of the novel's ending foregrounds the sacrifice of the subordinated partner. The ending reflects Troubridge's statement about her own subordination, "a life of watching, serving and subordinating everything" (39), to the greater genius of her partner. Yet the ironic treatment of Hilary's domination and Susan's sacrifice reveals that Hall was all too aware of the implications for the partner subordinated. As Hilary returns, Susan finds herself "slipping, slipping. She wanted to cry out, to clutch at any twig in passing" (*Forge* 315). In a parody of the marriage vow, Susan responds to Hilary's "you don't need to tell me any more" with "But I do, I do!" (315). Through their separation Hilary has readjusted his priorities, but he still does not fully comprehend Susan's need for subject status: "You're my Susan, and that's all that counts. What else could you be, do you think?" he asks blankly (315). For her part, Susan "rallied to one more supreme effort, her sense of self-preservation was strong" (315). But ultimately the two of them choose the chains of love. Cline emphasizes Hall's revaluation of commitment: "Although the fetters symbolism in her light-hearted work *The Forge* is a positive illustration of the empowering influence of commitments, nevertheless Hilary and Susan Brent often feel emotionally chained" (19). The novel's pat resolution ironically discloses that the problem *The Forge* poses—the conflict between vocation and relationship within a couple—has not been fully resolved.

· · ·

The comedy of *The Forge* gives way at the close to a grim realization that accommodation and sacrifice pose an incomplete solution to the self/Other inequality. The correctives tested—such as the articulation of the subject by the Other, the cross-identification of the protagonists, the introduction of a third-party mentor—are revealed to be necessary to communication, and a definition of the problem, but ultimately only hypothetical or ephemeral solutions. The coded lesbianism of the heterosexual couple suggests that, for Hall, the self/Other hierarchy is a problem, for the lesbian as for the heterosexual relationship. As Lacanian theorist Ellie Ragland-Sullivan notes: "Any of us who fashions our sexual *jouissance* into an ideology—heterosexists, heterosexuals, homosexuals, lesbians, married swingers, celibates, youthful experimenters, and so on—expresses desire with the force of a law imposed on others. Thus, any sexual ideology expresses a potential oppression of an other's desire" (68). Susan thinks, "Real genius can always surmount difficulties," but she identifies herself and Hilary as "Two geniuses in one small house, and not real geniuses either'" (*Forge* 238).

The Forge draws on comic romance conventions to probe the problem of subjectivity within the couple. Franks explains, "the couple is reconciled, having ostensibly learned that the multiplicity of attachments one forms, far from being impediments to self-expression, actually constitute one's sole ties with the real world. Further, freely chosen acknowledgment of these ties provides not only the source of all pleasure, but also the essence of identity, self-acceptance, and the ability to love," though she feels there is some doubt that the couple actually "develops or changes" (62). Neither partner in *The Forge* becomes a great artist during their separation, which suggests that perhaps the partners' problem may be one of personal deficiency in talent or dedication. The conventional ending of romantic comedy—the sacrifice of all for love—suggests a surprisingly complacent ideology. Hayden White argues that comic plots show "society . . . as being purer, saner, and healthier as a result of the conflict among seemingly inalterably opposed elements in the world; these elements are revealed to be, in the long run, harmonizable with one another" (*Metahistory* 9). The ending of *The Forge*, however, reveals a contradiction between a light breezy resolution of the comic romance plot and the gravity of the problem shown. The novel's resolution suggests that one partner in a relationship must choose between art and love.

Whereas the heterosexual-liaison novel foregrounds the woman's struggle with a male partner for subject status and sometimes compensates through fiction for the subordination of her real-life career, Hall explores the conflict between relationship and vocation for each partner within a relationship. Yet the novel ends with the typical resolution for female characters in comedy—the privileging of love over vocation, the choice Una Troubridge made in her relationship with Radclyffe Hall.[17] In dramatizing the nobility of her lover's sacrifice, Hall nevertheless reveals an insight into her partner's sacrifice that is never reached by her fictionalized counterpart, Hilary, thus creating a touching tribute to Una Troubridge.

Moreover, the parodic disparity between the limited insight of the lovers and the larger revelations of the novel suggests that, although Susan cannot achieve subject status within the novel (or within patriarchal society), the possibility may be envisioned outside of these constraints. If, as Case postulates, "the subject in heterosexuality cannot become capable of ideological change," then in creating a coded alternative to the heterosexual literary liaison, in placing women in relation to women rather than men, Hall may fictionally postulate a "feminist subject" who is "outside of ideology" and thus "capable of change"—rather than a "female" subject trapped within ideology (56).[18] Via the distancing effect of parody—and posterity—the fictional possibilities transcend the autobiographical and ideological realities.

(starting at the bottom, going counterclockwise) H.D., Richard Aldington in World War I uniform, Bryher in passport photo. All photographs courtesy of Beinecke Rare Book and Manuscript Library, Yale University—Aldington and Bryher photographs from the Yale Collection of American Literature.

CHAPTER FIVE

The Writer Self in H.D.'s Auto/biographical Fiction

> I thought I was someone but he calls me *Personne*, Nobody. I am nobody when it comes to writing novels. But I will find a new name. I will be someone. I will write these novels and re-write them till they come true.
>
> —H.D., *Bid Me to Live*

Julia Ashton, the protagonist of *Bid Me to Live*, suggests that writing may function as therapy, to resolve an identity crisis inextricably linked to the traumatic relationships that "named" her: she will "find a new name" (*Bid Me* 176). H.D. indirectly provides an explanation for Julia's rather enigmatic reference to truth achieved through rewriting in *The Gift*:

> The dream-picture focussed and projected by the mind, may perhaps achieve something of the character of a magic-lantern slide and may "come true" in the projection. But to "come true," it must . . . photograph the very essence of life, of growth, of the process of growing. . . . The dream, the memory, the unexpected related memories must be allowed to sway backward and forward, as if the sheet or screen upon which they are projected, blows and is rippled in the wind of whatever emotion or idea is entering a door, left open. (605–6)[1]

Projection (both cinematic and psychoanalytic) is a kind of vacillating textual representation that gives form to the unconscious. Julia presents the subject (more specifically the writer-subject) as constructed, written into being. In order to establish subjectivity, the author must project her self into being, "a new name"—in order to have a self, and as self-defense against the Other's construction.

H.D. returns obsessively to issues of identity in her fiction, focusing on the inequality of the subject/Other relationship through which the self is reflected and constructed. Among her fictional treatments are two full-fledged romans à clef, *HERmione* (1981) and *Bid Me to Live (A Madrigal)* (1960). Companion novels depicting consecutive phases of her early adulthood, they contain a variety of thinly disguised literary and auto/biographical relationships from this period. A third text, *Palimpsest* (1926), is a collection of three short narratives or novellas; the first of these novellas, called "Hipparchia" and set in classical Rome, presents a cultural displacement of this auto/biographical material.[2] The title *Palimpsest* establishes a narrative metaphor that underpins H.D.'s novelistic aesthetic: the overlapping, multiple versions of the same fictionalized relationships, the proliferation of Others, and the recursive, nonlinear therapeutic process of working through that characterize her fiction. Her emphasis on projected image as both the source and the manifestation of identity elucidates her view of the subject: psychoanalytic and cinematic projection represents the formative stage of identity. Another text, *Tribute to Freud* (1974), takes up the projection metaphor again, as H.D. and her companion, Bryher, share a mutual vision, imaginatively projected as a "dream-picture" on a wall in Corfu.

All these palimpsestic fictions are also to some extent Künstlerromanen (literally "artist novels," about the quest for artistic identity), but *Bid Me to Live* foregrounds the woman's struggle in a writing couple and her literary struggle within patriarchal culture. This novel best represents the literary-liaison subgroup of autobiographical fiction within H.D.'s oeuvre.[3] The overlapping nature of H.D.'s various treatments of literary liaisons and the lack of correspondence between the chronology of H.D.'s life and the novels' composition make any order of discussion somewhat arbitrary; the chapter is organized to correspond (roughly) to the sequence of H.D.'s various mentor-lovers: Ezra Pound and Frances Gregg, Richard Aldington and D. H. Lawrence, and finally Bryher (Annie Winifred Ellerman).

MULTIPLE MENTORS AND
PALIMPSESTIC IMAGES OF THE SELF

In *HERmione* H.D. fictionalizes her early twenties, the period when she lived at home after dropping out of Bryn Mawr, and Pound is cast as an early mentor figure, George Lowndes. This novel also presents alternatives to the male mentor, however, in the characters of the protagonist's mother and her friend, Fayne Rabb, who is based on H.D.'s youthful lover, Frances Gregg. In *Bid Me to Live* H.D. fictionalizes her life in London during World War I. Her persona is named Julia Ashton; her husband, Aldington, is depicted as Rafe Ashton. H.D. and Aldington were as yet unestablished writers when, through Pound, they met in London in 1912. During the summer of 1914 Amy Lowell introduced H.D. and Aldington to Lawrence (Firchow 53), who appears as Rico, the second male mentor in *Bid Me to Live*. These two romans à clef (*Bid Me to Live,* in particular) offer complex treatments of the literary liaison because of the plurality of the protagonist's male lovers and mentors as well as the extensive use of women mentoring figures.

H.D.'s daughter, Perdita Schaffner, states that *Bid Me to Live* was not so much a roman à clef as "straight autobiography, a word-for-word transcript" (186). However, the highly lyrical, impressionistic, metaphoric nature of the novel suggests that Schaffner's assessment, while perhaps accurate regarding the biographical details, may be naive from a literary standpoint. Fred Crawford points out that "after reading the renditions of Mecklenburgh Square by Aldington, Cournos, Lawrence, and others, H.D. was responding as well as recording" (233). Nevertheless, the novel does encourage readers, in the fashion of the roman à clef, to search out the "key," the series of correspondences between real and fictional personages. The *Bid Me to Live* manuscript does not provide a list of "coded names" and their prototypes, as does H.D.'s title page of the *HERmione* manuscript (DuPlessis, "Thralldom" 180), but many of the people depicted in *Bid Me to Live* actually annotated their copies of the novel with just such a key. Contemporary reviewers and even minor characters in the novel such as writer John Cournos (fictionalized as Ivan Levsky) noted the correspondences when the novel was published.[4]

Given H.D.'s bisexuality and her forty-year relationship with Bryher, those familiar with H.D.'s biography may wonder at the plethora of fictionalized heterosexual relationships in *Bid Me to Live*. The heterosexual orientation is also surprising because the roman à clef fictionalizing the earlier part of H.D.'s development—*HERmione*—was inspired by a lesbian union and portends a woman's language, intimating further development of this expression in H.D.'s auto/biography (though perhaps the order of composition, since *Bid Me to Live* was composed—or at least begun—first, plays some part in this progression).[5] Friedman and DuPlessis find H.D.'s decision to fictionalize her heterosexual rather than homosexual relationships to be motivated, at least in part, by the social taboo on lesbianism: "In what she chose to publish, H.D. excised or deflected attention away from Gregg and Bryher, both of whom played crucial roles in H.D.'s personal and poetic development" (9).

> In print, therefore, H.D. could examine her identity as a tormented heterosexual seeking non-oppressive relationships with men, the culturally approved love objects for women. In focusing on the heterosexual script, she muted often to the point of invisibility her lesbian bonds with women. In private, however, in unpublished manuscripts "safe" as the diary where so many women's forbidden thoughts have found a half-life of secret articulation, H.D. explored her passion for women and its relation to her artistic identity. (Friedman and DuPlessis 9).

Oddly, however, even in an unpublished work, "Compassionate Friendship," H.D. lists exclusively men when she identifies her "initiators" as Pound, Aldington, Cournos, Lawrence, Cecil Grey, Kenneth MacPherson, and Walter Schmideberg (Robinson 317). H.D.'s critics evaluate the contribution and influence of these mentors variously.

Perhaps most relevant to the male mentors in *Bid Me to Live* is DuPlessis's argument that "H.D. returned constantly to a pattern of personal relations that she found perplexing and felt to be damaging to herself and other women: thralldom to males in romantic and spiritual love." DuPlessis characterizes this thralldom as "love between unequals" ("Thralldom" 178). This protest against an inevitable inequality in the heterosexual romantic-literary mentorships is an essential component in modernist women's literary-liaison fiction (see Introduction). DuPlessis, who perceives a pattern of thralldom in many of H.D.'s texts, claims, "Lesbianism *per se*—whether platonic or actual— was not for H.D. a sufficient strategy of solution to the cultural problem posed by males" ("Family" 70).[6] It would seem that H.D.—like West and Hall before her—felt she had some unfinished business with the patriarchal culture within which she wrote and published.

A Lacanian reading suggests that the H.D. persona is recurrently cast in unequal heterosexual relations in order to emphasize the writer's conflicts within the hegemonic self/Other dyad. Her protagonists do not achieve a fully developed and independent artistic identity in relation to the Other because such a wholeness is not possible:[7] "The more the self attempts to guarantee a reading in terms of the self's plenitude and wholeness[,] the more insistently questions of its division and fundamental lack return. And as surely as her writing proposes a reading of the female self in terms of unity, it undermines that reading because it represents the self by means of a structural opposition of wholeness and division" (Buck 10).[8] Because H.D. was psychoanalyzed by Freud, and she thought in psychoanalytic terms throughout her career (concurrent to her mythological preoccupations), it is not surprising that her fictional autobiographies lend themselves to Freudian/Lacanian readings.[9]

In his analysis Freud viewed H.D. as arrested at the preoedipal stage. H.D. wrote Bryher in March 1933, "Freud says mine is absolutely FIRST layer, I got stuck at the earliest pre-OE stage, and 'back to the womb' seems to be my only solution. Hence islands, sea, Greek primitives and so on" (Friedman, *Psyche,* 132).[10] Translated into Lacanian terms, *Bid Me to Live* depicts a preoccupation with the struggle for subject status and the paralysis that comes with realization that the wholeness of the self is inevitably illusory. Diana Collecott finds Lacan's theories useful to discuss narcissism and "self-reflection" in H.D.'s poetry: "For the female subject, and especially for the female writer, this entry into patriarchal language involves not only the loss of the feminine imaginary, but a double exile from the self. . . . Some of H.D.'s poetry can be read, then, as a doomed attempt to reinstate the female subject and heal the linguistic division between signified and signifier by means of the 'hieroglyph' of the female body" ("Images" 350).[11] Lacan's definition of the mirror-stage transition is also reminiscent of H.D.'s description of projection quoted earlier from *The Gift:* it "manufactures for the subject, caught up in the lure of spatial identification, the succession of phantasies that extends from a fragmented body-image to a form of its totality[,] . . . to the assumption of the armour of an alienating identity, which will mark with its rigid structure the subject's entire mental development" (Lacan, *Écrits* 4). H.D.'s multilayered images of the self illustrate this spatial process of identity formation.

HERmione: THE SEARCH FOR AN IMAGE

HERmione presents two paradigms of the couple (lesbian and heterosexual) and the first stage in the professional development of the writer—discovery of vocation. Critics have argued that Fayne Rabb functions as a muse for Hermione Gart, and although this is a significant alternative to the hierarchal heterosexual writing couple (male writer, female muse), the novel does not present a lesbian writing couple, a liaison in which both partners are writers (or artists). This omission is striking since both Frances Gregg and Bryher, H.D.'s most significant women lovers, were in fact both writers themselves.[12] Furthermore, as a Bildungsroman, *HERmione* focuses on identity and the discovery of vocation. It is a Künstlerroman only to the extent that it dramatizes the very early development of the artist, the birth of the writer within a coming-of-age story. Whereas *HERmione* dramatizes the period in America before H.D. went to Europe, prior to the emergence of her poet persona, "H.D. Imagiste," *Bid Me to Live* is a more fully developed Künstlerroman, taking up the narrative of the woman artist in adulthood, her struggle to write and achieve subjectivity within patriarchy.

In the beginning of *HERmione* the protagonist does not yet envision herself as writer or poet: "It had not occurred to Her to try and put the thing in writing (*HERmione* 13).[13] Characteristic of the premirror stage, Hermione has no image that can develop into a speaking self: "She must have an image no matter how fluid, how inchoate" (5). The ambiguity of "image" suggests her need for both personal identity and poetic inspiration. The fluid, chaotic imagery, used to depict a young woman still closely tied to her mother, evokes the presymbolic, the Kristevan *chora.* Hermione is associated with a caterpillar, an amoeba, an octopus, all protean images suggesting the fluid, dependent, dyadic infant. Susan Friedman, who emphasizes the "fusion" of Hermione and Fayne, notes that the *"Kunstler* narrative of *Her* is fundamentally pre-Oedipal" (*Penelope's Web* 116).

Hermione's status as a speaking subject is, nevertheless, foreshadowed grammatically. Several critics have noted the innovation of Hermione's nickname, which places an object ("her") in subject position.[14] Furthermore, Friedman and DuPlessis point out the equality and equivalence achieved when "her" refers to her two lovers: "With Pound, Hermione's nickname 'Her'—always grammatically awkward as a subject—signifies her object status within conventional heterosexuality. With Fayne, however, the nickname signals a fusion, one that gives birth to two selves, subject and object indistinct" (12). This argument is supported by passages such as Fayne's, "Drawn to you I am repulsed, drawn away from you, I am negated. You are not myself but you are some projection of myself" (*HERmione* 146). Such merging, which culminates in the novel as Hermione chants "She is Her. I am Her" (181) with regard to Fayne, is a way to dramatize the "healing of splits and fragments which Her feels in her passion" (DuPlessis, *That Struggle* 66).

Even in this early, presymbolic phase, intimations of poetic vocation are present in Hermione's impressions, which take the form of vivid images from visual and auditory senses: "The catch was that her perception was ahead of her definition. . . . The boom of the bee in her ear, his presence like an eclipse across the sun brought visual image of the sort of thing she sought for . . . it had not occurred to Her to try and put the thing in writing" (*HERmione* 13). The realization that she has not written her perceptions establishes the possibility of doing so. Early in the text writing is inextricably associated with both George Lowndes, Hermione's mentor, and Eugenia, her mother. When Hermione tells her mother of George's marriage proposal, Eugenia replies that she believes George is "actually *teaching* you words, telling you what to say" (*HERmione* 95). As Deborah Kloepfer points out: "The source of all this talking, however, is greater than just George Lowndes; it is the entire patriarchal, symbolic economy 'outside' of female experience and design and far distant from the voice and rhythms of the maternal body" (26).

Eugenia is in some sense the powerful mother, associated with Demeter (*HERmione* 89–90), a mature maternal power seen by her daughter as a "poet" who creates original images (126), and as one whose words "had more power than textbooks, than geometry" (89). Eugenia encourages Her to write, but she views her daughter's production critically and disparagingly as "dear little stories" (80). Susan Friedman views Hermione as undergoing a process whereby she "connects with the lost mother, the powerful mother layered beneath the powerless mother" (*Penelope's Web* 124). As the narrative unfolds, the protagonist vacillates between two lovers, George Lowndes and Fayne

Rabb, with the latter emerging more triumphant. However, it is the male lover who vies more forcefully with Hermione's mother for the role of mentor.

Hermione at first identifies with Undine, the voiceless mermaid in the Hans Christian Andersen story (*HERmione* 112 and elsewhere). The process of coming into language entails separation from the mother and the presymbolic, a process that Fayne, as a woman, seems to understand. Fayne tells her friend that she has an "octopus intelligence" (71) and that "You are the sort of thing a caterpillar would be before it were born" (144). George on the other hand, knowing only the symbolic, cannot understand the separation Hermione is painfully undergoing as part of her initiation into womanhood and writing; he continues uncomprehendingly "as if her mind was still one mind, not separated like amoeba giving itself another amoeba, a sort of birth, a sort of twin repeating itself" (120). In an effort to communicate to George the pain and loss of her incipient separation from the presymbolic, she makes reference to his own mother as a poet or namer: "Your mother called me Undine" (120).

Naming is particularly significant in *HERmione* as a Bildungsroman, a novel of identity; it is a linguistic activity that marks the entrance into the symbolic. Hermione observes, "Names are in people, people are in names" (*HERmione* 128). She cannot be called Mrs. George Lowndes, Friedman points out, because as his wife, "she would be *his* poem, no longer a poet in her own right" (*Psyche* 41). Friedman also points to H.D.'s appropriation of Pound's nickname for her, Dryad, which she took from his poems into her writing: "In *HER*, H.D. wittily inserts Pound's lyric identification of her as a tree-nymph and muse into her own lyric characterizations of Hermione." Friedman notes that "trees become the motif of Hermione's autonomous self. Trapped as a 'tree' in Pound's lyrics, H.D. frees herself by reclaiming 'treeness' for Hermione in her own text" ("Rescriptions" 31, 33). Hermione, a proto-poet, engages in naming, designating herself as a tree and George a "midge under peony" (*HERmione* 73); shortly after meeting Fayne and not knowing her real name, Hermione decides, *"Her name is Itylus"* (81). Since Fayne is presented already as a sister figure, a Philomela to Hermione's Procne, her role as Itylus in the myth suggests she functions as an instrument of revenge on George (the Tereus figure), perhaps by revealing the women's love for each other.[15] Friedman argues that the "significance of words and naming in *HER* can be read as H.D.'s rewrite of Pound's poem ["Ortus"] celebrating his role in the origins of her identity" ("Rescriptions" 36), an argument that foregrounds the retaliative aspect of the fictionalized literary liaison.

George and Hermione are competitors as writers representing different, gendered styles. For George,

> Writing was an achievement like playing the violin or singing like
> Tetrazzini. It had, it appeared, nothing or very little to do with the fact
> of cones of green set within green cones. Writing had somehow got con-
> nected up with George Lowndes who even in his advanced progress
> could make no dynamic statement that would assure her mind that
> writing had to do with the underside of a peony petal that covered the
> whole of a house like a nutshell housing woodgnats. (*HERmione* 71)

Hermione's mind moves expansively and visually, creating elaborate
metaphors to describe her imaginative perceptions whereas George's
mind progresses dogmatically; he views writing as an acquired craft,
evaluated in societal terms such as "advanced progress," a technology
in opposition to the freedom of imagism. His approach is criticized for
lack of imagination when Hermione concludes that, for George,
"Writing had no mere relationship with trees on trees and octopus
arms that reached out with eyes, too all overseeing" (72). Implicitly
contrasting two approaches to writing, H.D. also demonstrates that
George violates the central precept of imagism: direct treatment of the
thing, to present rather than represent an object as image.

George encourages Hermione, but he is of limited value to her as a
mentor because he draws his view of writing exclusively from the
symbolic. Hermione's entrance into the symbolic, the male economy
of language, is described as a movement into a realm of restriction:
"Her discovery was a gambler's heritage. She did not know that all her
life would be spent gambling with the stark rigidity of words, words
that were coin; save, spend; and all the time George Lowndes with his
own counter, had found her a way out" (*HERmione* 75). The imagery
links George's evaluation to the measured values of patriarchy, as is
emphasized in the previous description of his attitude toward writing
as "achievement"—with only a hint about a possible "way out."

H.D. creates several variations of the story of Pound's "discovery" of
her ability to write poetry. In *HERmione,* after reading some of her work,
he tells her *"this   is   writing"* (*HERmione* 149; spacing in original).
Hermione faces George "across a forest jungle" and mentally answers,
"Love is writing" (149). This equation may be ironic in view of the
story yet to unfold, but it nevertheless refuses to separate the two integral components of the literary liaison. George's fictional statement resembles the biographical account, recounted by H.D. in *End to Torment,*
when Pound says, more personally, "But Dryad . . . this is poetry" (*Torment* 18). In *HERmione* George tautologically states the obvious, merely
identifying the writing he reads as writing. In the biographical version
Pound makes a more specific, aesthetic evaluation. The novel's version,
then, is less laudatory in its presentation of the mentor than the biographical one, revealing the repressed anger and desire for vindication
that characterize the fictionalized literary liaison. H.D.'s autobiographi-

cal *End to Torment* (albeit also a kind of fiction or self-construction) associates destruction and violence with her mentor's editing. In two instances she uses the word "slash" (*Torment* 18, 40) to describe Pound's subsequent treatment of her poetry, and the words "scrawled" (18) and "scratched" (40) to describe his careless, impetuous inscription of her new name at the bottom of the page. *HERmione* goes further in critiquing the mentor when George defines Hermione as a bad writer; he becomes a negative facilitator, an obstructor, to her discovery of vocation. He ultimately denigrates her work—saying in his "Uncle Sam" dialect, "Your pomes [are] rotten" (*HERmione* 167)—but is unable to answer her question about how they are deficient.

Nevertheless, despite the implied criticism of George Lowndes as mentor, the novel makes clear that what Hermione seeks in George is generalized rather than individual: "She wanted George as a little girl wants to put her hair up or to wear long skirts. She wanted George with some uncorrelated sector of Her Gart, she wanted George to correlate for her, life here, there. She wanted George to define and to make definable a mirage, a reflection of some lost incarnation, a wood maniac, a tree demon, a neurophatic dendrophil" (*HERmione* 63). George is criticized for knowing only the symbolic yet Hermione must learn from him—or someone else initiated into the symbolic—the defining activity of language. H.D. intimates that the presence of the Other is necessary to achieve subjectivity, which cannot occur when the writer is solitary: "There was that about George, he wanted to incarnate Her" (64).

H.D. uses the Pygmalion and Galatea myth to develop her exploration of the self/Other dyad and her critique of the traditional hierarchy of mentorships (*HERmione* 138). In contrast to H.D.'s treatment of the Philomela and Procne story, hegemony is unavoidable in this retelling: everyone wants to assume the role of Pygmalion (the subject) and no one wants to play Galatea (the Other). As Hermione attends a Philadelphia performance of *Pygmalion* in which the titular role is played by Fayne, the essential inequality of mentorships is revealed. Each woman seeks a Galatea of her own: "Curtains part as I look into the eyes of Fayne Rabb. 'And I—I'll make you breathe, my breathless statue.'" "'Statue? You—*you* are the statue'" (163).[16] As Shari Benstock points out, "each woman wants to make the other the object of desire. . . . Each would assume the patriarchal prerogative: neither wants to take the woman's part as the object of desire. The division of woman against woman is represented by an internalized and inscripted patriarchal code" (346). This point is reinforced in *Asphodel,* when Hermione mentions that she saw Fayne play Pygmalion in a "play called Galatea" (*Asphodel* 67). George, of course, assumes that the "patriarchal prerogative" bestows the role of Pygmalion upon him. He sees Hermione as an object to be articulated by others—by himself as poet—rather than a poet herself: "George said you are a poem though your poem's naught" (*HERmione* 212). In the Pygmalion episode represented in *HERmione,* H.D. does not present an egalitarian lesbian writing couple in her fiction any more than Hall does in *The Forge:* because the writer/subject needs a reader/Other, the potentially egalitarian dyad results in hierarchy.

In his role as lover, as in his role as poet, George has the effect of erasing Hermione's subjectivity; his erotic value is figured in images of *obscuring* trees and *erased* concentric circles: "George could never love a tree properly. . . . Kisses forced her into soft moss. Kisses obliterated trees, smudged out circles and concentric circle and the half-circle that was the arch (she had seen) of a beech branch sweeping downward. The kisses of George smudged out her clear geometric thought but his words had given her something" (*HERmione* 73).[17] The words, the poetry they share—in this scene a line from Swinburne—inspire Hermione, though his desire effaces her. H.D. repeats the circular imagery in her biographical account, retrospectively predicting what Pound's effect on her poetry would have been: "Ezra would have destroyed me and the center they call 'Air and Crystal' of my poetry" (*End to Torment* 35).

As the lover who replaces George in the second half of the novel, Fayne stands in a complex, ambiguous relationship to Hermione's discovery of her vocation. Fayne's role is that of an intermediary: as a woman she retains access to the imaginary (the domain of Eugenia, the powerful mother), but as an Other she provides the separation Hermione must achieve. Many critics have viewed Fayne as a muse; Friedman, for example, argues that Hermione rejects "her entrapment as a muse for [George's] poems" and that in Fayne "Hermione has found her muse" ("Rescriptions" 29, 35); she also contends that Fayne is not threatened by Hermione's writing. Several of H.D.'s critics also argue that Fayne functions as a muselike initiator into language. Benstock emphasizes that language "itself is in some sense the 'subject' of *Hermione*—the vehicle through which identity is expressed and also the mechanism that distinguishes subject from object, self from identity. But the text also mirrors woman's relation to language in Hermione's effort to become the subject of her own discourse. She struggles to say 'I,' to replace the third-person pronoun by the first" (337). Kloepfer contends that the "other phase of Fayne's influence is linguistic. She takes the language within which she and Hermione are forced to operate and begins to manipulate it, reinvent it, disturb it, replacing conventions of syntax and representation. . . . In Fayne's first conversation with Hermione she challenges Hermione's intellectual discipleship to George Lowndes" (125). If, however, as DuPlessis argues, "Her's accrued authority comes from the saturation in related sources of Otherness: maternal/sororal mirror in and access to a visionary level of language which the novel repeatedly traces" (*That Struggle* 62), then Hermione gains authority from Fayne's status as Other. Fayne's value as a muse to Hermione subjugates Fayne as a speaking subject. If neither Fayne nor Hermione wants to be Galatea, by analogy, neither should want to play the role of muse. Since a muse functions as inspiration, not an equal writer or a competitor, if Hermione rejects the role of muse to George only to bestow that role upon Fayne, her act denies *Fayne* subject status.

My reading of Fayne as a mentor figure is less celebratory than readings that focus on *HERmione* as an individual text rather than, as I view it, part of a series of palimpsestic auto/biographical fictions. Viewing the novel not by itself but in relation to *Bid Me to Live* and other mentor-themed works in H.D.'s oeuvre, the text seems less conclusive, less celebratory than when considered by itself. The ground it covers for the female protagonist, as lover and writer, is traversed again and again in texts composed and revised over a period of years. Moreover, while George competes with Hermione *as a writer*, an agent of writing, Fayne places herself in direct competition with Hermione's *writing* in a sometimes inhibiting relationship. Fayne complains that Hermione has many interests: "And this—this *other*—" while Hermione answers "Other? Do you mean my writing?" (*HERmione* 161). Hermione's (mis)understanding of Fayne's statement reconfigures the subject/Object hierarchy by making the writing itself the Other. However, Fayne's response denies Hermione's interpretation and is ambivalent: "No. Your writing is nothing really. It is the pulsing of a willow, the faint note of some Sicilian shepherd. Your writing is the thin flute holding you to eternity. Take away your flute and you remain, lost in a world of unreality" (*HERmione* 161–62). Fayne affirms Hermione's naming of herself as a tree (willow); she confirms the lyric quality of her writing (flute) and her ability to inspire others (as a shepherd). At the same time, her equivocal description emphasizes the weakness and fragility of Hermione's writing, echoing Eugenia's reductive view of Hermione's "little stories" (80). It suggests that there should be a self, external or supplemental to the writer self, without which she is lost. The rescription of Hermione's Other as Fayne, depicted in mirror images of identity, presents an alternative to both the patriarchal mentor and the powerful mother; Fayne is an initiator into language and a facilitator, in relation to the first phase of the writer, the discovery of vocation. At the same time, she is neither a writer herself nor a collaborator with Hermione.

In a dramatic gesture that signals her progress toward poetic identity, Hermione finally insists that she has words, that she is indeed not voiceless: "for Undine . . . sold her sea-inheritance and Her would never, never sell this inheritance, this death-inheritance of amoeba little jellyfish sort of living creature separating from another creature" (*HERmione* 120). Although her encounter with George taught her "words," the prerogative of the symbolic, she will retain the "inheritance" of Eugenia, the presymbolic, mediated by Fayne. The last pages of the novel show her "leaving her wavering Hieroglyph," a nonlinear alternative kind of writing, "[u]pon white parchment" of snow, with the meadow like "a piece of outspread parchment" below her (224), a pictorial writing that mediates between the nonverbal and the symbolic.

This discovery of Hermione's solution to the woman writer's dilemma is presented equivocally, however, when the fate of the Other within the couple is considered. For Friedman it is the replacement of "heterosexual love" by "lesbian love" that allows Her to write by inscribing "a form of desire compatible with women's creativity" ("Rescriptions" 29). Friedman and DuPlessis, reading the novel as a celebration, argue that the end shows Hermione beginning "her autonomous life as writer by writing a track into the snow" (Friedman and DuPlessis 13). Their use of the word "autonomous" nevertheless highlights the problem of the writing self within the couple. Despite the ending in vocation, the novel does not culminate in the relationship of writers that could possibly emerge from such a lesbian liaison. Instead it ignores Fayne's fate as a speaking subject.

The solution offered by the woman-woman bond, though compelling in this narrative, is interrogated by the ambiguity of the novel's ending. Although the ending draws together the major issues of writing and lesbian love—as Hermione returns home to hear Mandy, the black servant, announce that "Miss Fayne [is] all alone upstairs in your little workroom" (*HERmione* 254)—the novel does not resolve the issue of what kind of relationship, if any, Fayne and Hermione will have in the future. The meeting occurs after Hermione has suffered a breakdown caused, at least in part, by Fayne's betrayal of Hermione with George. And just prior to the announcement of Fayne's presence, Her has decided she is "at one with herself, with the world, with all outer circumstance" (234), suggesting the achievement of independent identity and autonomy characteristic of the Bildungsroman rather than the reviving of a relationship. Fayne's presence in Hermione's workroom may signal a facilitator's role, or, given Fayne's previous ambivalent assessment of Hermione's writing, it may suggest further complications and an inhibitory role. The issue is opened again for investigation in *Asphodel,* the sequel to *HERmione,* as Robert Spoo notes: "The ambiguous image of Fayne Rabb waiting alone in Hermione's 'little workroom' at the end of *Her* is clarified in *Asphodel,* where Fayne indeed continues to blight Hermione's artistic hopes and her emotional life, just as George Lowndes has done" (xiii). The issue is also reopened in *Bid Me to Live,* the Künstlerroman and roman à clef that takes up the story of H.D.'s biographical chronology after *HERmione* and returns again to the self/Other dilemma by placing its protagonist in relationships—this time with two male mentors.

THE FEMALE SPEAKING SUBJECT IN *BID ME TO LIVE*

HERmione illustrates the writer's discovery of language, preparing for the woman writer's struggle to write within patriarchal culture—the subject of *Bid Me to Live,* the roman à clef of H.D.'s personal and artistic struggles circa 1916–1919. To some degree this novel was written in response to a mandate by Freud, who suggested to H.D. "a therapeutic writing of events without embellishment or distancing masks" (Friedman, *Psyche* 30). Thematically *Bid Me to Live* is (like much of the other liaison fiction) the story of conflict between the roles of poet/writer and woman. Friedman describes both this novel and *Palimpsest* as painfully portraying "gifted women whose intellect and creativity make them sexually undesirable to men who ultimately reject them for stereotypically feminine and erotic women" (*Psyche* 36).

The possibility of the female speaking subject, explored in *HERmione,* recurs in *Bid Me to Live,* but with an important difference. Julia describes a concentric sketch she has made with herself at center—a self-conscious metaphor for her own subjectivity within her writing in general and her fictional auto/biography specifically:

> She was only blocking in the stone-face that had no intrinsic value, like a plaster-cast face of faun or satyr in a drawing-school. She blocked round it, it gave her a sense of continuity, it gave her her own proportion, placed her in the centre of a circle, which she measured, mock-professionally, with a pencil held before her. When she squinted at the pencil, she was not so much seeing the thing she was about to block in roughly, as making a circle, with a compass, for herself to stay in. (*Bid Me* 34)

The sketch puts a woman artist at the center, rather than those who claimed the status of subject during H.D.'s lifetime or who were viewed as such by the public (Pound, Aldington, or Lawrence). It is paradoxical that the sketch simultaneously embodies both restriction and the freedom of self-expression. Julia claims that this process "gives one a sort of vantage point—to get into the circle—I mean—" (*Bid Me* 35). The figure represents Julia's *potentiality* as a speaking subject, but she still works "mock professionally," still needing enclosure—protection by and from her male writer-lovers, such as Rafe, who accompanies her in this scene. The language of calculation ("proportion," "compass," "measured"), words similar to those used by George in *HERmione,* emphasizes the threat of the patriarchal limitations she risks as a woman writer who is planning her entry into the "circle" of the symbolic but wishing, nevertheless, to retain the presymbolic.

As with other women in literary liaisons (West and Nin in particular), writing embodies desire and is the catalyst that brings the lovers together. Julia describes poetry as having "brought Rafe to her, in the beginning" (*Bid Me* 59). Biographers describe H.D.'s early marriage as one based on mutual respect and equality, centered around writing: "A significant part of Aldington's and H.D.'s attraction for each other was their independently arrived at but shared ideas of poetry" (Zilboorg, *Aldington* 16). John Cournos believed that H.D. and Aldington embodied the egalitarian ideal: "Here were two poets, man and woman, who were happy together and worked together" (quoted in Hollenberg 129). Caroline Zilboorg notes, "H.D. responded to [Aldington] as a colleague, an equal, and a romantic partner" (*Aldington* 9), and defines the relationship as "unquestionably a love match of equals" ("Influence" 26). In H.D.'s fiction, literary interest adds a dimension to the partners' love for each other, distinguishing their marriage from Rafe's affair with his sensual mistress Bella, to whom he writes love poems but with whom he cannot share poetry as an equal, as a writer.

In *Asphodel* the Aldington character, Jerrold Darrington, is described in terms that reiterate the linguistic initiation provided by H.D.'s previous fictionalized mentor, George: "Darrington had given her words and the ability to cope with words, to write words. People had been asking her (just before the war) for poems, had written her saying her things had power, individuality, genius. Darrington had done this" (*Asphodel* 114). Darrington may even be a corrective to George, a more generous mentor: "He had given her books and said her poems were something. *You are a poem though your poem's naught.* He hadn't said that. . . . Someone, something wanted her to write. For writing and life were not diametric opposites" (76). With an intertextual warning H.D. repeats George's words from *HERmione.* The italicized repetition is ominous; if George can give words and then use them to inhibit the woman poet, so can Jerrold Darrington or Rafe Ashton.

In real life Aldington valued H.D.'s poetry, and in his public evaluations he subordinated his own poetic talents to hers, describing H.D.'s work as "the only modern English poetry I really care for. Its austerity, its aloofness, its profound passion for that beauty which only Plantonists know, make it precisely the kind of work I would like to do myself, had I the talent" (Zilboorg, *Aldington* 35). In his autobiography, *Life for Life's Sake* (1941), Aldington publicly gives the utmost praise to H.D. as poet and treats their personal relationship with discretion, only mentioning it in passing: "I would say of H.D. that she was more distinguished . . . than Ezra, both as a person and as a mind. I have never known anybody, not even Lawrence, with so vivid an aesthetic apprehension. Lawrence was more keenly aware of the living world, but he was almost blind to the world of art. To look at beautiful things with H.D. is a remarkable experience. She has a genius for appreciation" (111). Aldington also describes H.D.'s poetry as "the expression of a passionate contemplation of the beautiful" (112). When asked to contribute an essay about upcoming young writers in 1919, Aldington named H.D. along with such male notables as Joyce, Eliot, Lawrence, Huxley, and Proust (219). These copious laudatory public statements suggest the degree to which Aldington tried to shape H.D.'s professional image. At the same time, H.D. herself was fully conscious that her identity was a social construction. Her preoccupation with image as identity is supported by Collecott's analysis of her attitude toward photographs of herself. Collecott claims that H.D. "carefully controlled the use of photographs of herself that might conflict with her chosen *persona* as the poet H.D." ("Images" 339n. 53). H.D.—and her lovers— deliberately constructed the legendary "H.D. Imagiste."

The preoccupation with a constructed identity in *Bid Me to Live* illustrates the Lacanian notion that "subjects are themselves produced through symbolic relations" (Henriques et al. 214), demonstrating the causal relation between writing and subjectivity, what Gilmore calls "autobiographics." Julia says, "When I try to explain, I write the story. The story must write *me*, the story must create *me*" (*Bid Me* 181). In the novel the relationship of writing to subject status is conveyed by the ambiguous treatment of the act of writing letters; Julia comments flippantly, "as if it mattered that Rico was writing her, that she was writing Rico" (54). Through this chiasmus, letters symbolize a reciprocal act through which the Other "writes" the subject into existence. Early in the novel Rafe brings Julia's letters back to her for safe-keeping when he returns to the front. Letters, the characteristic genre of lovers and courtship, serve not only as the means to exchange affection but also as drafts or warm-ups for writing poetry—and thus artistic identity. Julia tells Rafe, "Writing letters to you and writing poetry go along in the same sort of groove, I mean when I get into the mood of writing a letter, I feel I can rush headlong down the proverbial cliff" (*Bid Me* 44). Julia's metaphor associates an element of danger and excitement with writing and the relationship. Within a letter to Rico, Julia composes a text that clearly prefigures H.D.'s "Eurydice"—first drafting the poem in prose, signaling the transfer of her affection and the construction of a new self in relation to a new Other. Friedman argues that H.D.'s "rescription" of her male "initiators" Joyce, Lawrence, and Pound "connects sexuality and textuality with herself in the position of the subject" ("Rescriptions" 37).

The possibility of a liaison that might include two productive writers is implied in the description of the way, earlier in their relationship, Julia and Rafe sketched together in a complementary activity resembling collaboration. Their sketches, however, each embody a different style:

"his drawings were niggling and tight, hers better conceived but vague in outline"; they "complemented each other, even in their crude sketches; 'Between us we might make an artist,' he said" (*Bid Me* 33–34). Rafe and Julia are connected as an interdependent unit: "Siamese-twin mangled tentacles still bound Rafe-Julia together" (47), an image of a self unable to exist autonomously and self-sufficiently, joined in tortured alliance of shared flesh and blood. The novel's numerous dyadic figures of doubles, mirror images, and complementarity also foretell and inscribe the separation of Lacan's mirror stage:

> the mirror represents the moment when the subject is located in an order outside itself to which it will henceforth refer. . . . But if there is division in the image, and instability in the pronoun, there is equally loss, and difficulty, in the world. . . . Symbolisation starts, therefore, when the child gets its first sense that something could be missing; words stand for objects, because they only have to be spoken at the moment when the first object is lost. For Lacan, the subject can only operate within language by constantly repeating that moment of fundamental and irreducible division. The subject is therefore constituted in language *as* this division or splitting. (Rose, "Introduction II" 31)

The image of Julia and Rafe as Siamese twins suggests simultaneously both division and false wholeness, the very incompletion of the self.

The novel's depiction of the early phase of the marriage equivocally counterpoints the triumph of independence (Lacanian separation) with the grief over loss. This ambivalence is expressed as the gratitude of the "child" for the "object" it is destined to lose: "But walking for the first time, taking the first steps in her life, upright on her feet for the first time alone, or for the first time standing after death (daughter, I say unto thee), she faced the author of this her momentary psychic being, her lover, her husband. It was like that, in these moments. She touched paradise" (*Bid Me* 18–19). The tension in the relationship is between the need for the other and the ultimate need to free herself, to detach herself from the "author" of her "momentary . . . being." Julia is represented as a toddler, suggesting her initial shaky image of her self as a writer. The lover-husband replaces the mother, but the resultant loss and inevitable fragmentation are implied in the word "alone." Julia and Rafe cannot be equals if he is the "author" of her existence; yet H.D. recognizes the dependence—the connection—necessarily entailed by the Other's construction of the subject.

Reminiscent of Elizabeth Barrett Browning's "Sonnets from the Portuguese," an initial phase of the fictionalized relationship celebrates the regeneration of the woman loved (H.D. and Elizabeth Barrett Browning were both several years older than their husbands). H.D.'s couple, however, not only fails to live up to the Browning ideal of equal lover-writers (perhaps itself a dubious projection) but also embodies a self-conscious low-culture parody of it: "They might have made a signal success of their experiment. They made a signal success of it, but in the tradition not so much of Robert Browning and Elizabeth Barrett as of Punch and Judy" (*Bid Me* 11). Their failure issues from competitiveness and their mutual desire for autonomy: "They both wanted to be free, they both wanted to escape, they both wanted a place where they could browse over their books" (11). Both seek subject status; as in *HERmione*, both partners want the role of Pygmalion. In her letters H.D. described a similar need for autonomy. On January 14, 1953, long after their liaison had ended, she wrote Aldington: "I just had to do my own stuff and was from the first, even with Ezra, in danger of being negated by other people's work. I speak of this, in regard to DHL [D. H. Lawrence] in the book. I would like to have given my gift to someone but it was just not possible, no one could 'take it,' in several senses of the phrase" (Robinson 349).

Julia realizes she cannot have a relationship with the Rafe she previously loved without negating his chosen development; he is moving, devolving, she feels, away from poetry: "I can not hold the poet to what he had and live" (*Bid Me* 46). The marriage is tied inextricably to the literary dimension of the relationship, emphasized as Julia obsessively returns to the image of a past husband who was a poet: "She had married him when he was another person. That was the catch, really" (16). Julia sees the former Rafe in "the old days when a young poet had been her lover" (134). Unspoken in the novel is her realization that their personal relationship cannot accommodate her role as an autonomous writer—not writing for Rafe or as Rafe thinks she should write. Such autonomy makes the woman writer less real, less tangible for the male lover—leading to the bifurcation, and ultimately to the transfer, of his physical love. His refrain "I love you, I desire *l'autre*" (56 and elsewhere) reveals that Rafe does not desire an equal but an Other to reflect his own desire. Friedman describes a similar dynamic in the H.D.-Aldington marriage: "Aldington apparently told Yorke [his mistress] that H.D. could not bring him happiness because she 'had no body.' . . . His choice of a 'feminine' woman . . . may have reinforced the cultural stereotype of intellectual, gifted women as asexual, emotionally bold and unfeminine. H.D.'s vulnerability as a woman arose out of her internalization of these dominant cultural norms and Aldington's expression of them" (*Psyche* 38).

Mentorship dialogues, a convention of the literary-liaison novel, reveal how Rafe's criticism and Julia's resistance are internalized, how they become part of the self. At first Julia responds defensively to Rafe's criticism of the drafted poem she sent to Rico. She said, "I saved that only for the other-side of the page, the paper. I kept it for the other-side of the page, for the paper" (*Bid Me* 54). Julia's defense implies there is something of value that he does not see as writing: the blank page, the "other side of the story," a *parler femme*. As the "dialogue" continues, Rafe's critique of the poem is spoken out loud, while Julia responds to him silently, through internal monologue, only in her mind. Inaudible to Rafe, her response articulates her resentment and resistance: "'There aren't eight furies and why unglorified furies?' he said. There were eight furies, there were eighty furies, everything was unglorified. She didn't say anything. It didn't really matter" (54). The mentorship "dialogue" is presented asymmetrically as two monologues, one spoken, one silent, yet interrelated.

The use of a silent response in this mentorship "dialogue" emphasizes the communication gap between the languages of male and female writers. Rafe's insistence on fidelity to fact negates Julia's imaginative self. To criticize the accuracy of her mythological associations is petty in this context, and antithetical to inspiration; as a result of it, Julia "feel[s] no Muse" (*Bid Me* 54). As Joseph Milicia points out, Rafe's criticism of the Eurydice sequence has a "personal motive" and is "colored by his jealousy of Rico" (293–94). The fictional depiction of the H.D. character's reactions to criticism make Julia more passive than H.D. was in reality. Indeed both Julia in *Bid Me to Live* and Her Gart in *HERmione* are remarkably passive.[18] Passivity and silence can nevertheless be subversive strategies for women writers. At one point H.D. uses the juxtaposition of blank space in the text to articulate Julia's response to Rafe's criticism. As he critiques her prose draft of "Eurydice" ("'You might boil this one down,' he said, 'about quarter the length and cut the *clichés*'"), his criticism is followed by a visual representation of Julia's response. His words are surrounded by blank space on the page, and following the space, a repetition of the self-serving clichéd refrain with which he describes his dichotomized concept of woman, "I love you, I desire *l'autre*" (*Bid Me* 56).

Aldington assumed a similar role, the censoring mentor. He designated himself H.D.'s editor and insisted on checking the grammar, spelling, and punctuation of all her manuscripts (Guest 101). In a letter written in September 1918, after she had taken up residence with Cecil Gray, Aldington wrote: "You don't need any reiteration of my admiration for your work (though, since we are being so devilish frank, it wouldn't hurt for you to improve your spelling & punctuation!)" (Zilboorg, *Aldington* 142). Aldington was concerned, as was Pound previously, with her "carefully fashioned literary persona" (181n. 5) and in his role as editor encouraged her dependence upon him, cautioning her, "don't submit your m.s. *ever* until I have been over it; you make little careless errors in spelling & syntax &c which fools pick up as a weapon against an original artist. Remember, H.D. cannot afford to be anything less than perfection" (180–81). According to Friedman, H.D. "wrote angrily to Bryher about Aldington's 'psychotic' attitude toward her spelling" (*Psyche* xiii). His primary concern is her persona, through the creation of which he gratifies himself and reifies his own definition of the writer. Both Pound and Aldington may have found it easier to love H.D.'s literary persona (a creation in which they felt they participated, Pygmalion-style) than to love the flesh-and-blood woman ("I love you, I desire *l'autre*").

Aldington differentiated strictly between poetry and prose throughout their dialogues about H.D.'s work, and according to DuPlessis, even H.D.'s choice of genre was a subject of debate. In 1918 Aldington vehemently discouraged her from writing prose: "Prose? No! You have so precise, so wonderful an instrument—why abandon it to fashion another perhaps less perfect. You have, I think, either to choose pure song or else drama or else Mallarmian subtlety. Which will you choose?" (quoted in DuPlessis, *That Struggle* 34). Aldington's criticism of her prose appears again in a letter of December 17, 1918, in which he made several pointed suggestions for revision:

> This is a very lovely translation, unique, personal, vivid. No one but you could have done it. I have marked a few minor corrections of punctuation, spelling & grammar, chiefly to preserve you from the fools who will see that & nothing else. Work of your sort must be utterly impeccable. Certain lines from their concision are ambiguous—expand them a little & make your meaning plain, unless the original demands ambiguity. Avoid inversion, the staccato, & repetition "why, why" &c or use them very sparingly. Note that your use of "absolute" is incorrect & makes it a noun. (Zilboorg, *Aldington* 172)

As an editor-mentor Aldington tempers criticism with praise; he strategically suggests that his criticism is intended to protect H.D. from picky professional critics (such as himself). Zilboorg argues that although "Aldington's criticism . . . was often specific and authoritative . . . . H.D. was used to working closely with her husband and understood both the essential justice and the kind impulse" that motivated his criticism (*Aldington* 173n. 3). Zilboorg, however, as Aldington's biographer has a rather romantic view of his role in the relationship. Aldington, a modernist, seems surprisingly intolerant of experimentation, insisting on genre differentiation in an either/or fashion. It seems he viewed H.D.'s poetry as first-rate, and he encouraged her as long as she continued in this genre. "He acknowledged her superiority over the other Imagists, and mostly over himself" (Guest 35). But this support ceases when genre distinctions are violated. His praise is restricted to her poetry (the symbolic) rather than a mixture of genres—a pattern fictionalized, with some variation, in Julia's subsequent relationship with Rico.

One of the aesthetic choices H.D. makes in fictionalizing the marriage is to terminate it earlier than happened in her own life, linking it to the end of the mentorship and suggesting that, for Julia, Rafe ceases to exist as a writer when the romantic relationship between them is transformed into a professional one.[19] Julia's ambiguous pronouncement to Rafe, "You need not write anymore" (*Bid Me* 130), fuses—and confuses—his roles as poet and epistolary lover. If the text he has been writing is herself-as-writer, the pronouncement signals a break, a move toward independence. Later Rafe asks Julia to keep her letters to him safe while he is at the front (131), which may indicate his willingness to let her be the guardian of her self. This request marks the end of their romantic-literary partnership and the beginning of a purely literary one, where Rafe is merely Julia's reader, and her texts originate exclusively from within herself. In December 1917, as the relationship disintegrated, H.D. resolved not to answer Aldington's letters (Zilboorg, *Aldington* 53n. 8), a silence similar to the one Julia uses as a defense in *Bid Me to Live*.

The pattern of retaliation and conflict over possession of H.D.'s writing continued beyond the end of the marriage, however. After their liaison ended, Aldington may have had an adverse affect on H.D.'s ability to publish her work. Robinson describes the way his manner of contacting potential publishers for *Bid Me to Live* may have "soured all of the potential British publishers on the book" and hindered publication in England until after its American publication in 1960 (349). Although retaliation and vengeance often motivate auto/biographical novels depicting literary liaisons, H.D.'s portraits in *Bid Me to Live* are remarkably kind to those who hurt her (unless her presenting herself as passive victim is considered a strategy of revenge). In a letter written in May 1918 she expresses great loyalty to those fictionalized in the novel: "I can't explain about the *others*," she wrote to John Cournos. "I feel loyal to them. I should die if I allowed myself to resent all that has happened" (quoted in Hollenberg 142).

THE SPIRITUAL DOUBLE AS MENTOR

As in fictional auto/biographies by West and Nin, *Bid Me to Live* dramatizes the protagonist's transition from one relationship to another. The transition is marked by an exchange of letters early in Julia's relationship with Rico (the fictionalized D. H. Lawrence). The new liaison evokes many of the same conflicts, issues, and literary activities as her marriage to Rafe, especially the emphasis on writing the Other and the construction of a writer's aesthetic and identity. Julia signals the transfer of her affection by hiding her poems from Rafe and sending them to Rico. The increasing alienation she is experiencing within her marriage is dramatized when she places her own poems in a *"cache"* behind the "tops of the French" books in the bookshelf: "It was something secret, something hidden, you might say, even from herself" (*Bid Me* 59). The position of the poems, behind the *Mercure de France*, represents her obscured position as a woman writing within the male order. At the same time, by placing the originals of the poems she sent to Rico with published (public) writing, she crosses the private, personal boundary of Rafe's criticism and, seemingly unconsciously, moves herself toward public, professional status. As a second male mentor, Rico seems at first to offer a more sympathetic alternative to the difficult, oppressive mentorship with Rafe. In some ways Rico portends for Julia an intensification of her own gender: his spiritual (and thus desexualized) nature resembles her own, in contrast to the ultramasculine Rafe. A relationship between these affined partners would create, it seems, a different kind of putative wholeness for the partners as a writing couple. Julia's relationship with Rico echoes that of Philip and Hipparchia in *Palimpsest*, as well as that of Hermione and her brother, Bertrand Gart, which is desexualized by the incest prohibition and figured through twinning images—"like two hawk-moths, like two hummingbird beetles, like two long-throated cranes" (*Hermione* 17).

II.D.'s emphasis on finding a double, either a feminine (Fayne Rabb) or a spiritualized (Rico) counterpart, in her auto/biographical fiction represents a movement away from thralldom, which encourages "a sense of mystery surrounding the motives and powers of the lover" (DuPlessis, "Thralldom" 179). Rico is presented as a double who (as in Zelda Fitzgerald's *Save Me the Waltz*) offers a tempting but deceptive illusion that the self returns to a past where it is in unity with the Other. The multiplicity of H.D.'s male mentors suggests different kinds and degrees of hierarchical relationships within patriarchy, establishing a gendered continuum that ranges from the incomprehensible masculine mystery of George and Rafe to the protagonist's more intuitive understanding of Rico and Fayne, grounded in similarity and likeness.[20] Yet Rico's apparent likeness to Julia represents similarity, not identity; eventually she finds in him yet another spokesman for and representative of patriarchal values that inhibit the woman writer.

In a transitional scene that is both retrospective and ironic, Julia and Rafe discuss drafts of her poems that are embedded in letters to Rico. As the marriage falters, "it was poetry that gave back Rafe now" (*Bid Me* 58–59), though only temporarily. Although the poems sent to Rico suggest that the role of mentor-lover will be assumed by him in the future, the discussion of poems momentarily rescues Julia and Rafe from their sexual impasse and restores them to the literary realm they still share. The letters, however, use a coded language, a private symbolism common to Julia and Rico, from which Rafe ultimately will be excluded:

> "I didn't particularly write it for Rico," she repeated, seeing the pale face, the burnt eyes, the words that flamed alive, blue serpents on the

page that Rico wrote her, that were just ordinary letters that you could chuck across a breakfast-tray to any husband, but that yet held the flame and the fire, the burning, the believing. (52)

Julia and Rico, as poets sharing a genre, have an affinity that is reflected in a similar spiritual imagery and a sort of interchangeability associated with the two (their prototypes shared the inverted initials, H.D./D. H.). Descriptions of Julia's writing draw on the fire imagery associated with Rico: his letters "were burning in her head" (54); Julia's handwriting in a letter is described as an "uneven lightning of her lines [which] reached in long, short lines across paper. Sheet lightning. Blue lightning" (55).

As a reader, Rafe is now reduced to a mundane domestic figure, superseded by Rico because of the latter's function as spiritualized Other, Julia's double. Julia believes this affinity produces a superior desire and creativity to the gender opposition experienced with Rafe: "the flame and the brand of this gift that Rafe and Julia had had between them was a secondary refracted light, the light of a second reflection of the rainbow, not the blaze and the blue-flame of the sun-shelf. Rico" (*Bid Me* 52). This new relationship is reciprocal, potentially egalitarian, in that as doubles she imagines "they would burn out together," and because "they were both free, equal too, in intensity, matched, mated" (58–59).

The letters represent Julia's cerebral desire for Rico. Friedman argues that "H.D. felt more akin to Lawrence as poet than Lawrence as novelist or essayist" ("Rescriptions" 27). Julia prefers Rico's letters to his novels because the letters put her in touch with a part of herself that is essential to poetic creation. She asks, "Why, in your interminable novels, do you not write—to someone, anyone—as you write me in your letters?" (*Bid Me* 164). She contrasts his work in different genres: "Perhaps I caught the *gloire* from you. Was it your way of thinking? But it isn't in your books, it was in your letters sometimes" (176). This contrast between Rico's letters and novels again raises questions of gender and genre. Milicia argues that "the great importance of letter-writing" in *Bid Me to Live* derives from a "philosophy of art" that privileges "'expression' rather than crafted form" (296). More significant for Julia is that letters are a personal genre, perhaps a women's genre, that facilitates the drafting and exchanging of poems, a reciprocal act that attempts to break down barriers between subjectivities.

Rico's ability to cross gender boundaries and write in the feminine genre of letters is a quality Julia appreciates but one that he denigrates and cannot acknowledge in himself. Teresa Fulker sees Rico as mediating the feminine for Julia: "She comes to realize that his power (which he still possesses) comes from a very feminine source. He has access to this source through [his wife] Elsa, but he also incorporates it within himself" (76). Rico is silently sympathetic about maternal functions, about the dead child Julia mourns throughout the novel—"It is true he cared, not speaking, when the child died" (*Bid Me* 140)—abandoning, momentarily, his masculine prerogative of speech. In his sympathy with Julia's loss of her child, Rico becomes, through the birth imagery, a kind of mother to Julia (Fulker 64n. 14; 77). This nurturing role is evinced by Julia's choice of a hiding place for Rico's letters, inside a jewelry box where she also keeps her mother's portrait (*Bid Me* 58), and may provide, in a suggested incestual relationship, a reason for Rico's rejection of Julia's very tentative move toward a physical relationship.[21]

Julia discovers gender-crossing through her relationship with Rico and considers this crossing to be a "loophole" in the impass of gender roles—that "one might be an artist, then the danger met the danger, the woman was man-woman, the man was woman-man" (*Bid Me* 136). Critics have argued that this proposition comprises a suggestion of androgyny that is either a transitional or a final solution to problems of gender and identity confronted by H.D. in her writing.[22] Friedman, for example, finds a shift from conceptualizing the "loophole" as androgyny in *Bid Me to Live* to "an androgynous lesbian identity in *HER*," privileging order of composition in the evolution of H.D.'s gendered literary solutions ("Rescriptions" 38, 39n. 9). It is true that in *Bid Me to Live* the androgynous literary couple seems to present an image of wholeness: "Each two people, making four people," and "the woman gifted as the man" (*Bid Me* 136). Further, H.D.'s suggestion of gender-crossing may go beyond the static idea that each sex contains complementary elements of the other. Her syntax, especially the chiasmus "man-woman . . . woman-man," creates a flexible, kinetic conception of sexual duality, traveling back and forth between sexual elements within the self. This motile inversion embodies the difference of the affined double from both the ultramasculine male mentor (Rafe) and the woman mentor-muse (Fayne). Such active gender-crossing, moreover, destabilizes hierarchy within the couple.

Rico is characterized by contradictions, nevertheless. Although he exhibits gender-crossing in his relationship with Julia, he advocates gender polarity ("man is man, woman is woman"). Julia rejects his stated aesthetic—his gender polarity and the gender specificity of his literary practice. Rico's aesthetic would forbid her to "trespass" (*Bid Me* 176) in the male domain of the symbolic and would deny her an imaginative movement and gender freedom that he grants himself:

> This man-, this woman-theory of Rico's was false, it creaked in the joints. Rico could write elaborately on the woman mood, describe women to their marrow in his writing; but if she turned round, wrote the Orpheus part of her Orpheus-Eurydice sequence, he snapped back, "Stick to the woman-consciousness, it is the intuitive woman-mood that

matters." He was right about that, of course. But if he could enter, so di-
abolically, into the feelings of women, why should not she enter into
the feelings of men? (62)

As subject, Rico grants himself a transcendent gender, an omniscience
he denies Julia, whom he views as man's Other. DuPlessis notes that
Rico "censors and controls her artistic work. Her aesthetic options (of
voice, subject, gendered perspective) are shaped by her personal need
to please him" ("Thralldom" 183). As her double, Rico senses the importance of the "woman-consciousness," but he relegates Julia exclusively to the presymbolic (the "intuitive"), and permits himself the
imaginative license of both the symbolic and the presymbolic.

   H.D. nevertheless follows Rico's advice in "Eurydice" (the origins of
which are traced in her fictional argument about the poem), and she
limits the poem's point of view to the mythical woman. Although his
recommendations are socially and ideologically restrictive and provoke Julia's anger, they facilitate her cultivation of a sort of *écriture
féminine*, writing the presymbolic *chora*, and foreshadow Hélène
Cixous's admonition that "women must write woman, and man man"
("Medusa" 877). Apparently sensing the advantage of the woman's
view in this particular instance, Julia's resentment is displaced in the
actual poem to a related issue, a woman's anger at being betrayed by
masculine self-interest:

> So for your arrogance
> and your ruthlessness
> I have lost the earth,
> and the flowers of the earth,
> and the live souls above the earth,
> and you who passed across the light
> and reached
> ruthless . . . ("Eurydice," *Collected Poems* [1917] 82–89)

A passage in *Bid Me to Live* echoes the sadly defiant tone of this poem:
"My work is nothing. But, Rico, I will go on and do it. I will carve my
pattern on an altar because I've got to do it" (164). The poem's defiant
tone protests the speaker's exclusion from the "earth," the symbolic,
and her relegation to the "underworld" of women's creativity. This
poem, therefore, explores the consequences of Rico's admonition. It
does not, however, represent a full or permanent solution to the problems of the woman writer in patriarchal society but articulates the
anger that often develops within the heterosexual, and emblematic,
literary liaison.

   Kloepfer finds that *Bid Me to Live* moves away from "the appropriation of the male sphere" and instead "attempts rather to find a space

beyond or anterior to male-female polarity, a space that precedes gender (or at least gender-consciousness)" (91–92). This anterior space
might be conceptualized as the presymbolic—the antecedent of gender (preceding its articulation)—and excludes the male (the symbolic).
Rico, though himself threatened by sexual division, provides Julia
with a greater sense that she has regained the wholeness of the
presymbolic (the maternal *chora*). Through the Rico episode, the novel
considers the presymbolic as the proper realm of woman's creativity.
Yet it foregrounds the woman writer's loss of the presymbolic and/or
exclusion from the symbolic.

Julia's literary liaisons, paradoxically, both inspire and paralyze her
as a writer. They provide the content for poems, her emotional reactions to relationships, but those painful emotions must be subjugated
before she can write them. Rico is associated with an oxymoronic spiritual fire that acts as a muse: "He is part of the cerebral burnings, part
of the inspiration. He takes but he gives," Julia observes (*Bid Me* 67).
Julia is cinematically inseminated when Rico "projects" a poem "in
her, or out of her" (81).[23] The two prepositional alternatives ambiguously refuse to locate the inspiration in subject or Object but emphasize the evocative, narcissistic function of a muse—to develop what is
already present in the poet. A psychoanalytical reading of the term
projection suggests the interdependence of subject and Other, since
"the subject sends out into the external world an image of something
that exists in him in an unconscious way. Projection is . . . a mode of
refusal to recognize (méconnaissance) which has as its counterpart the
subject's ability to recognize in others precisely what he refuses to acknowledge in himself" (Laplanche and Pontalis 354). Rico thus facilitates both Julia's recognition of her own image and a projection of
material from the unconscious into her poetry.

Dianne Chisholm notes that Freud derived the term *projection* from
early cinema (*Poetics* 92); Laplanche and Pontalis point to the resemblance between the psychoanalytic and the cinematographic usages
(354). The intangibility of both processes suggests that it is not the
physical Rico who is necessary for Julia—"the Rico absent was nearer
than the Rico present" (*Bid Me* 81)—but the projection or discovery of
the "woman-man" within herself (the Lacanian "discourse of the
Other") that Julia has retrieved through her gender-crossing encounter with her affined but opposite sex double, Rico. The Lawrence-
Rico character is transcribed as the absent Orpheus, which denies him
materiality and subject status (see *Bid Me* 51) while granting them to
Eurydice. Such a strategy might be viewed as an answer to Freud's suggestion, paraphrased by H.D., that "women did not creatively amount
to anything or amount to much, unless they had a male counterpart
or a male companion from whom they drew their inspiration." The
contextualization of this passage shows H.D. torn between being

"rather annoyed with the Professor" and suspecting that perhaps "he is right" (*Tribute* 149).

Rico is valuable to Julia as a muse but his value as mentor is as equivocal as Rafe's, though for different reasons. Julia resents the way he gives her advice on her life (to "kick over [her] tiresome house") but not her art: "when it came to one, any one, of her broken stark metres, he had no criticism to make" (*Bid Me* 80). When he ignores her writing, Rico negates her existence as a speaking subject. Yet Julia also ignores (or Rico feels she ignores) his writing: "There was all of me in the manuscript which you didn't even trouble to write me about," he thinks (77). In her own notes on *Bid Me to Live*, H.D. stresses the reciprocity of the relationship: "In Madrigal, Julia Ashton finds a companion, creatively her equal or superior. But she sacrifices him or is sacrificed by him" (*Bid Me* 205). The ambiguity of the sacrificial possibilities (connected by "or") is reminiscent of the "syntactical balance" of constructions in *HERmione*. The equivocation of the construction emphasizes that Julia and Rico are doubles, in some sense interchangeable, and as such, the hierarchized roles of the mentor-protégé relationship are crossed and recrossed.

At the same time Julia resents that he ignores her writing, she finds that when he offers criticism much of it is useless because it reflects only a traditional aesthetic. Resembling the editorial Rafe, who corrects the number of her furies, Rico argues that her mythical associations are imprecise as devices of characterization, creating "graven images" rather than realistic personages. "You are right," she responds to him, mentally. "Rafe is not the Marble Faun, not even a second-rate Dionysus. . . . But you are right. He is not Dionysus, you are not Orpheus. You are human people, Englishmen, madmen" (*Bid Me* 164). Even as she acknowledges that he is literally correct, her response—in this interiorized mentorship "dialogue"—reveals the limitations of Rico's imagination (as in the novels Julia also finds lacking, implying a criticism of Lawrence). Here she concedes that they are not gods but are only human—and only Anglocentric at that. Thus, she responds with ridicule ("they are madmen"), and with the defiance of H.D.'s Eurydice, "I will go on and do it" (164).

The threat of appropriation posed by Rafe in her marriage recurs in Julia's brief but ultimately aborted relationship with Rico. In *Bid Me to Live* H.D. appropriates material that her protagonist fears will be seized by Rico for a novel of his own (164, 173). In a preemptive move, Julia writes in a notebook that is a replica of his (172). Fulker states that, having "finally escaped from Rafe's narrative, Julia resists being written into Rico's" (75n. 24).[24] It is, Fulker argues, to avoid "being subsumed into yet another masculine narrative" that Julia does not go up to Rico's room, leaving their relationship unconsummated (75).[25] Julia does not want to find Bella or Rafe in Rico's book. H.D.

herself writes them into *Bid Me to Live*, gaining an advantage she then lost when her novel was not published until many of its real-life prototypes were dead. Regarding the group at Mecklenburgh Square, Vanacker states: "A true battle of the autobiographies seems to have been taking place, with several members of the coterie determined to have their versions succeed for posterity" (116).

In *Bid Me to Live*, Rico ultimately assumes the crucial role of namer, preempting subject status for himself. The issue of representation and naming—of assigning a signifier to a signified—is significant to the H.D. legend, inaugurated by Pound's celebrated inscription, "H.D. Imagiste," at the end of the sheaf of poems she showed him. Such naming is central to the symbolic order. By all accounts H.D. was dissatisfied with her given name, Hilda Doolittle, and initially pleased with both Pound's approval and his designation of her as the defining poet of a new movement, a new –ism. Aldington claimed, "H.D. looked very much pleased by the praise Ezra generously gave her poem," but that, finally, she "disliked" the label with which he signed her poems (135). Pound's act was equivocal since he thus appropriated the role of namer and founder-of-movements for himself. But in *Bid Me to Live* this function is displaced onto Rico, who is described as a "prompter in the wings" and "an author in a play" (150). In the Genesis charade Rico plays the role of God and assigns parts to the other characters. The hierarchy implied is a parallel to that implicit in mentorships, including the subjectivity appropriated by the mentor: "And Rico, playing any part, but always, when he entered, taking for granted that his was the centre of the stage. His was the centre of the stage, however tiny the little act he put on" (150). The ability to name leads Rico to define Julia, and his evaluation reiterates Pound's definition of H.D., as Rico holds up the poems Julia has brought as her contribution to Mary Dowell's (Amy Lowell's) anthology: "'Don't you realise that this is *poetry*?' said Frederick [Rico], edging her away toward the far end of the room" (140). His definition names her as poet—as Pound's defined H.D.—but it serves to marginalize her, moving her to the "far end" of the writing scene.

A relationship with Rico could be destructive were it to follow the precedent of Rico's parasitic relationship with his wife, Elsa, who in Julia's view, "fed Rico on her 'power,' it was through her, in her, and around her that he had done his writing" (*Bid Me* 79). Elsa is the facilitative wife, "singularly protective of Rico's writing," while she also claims not to pay attention to (that is, participate in) his work (83). The danger of the liaison with Rico is not only that Julia will be drained personally, as a woman, but also that she will be contaminated as a poet, become infected by his style, and lose her distinct voice—a more proximate threat, as Rico is her double, than that posed by Rafe and his gender opposition. The threat is figured metaphorically as tuberculosis, an inner consumption, a wasting away of subjectivity from within: "I don't mean the T.B. would make any difference to me. Only, I am susceptible, would catch something. I would catch your manner-isms, your style of writing, your style of thinking, even" (176).

It is only when she leaves with the young half-Scot composer Vane (music critic, Cecil Gray)—a male facilitator who is not cast as a patri-archal oppressor, who has no desire to be either muse or mentor—and finds herself in an attic room in Cornwall, that Julia is able to write (*Bid Me* 165). Vane is not a writer; whereas Rico can name the plants in Cornwall, Vane cannot (145). Yet his deficiency allows Julia finally to assume subject status and the role of namer herself. In Cornwall Ju-lia becomes more than a translator: she describes her relationship with Greek as a desire to "coin new words" in this foreign language rather than merely "translate" what is on the page. Birth imagery in this sequence is associated with words and writing, illustrating Julia's recovery from the trauma of the stillbirth early in the novel, now giv-ing birth to her own texts.

The novel's last chapter is written as an internal monologue ad-dressed to Rico and articulates Julia's mourning for an abortive love affair, yet it is this chapter that most strongly dramatizes her arrival at a place where she can actually write. Rico's value to her as a double and as a mentor-model is attenuated by her rage at his articulated gender polarity ("man-is-man"), but he fulfills, to an extent, the men-tor's functions of muse and facilitator. Julia comes to see the move to Cornwall as a "gift" offered by Rico and materialized by Vane: "It was Rico who had brought [Vane] to the house and it was Rico ironically who had precipitated this. . . . Even if they were not the human ani-mals going two by two, yet they were two separate entities who had found each other, 'the Tree of Life,' as Rico had called her, and 'the Angel at the Gate,' as he had labelled Vane" (*Bid Me* 121).

The number of male mentors in H.D.'s fiction (*Bid Me to Live* in par-ticular) suggests that the problem is not so much with any individual male mentor as with the various recurrent manifestations of patriar-chal social relations within the heterosexual couple. Friedman argues that H.D.'s writing block in the 1930s, when, H.D. claimed, *Bid Me to Live* was primarily being "roughed out," was related at least in part to her "ambivalence toward 'literary' men" such as Pound, Aldington, Lawrence, Macpherson, and Dowding: H.D.'s "letters to Bryher in 1933 and 1934 demonstrate that the image of literary men, especially of those whom she loved, still haunted her and hindered her ability to write" (*Psyche* 37). H.D. provides her own interpretation of her dreams of literary men in May 1933—"book means *penis* evidently and as a 'writer,' only, am I equal in uc-n [unconscious], in the right way with men. Most odd" (*Psyche* 37). Similarly, in *Bid Me to Live*, Julia's fear is not exclusively personal but literary as well: she fears the Other will obscure her poet self. With Freud's help H.D. came to see that subject and object meet via the unconscious. Exorcising the internalized Other—the critical censoring voices that she internalized from her male mentors as part of her socialization and poetic apprenticeship—is a much more difficult process, however, as *Bid Me to Live* reveals.

SUPERIMPOSED AND
CINEMATIC IMAGES OF THE SELF/OTHER(S)

In *Bid Me to Live* H.D. uses extensive imagery of optical illusion—mirrors, the stage, cinema, and photographic slides—to suggest that the subject is never whole or perceived without the intervention of a reflective medium—generally the Other. Julia reenacts the Lacanian mirror-stage process of identity as she begins to see herself as split, defined by the bifurcation with which Rafe sees her, and which she has come to internalize as a split between herself, the spiritual woman, and Bella, the sensual woman. Julia sees herself and Bella as "a composite" for Rafe, a "reverse light-and-shade" (*Bid Me* 89). Standing face-to-face with Bella, "Julia felt that she was looking at herself in a mirror, another self, another dimension but nevertheless herself" (103). Bella tells Julia, "He loves my body but you tyrannize his soul—it's you he cares for" (102), and Julia reflects that "She and Bella were simply abstractions, were women of the period, were WOMAN of the period, the same one" (103). Although Julia views the opposite sex—Rafe, the sensual man, and Rico, the spiritual man—in a similarly dichotomized way, she surmounts this dichotomy through her poetry.

The multitude of characters passing through her room at Mecklenburgh Square gives Julia the impression that she lives on stage, in a "room open on one side" (*Bid Me* 90). The proliferation creates an early example of the ensemble characterization that is so popular in today's film and media. Milicia associates the "play motif" in the novel with the limitations and unreality of Julia's life, her "sense that everything passing before her eyes is a scene from a play, a dance or a slide projector" (284). Although Julia describes the magic lantern images as "pictures all on one plane or parallel . . . not dynamically exploding inside" (*Bid Me* 179), the image may also be read as signaling an actual fragmentation of the self, instead of the wholeness desired. The various quasi-theatrical roles assumed by the characters suggest their fragmentation and incompletion.

Julia must accept the reality that wholeness of the self is unattainable if she is to overcome her paralysis and write. Julia is, variously, "Mrs. Rafe Ashton" to society, "Anthea" to Rafe, "Person" to Vane. Vane's nickname for Julia is seen by DuPlessis as an effort at androgyny, a gender-neutral designation, but as she also notes, Julia herself interprets the name as the French *personne* or nobody/anybody: "Without the entrapment of sexual and spiritual thralldom, she questions whether she has any existence at all" (DuPlessis, "Thralldom" 184). Julia's comment to Rafe upon their decision to separate—"I thought, this way, you would be one person" (*Bid Me* 133)—seems to support an interpretation of "person" as a whole being, echoing Rafe's view of the masculine self seeking gender complementarity in the ultrafeminine Bella. Bella herself claims, however, that the process does not work, "he isn't all there, half of him is somewhere else" (102), implying that Rafe needs the companionship of Julia.

It is not gender opposition or complementarity, however, that creates wholeness. Through media images, from film in particular, the novel explores the deceptive "specular wholeness" of the self. As Silverman explains the function of cinematic representation:

> "secondary" identification is effected in large part through the incorporation of character representations. Those representations are taken into the self, and provide the basis for a momentary subjectivity—a subjectivity which is sometimes in contradiction to the spectator's previous structuration, but which is more often sufficiently compatible so as to create the illusion of continuity. (*Acoustic Mirror* 23)

Silverman's description suggests the process whereby a subject internalizes an image perceived by the Other. H.D.'s characters, in their ever-changing roles and musical beds, are in a sense interchangeable actors granted "momentary subjectivity" by their collective presence, providing a plurality of Others for the subject. The multiplicity of mentors in *Bid Me to Live* suggests a movement from romantic thralldom, the self as constructed by an Other, to social construction by collective Others. In *End to Torment,* H.D. describes how this collective function and serial process was first "evoked" by Pound but actually fulfilled by Frances Gregg: "When Ezra left finally for Europe, Frances came into my life. She completed or 'complemented' the Dryad or Druid that Ezra had evoked so poignantly" (53).

The ensemble of characters thrown together in the flat by wartime London are "superimposed upon one another like a stack of photographic negatives" (*Bid Me* 89) through which each self is both partially obscured by and partially illuminated through the images of others. The characters appear collectively to form a complete self. Collecott describes a scrapbook among H.D's papers at Yale's Beinecke Library that suggests a similar image:

> the one page in the Scrapbook that we can confidently assign to H.D. herself is a welter of superimposed images. Photographic prints and newspaper cuttings of the faces of D. H. Lawrence and Richard Aldington at different dates have been stuck on, torn off, recovered, set on top of one another. The manuscript of *Madrigal* or *Bid Me to Live* apparently

KING ALFRED'S COLLEGE
LIBRARY

went through similarly palimpsestic erasures and revisions, or (to use the terminology of post-Freudian criticism) deletions and substitutions. ("Images" 331).

Collecott goes on to describe *"Superimpositon"* as "H.D.'s characteristic method" (331). The palimpsest of overlapping lovers in *Bid Me to Live* comprises, characteristically, a verbal superimposition.

Julia's three heterosexual relationships are increasingly degendered, as she moves from the ultramasculine Rafe, to the spiritual double in Rico, to the brotherly Vane, a gradual movement away from the thralldom DuPlessis finds in her real-life relationships of this era. In her flight to Cornwall with Vane, with whom she passes as a "sister," the threats of gender polarity and writerly competition are removed; unlike the previous two relationships of the novel, this is not a literary liaison. Her relationship with Vane, allowing her the greatest contact with her uncontested self, creates the greatest sense of being her own "person."[26] As Vane takes Rafe's place in Julia's life, Julia realizes "she was herself now playing her own part in this curious mixed partners, dance of death" (108). This realization of her own complicity in the "play" is more complex and "real" in a Lacanian sense than any simplistic, and ultimately false, discovery of a purported real self. Rather, Julia realizes that the self is always constructed in relation to the Other(s), "it was a game, after all" (108). Julia rejoices that the house in Cornwall, an alternative to the "tired house of life" Rico urged her to throw over, is "invented for her" (161). Vane offers her the opportunity to choose the room she will write in. He poses an alternative to both the sensual husband and the spiritual double, an alternative that is figured as a transition rather than a destination: "But she had escaped, she had got away from four walls about to crush her" (110–11). According to Milicia, "the Cornwall experience cannot be an ultimate solution," yet the final chapter of the novel "develops an alternate possibility for Julia: creating art as a way of life" (293). In Cornwall Julia finally experiences her own potentiality: "rejoicing in herself, butterfly in cocoon" (*Bid Me* 151).

PARODY AND CULTURAL DISPLACEMENT IN "HIPPARCHIA"

Bid Me to Live is the most straightforwardly auto/biographical treatment of the traumatic stillbirth and infidelity H.D. experienced during the Mecklenburgh Square era, but it was not the first account to be finished and published. Years before she refined *Bid Me to Live* and finally published it (in 1960), H.D. had published *Palimpsest* in 1926. In "Hipparchia," the first story or novella of this trilogy, she presents a highly coded, quite different account of the autobiographical World War I material, displaced into the period of "War Rome" (circa 75 B.C.).[27] Freud probably was referring to this work, which he read prior to beginning his sessions with H.D., when he suggested she write the account that then became *Bid Me to Live,* "without embellishment or distancing masks" (Friedman, *Psyche* 30–31). The characters in "Hipparchia" are masked by different names and cultures, but to those familiar with *Bid Me to Live* and with H.D.'s biography, the central cast and plot strikingly rewrite the originals. Hipparchia, a Greek living in Rome, is the expatriated H.D., and a Roman soldier, Marius Decius, is Aldington, who becomes involved with Olivia (Dorothy "Arabella" Yorke, the Bella of *Bid Me to Live*). Hipparchia finds solace with Quintus Verrus (Cecil Gray, fictionalized as Cyril Vane). Notably missing is a D. H. Lawrence equivalent, although Hipparchia's brother Philip functions as brother-soul and double: he is "herself yet magnified" ("Hipparchia" 115, also 127).[28]

Bid Me to Live and "Hipparchia" both foreground the asymmetrical nature of auto/biography, the writer's exploitation of the relative authority of telling her own story in relation to that of the now silenced Other. The two texts use different techniques to achieve similar objectives, but H.D. (like West) uses a parodic depiction of the lover to expose and critique masculinist values. Whereas the novel achieves a great deal of sympathy for its protagonist by using exclusively Julia's perspective, "Hipparchia" achieves a similar effect by a limited omniscient point of view that discloses the partner's view; in this case, however, the limited omniscience reveals the often unsavory thoughts of Marius, creating sympathy for Hipparchia through the unsympathetic portrait of her male betrayer. Marius's thoughts reveal, for example, that his attention is caught by Olivia because "his taste coincide[s] with the general barrack preference" ("Hipparchia" 31). Although he at first sees Olivia as "common and inconsiderable, a peasant (frankly almost) a Sicilian" (31), he is eventually seduced merely by "the backtilt of a woman's head" (37).

The more coded cultural displacement of "Hipparchia" allows H.D. to present a more vindictive and gendered version of the events than she did in *Bid Me to Live.* The polarity between the spiritual woman and the sensual woman, for example, is more pronounced in "Hipparchia" than in *Bid Me to Live;* Hipparchia is characterized by fine "sensitive thwarted Patrician outreachings: Marble" and Olivia by "[h]eavy flesh and sensuous misdoings: porphyry" ("Hipparchia" 68). In this version the formerly implicit criticism of the rival is exaggerated into brutal parody. Whereas the H.D. character is exalted as a poet and a scholar, the sensual woman from *Bid Me to Live* (Bella) is here a courtesan (Olivia), grotesquely parodied. When Olivia seduces Marius she does so with "professional, skilled gesture" and "all the langorous professional appeal" ("Hipparchia" 44–45). Hipparchia is established, rather than an emerging writer like Julia Ashton: "You have chosen your career," Marius tells her. "It is no mean one here in

Rome" (11). She is the daughter of a classical woman scholar, also named Hipparchia, and (in a fictional compensation) her accomplishments are exactly those in which Aldington found H.D. inadequate: Hipparchia is "highly specialized in literature and grammar and the intellectual accomplishments" (13).

H.D. has been described as "the most decorous of authors," one whose "reticence clouds all her novelistic treatments of sex" (King, "HERmione" 342).[29] Yet her treatment of sexuality in "Hipparchia," although metaphoric, is graphically suggestive. The most devastating parody is reserved for Marius's body and his sexual technique. Hipparchia sees him as "fat, empty, like some overgrown tuberous vegetable" ("Hipparchia" 13). She wryly explains her reaction to physical intimacy with such a lover: "when one has slept perhaps on a rough estimate, one hundred and fifty times with one man, it is can you not see, somewhat of a shock, at the end, to find it has not been a man at all, merely a rather bulbous vegetable. No, I apologise, no cabbage but a turnip" (14). The awkward, halting syntax parodies the movement toward sexual climax; and the unflattering metaphor seems to extend its application to phallic sexuality more generally.[30] As Marius thinks of Hipparchia in her bedroom, his mental imagery of rape and murder foregrounds his own sensual incomprehension of her complex frigidity: "Plunge dagger into a gold lily. What more was she, had she in her most intimate encounters given him? You might as well plunge dagger into the cold and unresponsive flesh of some tall flower" (7). Whereas Marius is associated with masculine violence, Hipparchia is associated with a rare gold lily, an aesthetically pleasing object. According to Marius, Hipparchia is "no woman" (11) and lacks affection and human emotion (12). But Hipparchia's own thoughts reveal her frigidity exists only in relation to certain sex acts: she seeks "intimacy without intercourse" (92–93).

While much of the parody is at the expense of those who betray Hipparchia, it exaggerates and may illuminate material from *Bid Me to Live* and H.D.'s biography. In the novel, for example, Julia does not respond sexually to Rafe because of the stillbirth of her child and her subsequent fear of pregnancy: "I couldn't help being as you said— well—paralysed with fear—I mean, they told me at the nursing-home that I must not have another child—" (*Bid Me* 133). Although Rico's constant reference to Julia's "frozen altars" (*Bid Me* 55 and elsewhere) reinforces the idea of a temporary suspension of sexual response, Hipparchia is depicted as frigid, or perhaps untouched by Marius's kind of eroticism. Hipparchia is repeatedly described as "boy and girl alike" ("Hipparchia" 40), encoding H.D.'s bisexuality. Although we cannot know which version of this intimate matter is more accurate biographically, the impulse toward personal auto/biographical revelation seems to be given fuller play in "Hipparchia," the more coded version that is both more idealized than *Bid Me to Live* in terms of the protagonist's role as a writer, and more brutal in its treatment of the male lover's excessive and unattractive sexuality.

The criticism of masculine sexual violence, of which Marius is an agent, continues in the comparison of Hipparchia's two lovers' techniques; Quintus Verrus is characterized by a more diffuse erotic practice:

> Euripidean choros was perfected subtle breath of metre as the man beside her had perfected breath of loving. There had been no striving, no lacerating clutch and plunge, such as soldiers parrying, counter-thrusting, practice at their sword-play. This was a different matter . . . belonging to realms of columned porches, of temples, of temple corridors and to the curious lap-lapping that strove subtly, inreaching, hardly perceptibly moving, that was the langorous yet distinctly measured, equalizing, balancing movement of the inner tideless ocean. ("Hipparchia" 53)

Although she rejects the phallic eroticism associated with Marius and quickly tires of Verrus, Hipparchia's experiences with the latter convince her "[s]ome Aphrodite had recalled her, called her to the realm of womenkind" (52). This whole-body eroticism abates Hipparchia's frigidity, at least for a while. As in *Bid Me to Live,* the rejection of the ultramasculine man precipitates a movement toward freedom and new artistic possibilities. Hipparchia's highly developed artistic side compensates for her diminished sensuality: "She had apprehended poetry physically as she had never apprehended loving" (47).

The latter half of the story finds Hipparchia "established in Tusculum like any ardent pedagogue" with one goal: to "get the book done" ("Hipparchia" 98). Her book, left incomplete by her brother Philip, is an ambitious, interdisciplinary project: "a fervid compilation of poetry, religion and ethics" (98). Although this would appear to be a cross-gendered project, in fact, in "Hipparchia," culture itself is gendered: Greek as female and Roman as male. Thus, Hipparchia comes to believe it would be "absolute desecration" to translate Sappho into the Latin of her male captors. She decides to "quote it entire in Greek," her native language (100). The allusion to Sappho may hint at H.D.'s decision not to "translate" her lesbian impulses into published texts. Moreover, Nicoletta Pireddu claims that "the image of transposition as translation also acquires a first-rate importance to depict Hipparchia's mediating role between a male and a female language" (60). Thus it is significant that Hipparchia is bilingual, a scholar who can choose from two languages. An outsider, Hipparchia believes she can destroy Rome through gendered aesthetic choices and the act of writing: "If she wrote [the names of the Greek gods] often enough they would serve (as some Eastern charm) eventually to destroy Rome" (100). She believes she can overturn hierarchy, "the conquered must inevitably conquer" (103).

The practice of attributing gender to cultures and languages and the depiction of translation and bilingualism as gendered processes are emphasized in "Hipparchia," as in *Bid Me to Live,* where Julia's translations represent an intuitive, felt writing as opposed to an intellectual process:

> She brooded over each word, as if to hatch it. Then she tried to forget each word, for "translations" enough existed and she was no scholar. She did not want to "know" Greek in that sense. She was like one blind, reading the texture of incised letters, rejoicing like one blind who knows an inner light, a reality that the outer eye cannot grasp. She was arrogant and she was intrinsically humble before this discovery. Her own. (*Bid Me* 163)

This tactile, braille-like writing, brought into being (hatched) by female reproductive creativity, suggests the writing advocated by contemporary French feminists. In this sense, Julia and Hipparchia translate their bodies into writing. DuPlessis argues (though not specifically in relation to this text) that "translating is a way of infusing or transfusing one work into another; in another sense, using other poets' desires to state one's own means that desire is masked yet alleged" (*That Struggle* 12).[31] Translation is thus yet another palimpsestic technique, superimposing autobiography, gendered writing, and a literary tradition.

SERIAL COLLABORATION IN *THE TRIBUTE TO FREUD*

Through translating her bisexuality into her own texts, H.D. crosses the boundaries between homosexual and heterosexual. Her series of fictionalized mentor-lovers includes both women and men, precipitating Friedman to ask, "Does H.D.'s work, in short, belong squarely in the center of a lesbian tradition?" She notes that alongside "*Her, Asphodel,* and her love poems for Bryher are the prose and poetic accounts of a love for men, different in kind but equal in intensity" (*Psyche* 45). Ultimately, Friedman finds there is not yet enough biographical data to answer this question, and I would rephrase it, for study of H.D.'s fiction, to ask what she *contributes* to a lesbian literary tradition, specifically in relation to the fictionalization of Bryher and their literary liaison.

H.D.'s and Bryher's fictional depictions of each other are fairly similar in that their treatments are more romantic than literary—that is, they do not depict themselves extensively as a writing couple. Moreover, it seems notable that in Hall's, H.D.'s, and Bryher's homosexual-liaison fictionalizations, the female lovers are never treated with parody as male lovers are in the heterosexual-liaison texts. Although it is tempting to attribute this to a higher degree of affinity and a lesser amount of conflict in same-sex writing couples, and other critics have argued that this is the case (Koestenbaum, London), these instances also differ in a more pragmatic fashion, because the three writers fictionalize relationships that are ongoing. The heterosexual liasons, Nin's and West's, were ended by the time the relationships were written or published; Zelda Fitzgerald's marriage was certainly affected by her incarceration. Lesbian liasons nevertheless seem more often to produce novels in the genre of romance (see Chapter 4)—as Collecott also argues in relation to Bryher's *Two Selves* ("Lesbian Romance")—rather than fully developed literary-liaison fictions.

Bryher's posthumous reputation has not approached H.D.'s now canonical status as a poet, but Bryher herself wrote and published, often with her own resources, a substantial oeuvre including novels, memoirs, articles, translations, and book reviews (see Martin). H.D. and Bryher played various literary roles within their liaison, sometimes reciprocal, other times asymmetrical. Kloepfer summarizes Bryher's role as serving "alternatively/simultaneously as companion, muse, protector, antagonist, and lover in an intense and uneven relationship that nonetheless often provided the center for H.D.'s emotional and creative existence" (121–22). Bryher was clearly a facilitator and a patron, encouraging H.D. with both financial and emotional resources. In this role she, like Nin, used her considerable personal wealth to facilitate her partner's writing, as well as to assume power within the relationship (although as the daughter of a millionaire shipping tycoon, Sir John Ellerman, Bryher's wealth was far greater than Nin's as a banker's wife). Bryher used her extensive talents as financial manager to control a good portion of the family fortune, which she generously used to support a multitude of writers and cultural projects. H.D.'s biographers are not completely in accord on the extent of H.D.'s own personal wealth, though she inherited money both from her own family and from Bryher's father (Robinson 339), but Bryher's support seemed necessary for H.D. to allow herself to spend money on travel and personal extravagances, such as the flowers she loved.

As a facilitator, Bryher's contribution to H.D.'s writing was both practical and literary. She put H.D.'s poetic production before other needs that posed distractions for H.D. For example, she urged H.D. to place her daughter, Perdita, in a nursery shortly after her birth. She wrote, "I hope you will be sensible over Perdita and remember you were not given poetry to sit and worry over an infant in a solitary cottage. I am very jealous for your poetry" (Zilboorg, *Aldington* 197). Her jealousy is not expressed as romantic rivalry, not as a jealousy of but a jealousy for her art, for that which furthers H.D. as an artist. H.D. acknowledges her debt to Bryher poetically in the dedication to *Palimpsest:* "when all the others, blighted, reel and fall, / your star, steel-set, keeps lone and frigid trist / to freighted ships baffled in wind and blast" (n.p.). It is Bryher's faith in H.D.'s art that enables that art to deliver its freight. At other times, however, H.D. clearly felt Bryher's interest in her work was oppressive. While in psychoanalysis with Freud in 1934, H.D. wrote Bryher: "if you love me, and love my work, leave that to work its own will in its own way. . . . Let me write, then let me FORGET any writing. . . . Please for six months or a year do not probe me about writing" (Guest 218).

Despite her forty-year relationship with Bryher, H.D. minimizes her partner's role in her fictionalizations. Bryher is portrayed fleetingly near the end of two texts (she appears as Beryl in *Asphodel* and as Julia in "Hipparchia"), and also in *Paint It Today*. The depiction of the Bry- her character is romantic and magical in *Asphodel*, a sort of literary sav- ior: "Was it some sun-god on the rocks that had sent Beryl, for people don't come like that out of nowhere, not in 1919, asking to talk about poetry" (187). Spoo argues that H.D.'s portrait of Bryher as Beryl in *As- phodel* was idealized: "H.D.'s veil of Loves was as honest as it was inclu- sive—but here at the end of *Asphodel* flaws and inadequacies are lost in the glow of Beryl's eyes" (xv). Guest characterizes the real-life relation- ship as emotionally asymmetrical, with Bryher functioning, at least early on, as "admirer, a worshiper" (118). H.D. apparently used "her sexuality, strengthened by Bryher's fixation on her, to retain her hold over Bryher," though H.D. was not sexually attracted to Bryher (Guest 120). This speculative characterization may be supported by Perdita's perhaps ingenuous description of the couple as "platonic lesbians" (children never want to believe their parents have sex). Whatever the reality of their relationship, H.D. did not subject Bryher to the parody with which she treated Pound and Aldington in her fiction.

Although the female companion plays a much less pronounced role in H.D.'s fiction than in her life (through Frances Gregg and, most important, Bryher), "Hipparchia" intimates the significance of this figure by introducing her in the celebratory ending of the story. Hipparchia ultimately rejects both her male lovers as mentors: Verrus is finally associated with "shallow scholarship"; Marius is condemned for his failed attempts at trying to "help her with her verses" and is shown to be "one with all misdirected efforts" ("Hipparchia" 118–19). It is only after Hipparchia rejects her male lovers that Julia Cornelia Augusta arrives and is at first mistaken by Hipparchia for the poet Moreo. Julia is a historian who seeks "a suitable companion" (126), reminiscent of Bryher, who wrote historical novels set in classical times and who sought out H.D. in Cornwall. While Julia and her fa- ther are both interested in Hipparchia's manuscripts, Julia alone is able to appreciate the variety of her literary production: "Poetry. All your poetry. All those rare translations. . . . I know them all, all. They helped me to love Athens. All Greece, islands that no Romans ever yet saw" (131). After a period of doubt, Hipparchia comes to believe in an ecstatic writing that suggests, to contemporary readers, the physical exuberance of an *écriture féminine*. In the conclusion, Julia/Moreo bears the revelation that "Greece is a spirit," which Hipparchia has made others love as she herself loves Greece. The final line of the story bestows the promise of companionship, "I will come with you" (131). For DuPlessis this female-female bond constitutes the difference between Hipparchia and her mother: "Hipparchia thus exactly replicates an earlier decision made by the first Hipparchia, her mother, to reject the feminine, for her intellectual and poetic vocation, yet this vocation, as her mother enacted it implied a heterosexual identification with men" (*That Struggle* 47). DuPlessis argues that the mother-daughter conflict is finally resolved when "Julia's admiration and sisterly care also support Hipparchia's vocation" (48). Both *HERmione* and "Hipparchia" end with intimations of lesbian bonds as an attempt to resolve the self/Other hegemony.

In her turn, Bryher also depicts H.D. in her fiction. The final chapter of *Two Selves* ends with a brief but portentous fictionalization of her first meeting with H.D. The protagonist Nancy (the Bryher figure) anticipates meeting the poet (H.D.): "She was too old to be disappointed if an elderly woman in glasses bustled out. Poets, of course, were not what they wrote about. It was the mind that mattered." The novel, a Bildungsroman, ends climactically with Nancy's first view of the unnamed poet: "A tall figure opened the door. Young. A spear flower if a spear could bloom. She looked up into eyes that had the sea in them, the fire and colour and the splendour of it. A voice all wind and gull notes said: 'I was waiting for you to come'" (*Two Selves* 126). Although it is revealed in this chapter that Nancy has "dropped [a novel] on some publisher's [*sic*]" (119), she is not yet a full-fledged writer, nor does she enter a professional literary relationship with the unnamed poet in the novel. In Bryher's sequel, the autobiographical travel novel *West*, both the fictionalized H.D. and Bryher characters are subordinated to the presentation of America. Bryher blurs the equivalence of the real H.D. with her fictional counterpart by having Nancy praise the poetry of Pound, H.D., and Lowell, while she also creates a fictional counterpart to H.D. in the character of Helga Brandt. None of these depictions does justice to the complexity of their evolving relationship (they did not always live together, but they remained in close contact until H.D.'s death in 1961).

The reciprocal nature of their professional relationship is revealed through H.D.'s and Bryher's contributions to joint projects. In a chapter on their editorial collaborations, Marek argues that H.D. worked to foster "the spirit of collaboration" and to further "cooperative exchange" (103, 104). Marek characterizes their work as reciprocal, as "H.D. brought Bryher to the *Egoist*, the Egoist Press, and other literary connections, [while] Bryher provided H.D. with years of financial support and an entrée into the world of cinema through *Close Up*" (102). Marek ar-

gues that Bryher's role is obscured by her "characteristic modesty" and
that she did far more work than is reflected either in the contents of the
journal or in her own accounts in her memoirs (120).[32] Although
Marek's valuable study illuminates their editorial contributions, the degree to which H.D. and Bryher collaborated on their own individual literary projects has been less extensively documented by critics.

Of H.D.'s collaborative literary relationship with Bryher, Zilboorg
explains:

> H.D. was continuing her rewarding work on new poems and translations
> from the Greek, work she regularly discussed with Bryher who, in turn,
> was sharing with H.D. chapters of her own nearly finished [autobio-
> graphical] novel, *Development,* as well as her attempts at translation . . . .
> These exchanges were emotionally as well as intellectually quickening
> for H.D., and her letters to Bryher during this period reveal her excite-
> ment with this fresh burst of creativity. Certainly her relationship with
> Bryher nurtured her artistic work. (*Aldington* 191)

For her part, H.D. also encouraged Bryher in her work: "I think the
chapter [of *Development*]—really a good contrast. Do go on as well as
you can. We will try to get away somewhere *as soon as possible*—then
you must work. You will get ideas once away" (198–99). Their literary
collaboration, then, seems to consist of reciprocal encouragement and
conversations about their writing. Collecott describes the kind of "active collaboration" one might expect of their writing as taking place
in their photographical projects instead, where "they express a reciprocity between artist and subject rare in the history of photography"
("Images" 336). Laird describes a "partial collaboration" between the
two women (131) and an extensive "visionary collaboration" facilitating H.D.'s ironic response to Freud's analysis. Laird views H.D.'s *Tribute to Freud* as a "tribute to Bryher" as well (146).

Although H.D.'s auto/biographical fictions only fleetingly depict
Bryher as a writer, her memoir/tribute contains an episode where H.D.
presents herself and Bryher as engaging in a kind of literary collaboration. The "Writing on the Wall" sequence in *Tribute to Freud* is unique
in H.D.'s auto/biographical texts. In contrast to Rafe's critical response
"Not so good" to Julia's draft of the poem that became H.D.'s "Eurydice" (*Bid Me* 53), the words attributed to Bryher as she confronts the
writing on the wall, are unequivocally encouraging:

> I say to Bryher, "There have been pictures here—I thought they were
> shadows at first, but they are light, not shadow. They are quite simple ob-
> jects—but of course it's very strange. I can break away from them now, if
> I want—it's just a matter of concentration—what do you think? Shall I
> stop? Shall I go on?" Bryher says without hesitation, "Go on." (*Tribute* 47)

Bryher's role here is not merely facilitative; in this sequential collaboration she contributes "detachment," "integrity," as well as "support" (*Tribute* 72). Moreover, she actively takes up the work herself as H.D. becomes exhausted:

> But though I admit to myself that now I have had enough, maybe just a little too much, Bryher, who has been waiting by me, carries on the "reading" where I left off. Afterwards she told me that she had seen nothing on the wall there, until I dropped my head in my hands. . . . But as I relaxed, let go, from complete physical and mental exhaustion, she saw what I did not see. It was the last section of the series, or the last concluding symbol—perhaps that "determinative" that is used in the actual hieroglyph, the picture that contains the whole series of pictures in itself or helps clarify or explain them. (*Tribute* 56)

This serial collaboration is egalitarian and interdependent. Each partner completes her part of the work; both are essential to the whole. Bryher does not intervene—or even perceive the image—until H.D. has fully exhausted her vision; at this point Bryher begins to see where previously "she had seen nothing." Each woman's work is necessary to the other's—H.D. initiates the vision and Bryher's contribution provides the "determinative" key to interpret it. H.D. says "she saw what I did not see" (*Tribute* 84). In this way each woman is individually productive, each facilitates the work of the other, and a joint project results.

The description of the writing on the wall episode is couched in terms that suggest a subversive experience in which a preverbal visual hallucination is projected onto—or into—the patriarchal symbolic. H.D. describes the difficulties she and Bryher encountered while they were traveling in Corfu during a time of "political upheaval" and explains that people "expressed surprise that two women alone had been allowed to come at all at that time" (*Tribute* 74). She articulates their status as a couple in order to reject the way they were perceived by society, characterized as "alone" because they were unaccompanied by men: "we were always 'two women alone' or 'two ladies alone,' but we were not alone" (74). It is appropriate that the vision is set in Corfu because Greece is a culture gendered female for H.D. Collecott explains: "Greece was for H.D. the 'motherland,' home of female divinities and—to adapt Lacan—locus of the suppressed or lost world of female union" ("Images" 364). Freud in fact interpreted the vision they saw together as expressing H.D.'s "desire for union with [her] mother" (*Tribute* 44). The writing they en-vision links the nonverbal *chora* with the linguistic symbolic: it is "picture-writing" (*Tribute* 65).

In this narrative, H.D. returns to the issue of the self/Other hegemony within a same-sex literary liaison. She hints at the possibility of
a female writing couple in *Tribute to Freud* as an alternative to the heterosexual partners in her auto/biographical fiction:

> I knew that this experience, this writing-on-the-wall before me, could
> not be shared with them—could not be shared with anyone except the
> girl who stood so bravely there beside me. This girl had said without
> hesitation, "Go on." It was she really who had the detachment and the
> integrity of the Pythoness of Delphi. But it was I, battered and disassoci-
> ated from my American family and my English friends, who was seeing
> the pictures, who was reading the writing or who was granted the inner
> vision. Or perhaps in some sense, we were "seeing" it together, for with-
> out her, admittedly, I could not have gone on. (*Tribute* 48–49)

H.D.'s reaction to the writing on the wall is described as totally
sustaining. Both she and Bryher "see" the pictures and are thus
depicted as visionaries, granting both the traditional literary
glorification of poets. In her analysis of this sequence, Laird notes how
"[g]endered attributes are deconstructively crossed and criss-crossed"—
the "feminophallic" Niké and the "male-concentric" soldier's face, for
example (141). Their vision is "shared"; it transcends individual ownership (72). H.D. is vague about the source of the vision, as to whether
"that hand or person is myself, projecting the images . . . or whether
they are projected from outside" (*Tribute* 68), but she is not inseminated by a projection of the Other, as Julia was with Rico.

The exact nature and status of the writing-on-the-wall experience
itself is highly ambiguous, nonetheless. Susan Friedman characterizes
the experience as a "collaborative interpretation" ("I go where I love"
122). Ruth Hoberman discusses the writing on the wall as "the product of two women's minds collaborating, on contact, briefly, with a
mythic past" (98). The experience is characterized by H.D. herself as
writing on a wall; her account of it is eventually published as a literary
production, as H.D.'s tribute. The sequence might even be viewed as
an allegorical revelation of H.D.'s and Bryher's characteristic mode of
literary collaboration, with the Greek setting serving as a coded way
to suggest the lesbian origin of the collaboration.[33] At the same time,
if the account is indeed autobiographical, this kind of serial, sequen-
tial collaboration apparently never led to coauthorship (equal contributions to a jointly authored, published literary text) for H.D. and
Bryher. Laird notes that the published *Tribute* itself was not
coauthored (145). Moreover, although *Tribute* describes an experience
of collaboration, the experience itself—whether mythic, prophetic, or
autobiographical—is centered around a vision, not reality.

...

H.D.'s palimpsestic auto/biographical writings work through super-imposed variations of literary relationships and sexual liaisons. Ulti-mately, as with her description of the magic lantern slides, the effect she seeks is cumulative, and no one version suffices. Like the other writers in this study, H.D. emphasizes mentorship dialogues that re-flect the conflicting interests of the self and Other in the literary cou-ple. As with Hall, the alternative presented by H.D. for the literary couple in which both partners seek subject status is serial or sequen-tial—rather than simultaneous—collaboration. The H.D.-Bryher col-laboration is described by de Lauretis as an example of same-sex "en-trustment," a relationship based on mutual trust that exists "in full recognition of the disparity that may exist between them . . . not in spite but rather because of the power differential between them, con-trary to the egalitarian feminist belief" ("Triangle" 21–22). The con-cept of entrustment would seem to characterize the Hall-Troubridge li-aison, as well, and Hall's advocacy of accommodation. H.D., however, is the only writer in this study to hint at a model of companionate se-rial collaboration in which both partners create together, in close tem-poral proximity. The writing-on-the-wall episode in *Tribute to Freud* contains an intimation of what egalitarian collaboration might look like, though it is still a visionary experience in a foreign land.

Alternative Mentors
and Modes of Collaboration

The egalitarian romantic-literary couple is a prototype with tremendous appeal for readers as well as for writers. Public shock at posthumous revelations concerning the behavior of contemporary writing couples—at biographers' discovery of Nin's bigamy, for example—results from the force of disillusionment, the inevitable aftermath of the idealization of these couples as equal partners and as role models. Our emotional and erotic investment in such a model should not be underestimated. Biographers, critics, and readers are loath to relinquish this attractive image—a quite legitimate projection of our desire to overcome sexual hegemony. Yet each chapter of this study examines a distinctive story that challenges the ideal of the writing couple and presents a skeptical variation on the story of a woman's struggle within that relationship. The preceding chapters reveal familiar configurations in artistic-liaison fiction. Primary among them is the subject/Other dyad in the guise of a romantic couple enacting the plot of the Künstlerroman, the discovery of vocation and artistic identity. Although the auto/biographical struggle for artistic identity is often fictionally displaced to another profession (acting in West, dancing in Fitzgerald, painting in Hall), the conflict central to the literary liaison—a struggle with a critical and/or authoritarian mentor-lover—is not so much resolved as terminated through ending the romantic relationship. Such a conclusion is especially problematic for relational (rather than autonomous) life writing.

Literary-liaison fiction also depicts supporting players in relation to the women, alternative Others—rivals, oppressors, mediators, muses, mothers, and various mentor figures—who are external to the couple but who often comprise a third party to form triangular relationships. In these triangles the third party functions as a displacement for and/or projection of desire. Adding a third party to a couple, whether it be a kinder, gentler patriarch, a same-sex muse, or a powerful mother, is a technique to break apart, at least temporarily, the binary construction of the self/Other, even though the triangulation may serve, ultimately, to reinforce the dyad. This disruption also presents alternatives to the roles played within the couple. Where muses and supplemental, facilitative mentors proliferate through third-party tri-angulations, new kinds of relations are envisioned. Thus, the experimentation with another lover or a temporary escape to the Kristevan *chora* extends the possibilities presented by Lacan—imagining new configurations of the self and Other.

When the alternative mentors are women, the pattern often resembles that delineated by DuPlessis as a paradigm shift within the genre of the women's Künstlerroman from the nineteenth to the twentieth century: "the displacement of a thwarted woman in a heterosexual plot to an emergent daughter in a reparenting plot, where the daughter-artist extends and completes, in cross-generation collaboration, the unfinished artisanal work of her parent" (*That Struggle* 42). Mothers are often unacknowledged muses in liaison fiction, and the woman-woman bonds that sometimes emerge as homosocial or homosexual alternatives to the cross-gendered mentorship echo the formative prelinguistic model of the *chora*. Within the fictional plots told and retold in this study, reparenting occurs through an alternative dyad composed of a symbolic daughter and an often powerful mother-mentor figure. In West's *Sunflower*, Fitzgerald's *Save Me the Waltz*, and H.D.'s *HERmione*, mothers play major roles as mentors and muses—but also sometimes as obstructors. These variant mother-daughter couples not only revisit the presymbolic dyadic relationship, they also challenge heterosexual hierarchy.

One might wonder why these women writers, dissatisfied with their partners, did not simply strike out independently on their own. They remain, however, because the self can only be perceived in relation to the Other, or as Silverman explains, "no identity can be sustained in the absence of the gaze of the Other" (*Acoustic Mirror* 149). In fictionalizing the liaison and acknowledging the need for a reflected rather than an autonomous identity, these modernist women place the relationship and the real-life subject in the center of an ever-expanding frame of reference, which proceeds from the intimacy of the pair outward toward the larger culture. For these writers, then, the larger historical and social context of conventional biography is the social order within which they had to establish themselves if they wished to write publicly in the 1920s and 1930s. Often angry with their partners for their lack of support and appreciation of the women's writing or for their appropriation of shared autobiographical material, these women publicly interrogate the lover's role as writer but, admittedly, they often retaliate and revenge themselves using tactics of reappropriation. The anger of several of the women studied in this book, some of them first-wave feminists, targets the individual lover because of a frustration (which we can retrospectively historicize) with internalized inegalitarian structures of patriarchy that defeated their idealized relationships. Productive antagonism—the creative potential of women's anger—should not be underestimated.

The transgressive auto/biographical writers in this study wrote fictional auto/biographies to achieve presence as writers and to challenge the role of the subject in authorship by reinterpreting their relationships through the process of fictionalization. In *Sunflower* West posthumously achieved subject status in a fictionalized relationship; Nin's diaries brought her mass-market success as a writer and contemporary cult popularity. In *The Forge* Hall constructs a coded story of forbidden lesbian partnership; Fitzgerald tells a tale of frustrated struggle for self-definition in *Save Me the Waltz*. Nin and H.D. prefigure postmodern skepticism by retelling their stories in multiple versions, settings, and (con)texts. West and H.D. posit a constructed self through their self-proclaimed desire to write identity into "truth." Each auto/biographical fiction nevertheless presents variations—different solutions or conclusions—to the struggle for subjectivity with a writer partner. Nin, Fitzgerald, and H.D. depict figurative returns to the presymbolic. Yet for Nin such an encounter first creates a determination to write a feminine story, then to mediate that story for men/patriarchy. Fitzgerald's quest yields a somber comprehension of the limitations imposed upon women writing within patriarchy. H.D.'s multiple versions of the mentorship struggle eschew one fixed answer but produce, in the *Tribute to Freud*, a prototype for a more egalitarian collaboration than any of the other liaisons fictionalized in this study. West explores the acquisition of subject status through role-playing and acting, suggesting that destabilizing the self might be a strategy to evade definition by the Other. Hall's comic lesbian romance explores cross-attribution and identification with the Other to undermine self/Other hierarchy and to hypothesize sequential subject status.

These writers' common obsession with subject status in relation to the Other and their experiments with a destabilized self (and a decentered male self) link stylistically diverse works. By grouping these writers' autobiographical fictions, I hope to expand the canon of modernism, to open a space for seemingly more conventional but less appreciated texts of the modernist era—and conventional only when their narratives are compared with the currently privileged, nonlinear, stream-of-consciousness novels. The innovation of underappreciated novelists such as West and Hall is simply of a less evident kind. Autobiography is always a kind of metanonfiction, but these transgressive auto/biographical fictions pose a particular challenge to generic classification, crossing, and thus disputing, the binaries of fiction/nonfiction and of biography/autobiography.

. . .

This study raises several issues for further study—and perhaps some unresolvable questions. Is there, for example, any possibility of sustained equality in a relationship that is both professional and romantic? Does a same-sex collaboration offer alternatives to the hierarchy of patriarchal mentorships? Koestenbaum describes "egalitarian intellectual dialogue" in "male-male collaborations" (4). London presents images of productive female same-sex collaboration, and she expresses doubt about the equality of her cross-gendered partners. In comparing the Brontë children's gendered alliances, for example, London contrasts Branwell and Charlotte's collaboration, "a story of rivalry and gender difference, of hierarchical authority and struggles for independence" to the "seamless union of the Emily and Anne partnership" (44). Similarly, in the husband-wife pair William Butler Yeats and Georgie Yeats, she finds "conventional gendered hierarchies," including "Georgie playing 'psychic' to WBY's 'artist'" (184).

Much of the conflict experienced by the couples in this study derives from their competition for authority and source material: both desired the primacy of authorship in the same realm—fiction writing. Nonfictional collaborations and coauthorships have recently proliferated in the humanities—modeled by such notable pairs as Gilbert and Gubar or Ede and Lunsford—suggesting strategies that coauthors of fiction (or any fictional coauthors) might emulate. Scholars Linda Hutcheon and Michael Hutcheon describe a kind of alternative collaboration, which eschews the contested situation since the partners are specialists in different fields (comparative literature and respiratory physiology) and both are "outsiders" to the discipline of the shared project (in their case, opera). The method they advocate, based on their personal experience, is a "dialogical" model of collaboration (such as explored by Lunsford and Ede), a practice resembling "dinner table talk": "a loosely structured mode of collaboration involving multiple and shifting roles for each partner . . . where power and authority never disappear but are shared and sometimes contested" (Hutcheon and Hutcheon 63). Such shifting roles might also be achieved through de Lauretis's notion of "entrustment" (see below). The displacements of *Sunflower, Save Me the Waltz,* and *The Forge,* in transforming the role of writer to actress, dancer, or painter, may thus suggest the writers' awareness that for collaboration to replace appropriation the partners' authority must derive from different skills or expertise.

While the Lacanian self/Other paradigm presents a pessimistic outlook and a discouraging prospect for equality within a couple—or for any egalitarian writing collaboration—some of these writers' practices hint at alternatives to full coauthorship of the Gilbert and Gubar model, in which two writers consult about, draft, edit, and produce one work. Collaboration is not a discrete activity but a process, a continuum of activities. Accordingly, Laird distinguishes between "full collaboration," in which writers work together "at every stage of composition," and what she calls "partial" or "approximate" collaboration; she points out that the former is not necessarily "more equitable, or more mutually rewarding" (7). The practice I call "parallel play" in my discussion of West's and Wells's companion studies of Henry James, in which the partners each write individually and concurrently on the same topic or project, may be considered a kind of approximate collaboration—a precursor, or a potentially early stage of working together. Dorothy Richardson playfully advocates this alternative in her story "Seen from Paradise," in which lovers overcome hierarchy by remaining "as they were at the altar and at the wedding feast, side by side" (93). Sitting side by side rather than face-to-face and blocking each other's view, "each could relax and share a common spectacle, share, too, the sense of togetherness that is at its strongest when surrounded, on *neutral territory,* by fellow creatures" ("Paradise" 94).

Sometimes unequal relationships can nevertheless produce uncontested auto/biographies, as is suggested by my accounts of Hall's fictional and Troubridge's biographical accommodation, or of H.D. and Bryher's writing on the wall. "Entrustment," as conceived by de Lauretis, defines a kind of same-gender mentorship in which "one woman gives her trust or entrusts herself symbolically to another woman, who thus becomes her guide, mentor, or point of reference." Although de Lauretis does not suggest that this entrustment can exist in heterosexual couples, she notes that it exists in spite of disparate "social position" ("Triangle" 21). Her proposition thus allows for a productive same-sex relationship that is not fully egalitarian. As one example of this woman-woman entrustment, she mentions the experience of H.D. and Bryher in *Tribute to Freud* (22). While I view this experience as a largely egalitarian—though serial—collaboration, the partners were equals in neither financial matters nor in their status as writers. And although H.D. and Bryher shared the hallucination or vision of the writing on the wall, H.D. then published it autonomously in her *Tribute to Freud.* H.D. and Bryher also engaged in separate but parallel collaboration, each incorporating a condensed version of the originating moment of their relationship into a fictional text, "Hipparchia" and *Two Selves,* respectively. Models of alternating, partial, parallel, or serial collaboration may produce autonomous literary texts and provide independence for the self, while still permitting mutual influence and an opportunity for both partners to exploit auto/biographical material.

A further alternative to self/Other hegemony is the rather grim prospect of posthumous collaboration. In some cases collaboration results after the death of the beloved frees the Other to become the subject. This is part of the tradition of precursors, as Gubar suggests in her discussion of modern writers' transhistorical collaboration with Sappho, "Sapphistries." Gubar presents a model that is similar to that practiced by Toklas in her more personal, posthumous collaboration with Stein, as she published her auto/biographical *What Is Remembered* (1963), which might be considered a companion text to *The*

Autobiography of Alice B. Toklas. Kay Boyle's *Being Geniuses Together* is another interesting case in point. After Robert McAlmon's death, she composed chapters regarding her own life at parallel epochs, to be interpolated into his autobiography, previously published in 1938. Her work, published in 1968, listed him as author but she described the work as revised and "with supplementary chapters by Kay Boyle." In the prefatory note Boyle mentions nothing about her obvious desire to write her own story but claims it is her "hope that the present revision will do more than provide a deeply sympathetic portrait of a writer and publisher who deserves to be remembered for his unique qualities, but that it will as well help to accord to Robert McAlmon his rightful and outstanding place in this history of the literary revolution of the early nineteen-twenties" (McAlmon and Boyle xiii). Although she claims to foreground McAlmon, she adds her self-authored story to his, comprising a corrective to his autonomous text and intimating that his portrait must be considered in relation to hers.

The liaison stories in this book tell the relational, asymmetrical story of a couple and therefore cannot do justice to the man's point of view at the same time as they protest his repression of the woman's artistic identity. Although this study focuses on the implications of the self/Other hierarchy for women writers, there is need for a study of the consequences for men. The male partners in these heterosexual liaisons wrote their own auto/biographical fictions (and, in some cases, nonfictions), stories of bondage to femmes fatales and of partnerships with literary fantasy spirits, witchy harpies, and madwomen; they write of the pain of sexual betrayal, and of the triumphs and costs of hegemony. The relatively new subfields of gender studies, masculinities, and queer theory begin to provide theoretical models for how male fictions might be treated. Many of these studies, however, in focusing on same-sex collaborations fill in a neglected area of scholarship but nevertheless leave unanswered questions about the challenges to equality that are posed by heterosexual and bisexual collaboration.

• • •

The common ground in all the liaison stories, whatever the gender and sexual orientation of the authors, is the conflict between self and Other. There may be a tendency for the self always to see itself as origin of the creative work. As MacCannell explains, aggression "arises because the 'independent' ego ideal will always see itself as pitted against its fellows, or against the structure (culture, the communal situation) personified as yet another individual person, or Person" (69). Gilbert and Gubar's light-hearted spoof of their own collaboration, *Masterpiece Theater,* suggests that self-interest may lurk behind even professional, nonromantic, same-sex collaboration. Identifying themselves in egalitarian and indistinguishable form as "SG1" and "SG2," their fictional dramatic counterparts contest the source of even banal ideas, each claiming, "That was *my* idea" and "I thought *I* said that" (*Masterpiece* 40). Although patriarchy exacerbates hegemony, gender may be less of an obstacle than ego. As Ragland-Sullivan explains: "Neither sex is the negation of the other, but the obstacle to the other. Nor does homosexuality offer an ideal Good in relationships anymore than heterosexuality. Every person always confronts the Other beyond the other" (972).

It may be that self/Other hegemony persists in the liaison fiction, despite these writers' various strategies of contestation and resistance, because the texts are autobiographical. The generic intersection of fictionalized *autobiography* does not permit its authors to write entirely beyond the actual, beyond an ideology in which patriarchy (or patriarchies) persists. It is not surprising that these women are more successful in writing oppositionally, against patriarchy, than beyond it; it is always easier to articulate the problems of the status quo than to envision solutions external to it. Their persistent desire to create alternatives nevertheless attests to the subject's obstinate struggle for subjectivity and to the attractions of the transformative potential of fiction. The protagonists—and the texts themselves—depict a range of possibilities for the gendered, role-playing, cross-attributed, multiple, serial, or decentered subject, anticipating in some cases what we today call the postmodern self.

Notes

INTRODUCTION

1. The introduction's title is from Rebecca West, "The Art of Skepticism," *Vogue*, 1 Nov. 1952, 115.

2. I adopt Heidi Hartmann's definition of *patriarchy*, with some qualifications. She emphasizes that it is "the systemic dominance of men over women" (7): "*Patriarchy is not simply hierarchical organization*, but hierarchy in which *particular* people fill *particular* places . . . [a] set of interrelations among men that allow men to dominate women" (14). Hartmann's definition is complicated by differences among male patriarchs and the fact that women may function as agents of patriarchy or act in complicity with such dominance.

3. This lack seems ironic, given the recent designation of the 1920s (and 1928 in particular) as a "banner year for lesbian publishing" (Cook 718). Jeannette Foster argues that there was "a first peak in variant literature" between 1925 and 1935; she traces the change in English literature to the "relaxing of all sexual strictures" in the 1920s (154, 241). Sheila Jeffreys views the 1920s as a period in which literature was engaged in a "process of differentiating between innocent friendship between women and fully fledged lesbianism," culminating in the battle provoked by *The Well of Loneliness* in 1928 (125 and elsewhere). Lillian Faderman describes a change in "all types of sexual activity" in 1920s America and argues that as a result women had to reevaluate their same-sex friendships, previously viewed as romantic, for possible sexual attraction (327–28). See Bette London, *Writing Double* (esp. chap. 2), for discussion of women's writing partnerships as "lesbian," though perhaps nonsexual.

4. For an account of their marriage see Julia Markus, *Dared and Done* (letter p. 3). Dorothy Mermin focuses on Browning's complex role as facilitator of Barrett's writing, "The Domestic Economy of Art," in Perry and Brownley, *Mothering the Mind* (82–101).

5. Sandra Gilbert and Susan Gubar see the success of modernist women writers as producing anxiety for their male counterparts: the men defused anxiety about the "literary combat in which they often felt engaged" by using such strategies as "mythologizing women to align them with dread prototypes; fictionalizing them to dramatize their destructive influence; slandering them in essays, memoirs, and poems; prescribing alternate ambitions for them; appropriating their words in order to usurp or trivialize their language; and ignoring or evading their achievements in critical texts" (*No Man's Land* 1:149).

6. Jeffreys also points out that movements to further interests of homosexuals and the study of sexuality (even the movement in which Hall and Troubridge were active, the British Society for the Study of Sex Psychology) were focused on male homosexuals and often took a conservative view of women's rights (156).

7. Jayne Marek criticizes the "assumption of reaction, which informs several recent studies of modernist women's work," such as those by Shari Benstock or Gilbert and Gubar (13). Several recently published books on collaboration, often treating same-sex partners, may be a reaction against this earlier focus as well as a sign of the pervasive influence of composition pedagogy emphasizing collaboration and workshop teaching.

8. For classical antecedents of this model see Harold Bloom, *The Anxiety of Influence,* chapter 6.

9. A collection of essays by Teresa de Lauretis, Naomi Schor, Elizabeth Grosz, Diana Fuss, and others, *the essential difference* (ed. Schor and Weed), presents complex and persuasive responses to the simple opposition of constructionism to essentialism (of a socially fabricated versus an innate gender), including some history of this impasse within the feminism of the 1980s.

10. In calling this experience "Lacanian," I wish to designate not only Jacques Lacan but also those critics who articulate his ideas, and those feminists who reformulate his ideas, particularly the so-called French feminists Julia Kristeva, Hélène Cixous, and Luce Irigaray. Though not exclusively of French origin, this group of contemporary feminists is associated with theories of a woman's language or *écriture féminine,* a purported writing of the female body. One of the most detailed accounts of the mirror stage as a gendered experience is Kaja Silverman's *The Subject of Semiotics* (149–93). Derived from Freud, the mirror stage is, in various reformulations and articulations, part of many psychoanalytic and linguistic schemes for human development. Otto Rank, for example, calls the movement from the maternal to the patriarchal community the "second adult" or "mature" initiation (246).

11. As Marcia Ian elaborates in *Remembering the Phallic Mother,* the phallic mother "hardly resembles anyone's actual mother—except in one's own fervid imagination. . . . She is a fantasmatic caricature, and a caricature of the fantasmatic . . . our role model and the very 'type' of the autonomous self. By having a penis, she defies the psychoanalytic 'fact' of woman's castration, at the same time she attests to the 'fact' of every other woman's castration but hers; she is the girl who has everything and the one 'we' for that reason desire and wish 'we' could be" (8–9). Ian's formation draws upon the conception of the powerful, uncastrated mother first hypothesized as "phallic" by Freud; she argues that the phallic mother "bears" and "is" the fetish and arouses ambivalent feelings (9).

12. In addition to the French feminists mentioned previously, suggestive definitions of *écriture féminine* may be found in Silvia Bovenschen, "Is There a Feminine Aesthetic?"; Maria Minich Brewer, "A Loosening of Tongues"; Christiane Makward, "To Be or Not to Be . . . a Feminist Speaker."

13. Feminists are undecided as to whether a Lacanian-derived approach facilitates or is antithetical to the personal, psychological, and social change implicit in a feminist ideology. Lacan has sometimes been dismissed, along with the French feminists who adapt his work, as merely essentialist, and thus a blocking agent to feminist change. Juliet Flower MacCannell calls this "killing the messenger who brings the bad news" (3). Lacan's work is certainly informed by some of the limiting notions of gender against which second-

wave feminists protest. Although feminists of this era have often eschewed limiting definitions of "woman" and gender, they too must rely upon a nominal essentialism in order to define women's place in the status quo and to articulate contemporary objectives for change. Psychoanalytic theories may present themselves as descriptions of innate processes, but they are also always evolving and revisionary (Kristeva revises Lacan, who revises Freud—who revises Freud—and so forth). See MacCannell for distinctions between Lacan and Kristeva (29 and elsewhere). Other feminists defend Lacan's theories from charges of essentialism. Diana Fuss, for example, points to the significance of Lacan's work for theories of social construction (*Speaking* 6–12).

14. Rebecca West's given name was Cicely Isabel Fairfield; Radclyffe Hall's was Marguerite Radclyffe-Hall; H.D.'s was Hilda Doolittle.

15. Anaïs Nin is frequently dismissed for her essentialist notion of the feminine woman. Her style of feminism was popular in the 1970s, however, and she argues for change in women's roles, opposing the patriarchy that she defines as being "like men." Rebecca West, though a suffragette, has been disparaged for the more accommodating feminism she cultivated as she grew older. For an analysis of her "paradoxical feminism" and her equivocal treatment by feminist critics, see Ann Norton, *Paradoxical Feminism*.

16. This choice represents the kind of collective identity that is necessary for any struggle against a dominant force. For an excellent discussion of the necessity of classification for identity politics, see Diana Fuss, "Reading like a Feminist."

17. Only the initial part of his first clause applies unequivocally to the liaison autobiography, which does not limit the subject to "his own existence" but more broadly conceives a self within a relationship. (Unless otherwise noted, italics within quotations are always from the original.)

18. The reference in Fleishman is to Lejeune, *L'Autobiographie en France* (Paris, 1971), 25, 28.

19. The title of the journal *A/B: Autobiography Studies* similarly suggests this dual focus.

20. For accounts of H.D.'s collaborations with women editors, see Marek, *Women Editing Modernism*. Cyrena N. Pondrom discusses their correspondence and finds that they document "a supportive community of female writers" (Pondrom 372).

21. Avrom Fleishman recasts Freud's "Where id was, let ego be."

22. The current interest in collaboration has fostered two recent journal issues with forums or clusters of articles devoted to the topic, in applications beyond composition. Both these journal issues serve as excellent introductions to the topic: see *PMLA* 1116.2 (2001) and *On Collaborations* in *Tulsa Studies in Women's Literature* (fall 1994 and spring 1995).

23. Louise DeSalvo takes her title from Anthony West's statement about his own conception; he claimed that his mother maliciously "became pregnant to solidify her relationship with Wells" (DeSalvo 9). The son produced by the Wells-West liaison was an initially unwilling—and always bitter—third party in their antagonism, which he ultimately appropriated for himself (see the chapter on West in this study).

24. The other three professions studied by Levinson were hourly workers, executives, and academic biologists. His work is valuable in its breadth and theoretical nature; most studies of cross-gender mentorships focus on narrow and specialized groups in business, education, and other individual

professions. For an overview of research on mentoring see Jeanne J. Speizer, "Role Models, Mentors, and Sponsors."

25. Kathy Kram devotes a chapter to "Phases of a Mentor Relationship" in *Mentoring at Work.*

CHAPTER 1

1. Portions of this chapter previously appeared in *Tulsa Studies in Women's Literature* 14.2 (1995): 309–24, and in *Frontiers* 15.3 (1995): 167–85.

2. Wilson went on to mentor and marry Mary McCarthy, "reputedly locking her in a room until she wrote a story" (Sheehy 37).

3. Linda Philip-Jones mentions this aspect of mentorship as a derivative of the classic patronage system (86–87).

4. See Gunther Stuhlmann's note in Nin, *Nearer the Moon* (114–15), and his note in Miller, "The Diary of Anaïs Nin" (14).

5. Wendy DuBow, for example, argues that Nin constructed a "dichotomy" between her identity as artist and her identity as woman, and that her ultimate "allegiance to this dichotomy cost her potential supporters" (23). More recently Diane Richard-Allerdyce defends Nin from charges of essentialism while at the same time placing her writing within a tradition of *écriture féminine* (12). Using a Lacanian approach she argues that Nin saw the sexes as "opposites . . . but functions of each other" (27) and that "gender distinction" is the result of "a secondary (rather than a primary) signification" (174n. 25).

6. The publication of the erotica (*Delta of Venus* in 1977 and *Little Birds* in 1979) may initially have contributed, as did her work in the diary genre, to her exclusion from the canon. However, the erotica is finally beginning to attract serious critical attention.

7. Determining the amount and kind of influence these official and unofficial editors had on Nin's work is important scholarly work yet to be undertaken. According to Noël Riley Fitch, Nin and Miller's mutual influence was extensive (*Anaïs* 119). Not only did Miller make detailed suggestions on Nin's draft of *House of Incest,* but Otto Rank proposed its conclusion (*Anaïs* 161–62, 181). Fitch uses a revealing biological or botanical (that is, reproductive) metaphor to describe Nin and Miller's "pollination of each other's intellectual and artistic capabilities" ("Literate Passion" 156). Other critics attribute much influence to Nin's official editors. Deirdre Bair describes Rupert Pole and Gunther Stuhlmann as editor-collaborators, posthumously revising Nin's diary: "The two men argue their positions and points of view until both are satisfied with the text" (*Nin* 516). Fitch claims that the "presence of [Stuhlmann's] name on the title page and cover of each diary" reveals the extent of his revisions of Nin's published diaries (*Anaïs* 375). Various critics' disagreements about the extent to which others affected Nin's published works are influenced by their choice of biographical or literary approaches, their sympathy with or antipathy to Miller, and the degree of romanticism they attribute to the Nin-Miller relationship. Nin's ambiguous standing as a noncanonical, or even perhaps a cult, writer seems to make true scholarly assessment particularly difficult. But as Fitch observes, Nin and Miller's "romantic rebellion appeals to a growing number of admirers" ("Literate Passion" 170).

8. This classification is complicated, however, by the license permitted by fiction. Jason notes that Nin claimed "to protect" the identities of the same

people in the diary that she "exploit[ed]" in her fiction: "Certainly those people knew who they were" ("Another Veil" 203).

9. The June story was also published as an excerpt, with the title "Hans and Johanna," in *Anaïs: An International Journal.* The journal editor explains that it was deleted from all subsequent editions of *Winter of Artifice* (Stuhlmann note in Nin, "Hans" 3). Nin claimed she had a "special version" of the novel made to delete the story of Henry and June so that her husband, Hugo, and her lover, Gonzalo, could read it (*Nearer the Moon* 305). Since the excerpt ("Hans and Johanna") is shorter than the original in *Winter of Artifice* ("Djuna"; 1939), I discuss "Djuna," which I consider a significant draft for the other versions of the June story under study. I do not treat the versions of the June story in Nin's five-novel roman-fleuve, *Cities of the Interior,* because I consider these later examples overworked, and less interesting than the early ones from both an artistic and an autobiographical standpoint.

10. Critics have been as puzzled by the writers' depiction of June as Nin and Miller were puzzled by the original. The "real" June was elusive, indeed. Stuhlmann reports that very few facts have been substantiated. We know that her family was immigrant and Jewish; that they changed their name from Smerth to Smith; and that June was born in Bukovina, Eastern Europe, in 1902 (122–23). Most critics see her as a femme fatale—at once fascinating, elusive, deadly. For Gary Sayre the June character in *House of Incest* (Sabina) embodies a "carnivorous, incestuous" desire that will destroy the narrator if she continues to identify with her (47). Oliver Evans sees Sabina as "*naturally*" destructive in contrast to the narrator, the "earth-mother archetype" (31). Evelyn Hinz considers the June figure in the diary to be one-half of Nin's literary dilemma: June is the half that creates illusion, Miller the half that exposes it (*Mirror and Garden* 102). Marie-Line Pétrequin argues that June represents Nin's repressed desires and a "'male' quality" (49). The maternal qualities emphasized here are to some extent, though in an archetypal rather than a psychoanalytical context, remarked upon by Stephanie Demetrakopoulos, who describes June as a mixture of both "an aspect of archetypal femininity, which is implicit" in Nin and Erich Neumann's "Terrible Mother" (124–26).

11. In her study of Nin's erotica, Karen Brennan makes a similar point about Nin's comfort (relative to that of Miller) in being herself "a spectacle for the gaze of a man," as she performs (writes) for the collector after Miller refuses (67ff). Brennan's discussion of the "paradox of the female writing spectacle," gendered authorship as it draws upon the issues of the female gaze, "double identification," and voyeurism, as well as Nin's ambivalent complicity, intersects in significant ways with the argument presented here. Brennan and I differ markedly, however, in our choice of primary text and our conclusions.

12. In Nin's original sequence of diaries, the volume entitled "June" apparently preceded that entitled "Henry." See Rupert Pole's preface to *Henry and June.*

13. Rachel Blau DuPlessis also makes this point in associating "underworld language" with the lost Etruscan ("Etruscans" 275).

14. The version of the encounter published in *Henry and June* is similar to this one from the *Diary.* The major differences are that, in *Henry and June,* the version is broken up into short paragraphs and the judgmental sentence "She killed my admiration by her talk" is not present, suggesting that it may have been added when the original diary was edited for publication in 1966.

Another significant difference is that, in the final paragraph, the narrator claims she is "like a man" in loving June's "face and body" (*Henry and June* 14). Although the editor, Nin's long-term lover and literary executor Rupert Pole, claims the volume is edited to focus on Henry and June, the degree to which the editing might have altered this kind of passage remains unclear.

15. Among those critics who first noted Nin's anticipation of French feminism are Ellen G. Friedman ("Anaïs Nin" 347), Margret Andersen (263), and Sharon Spencer (165, 171).

16. Ellen Friedman makes this point about both *House of Incest* and *Winter of Artifice* ("Anaïs Nin" 345).

17. Bair attributes the biographical suggestion of visiting an exhibition to Nin's cousin, Eduardo Sànchez. She claims Nin then asked Miller to recommend a specific brothel (*Nin* 130).

18. While Judith Roof concedes that Nin "gains some essential knowledge about female sexuality" in this scene (2), she reads the rue Blondel sequence as one of only fleeting "authenticity," which ultimately "defends against lesbian sexuality" (3).

19. DuPlessis believes this contradiction, "between the desire to please, making woman an object, and the desire to reveal, making her a subject," is resolved by the diary "as form and process" ("Etruscans," 280).

CHAPTER 2

1. The double standard was part not only of Wells's marriage but also of his romantic affairs, which were not always monogamous. For example, although Wells was unfaithful to West, he wrote her: "Please love me and be faithful to me. It is much bitterer and more humiliating for the male and I can't bear the thought of it. I love you and want to keep you anyhow, but I know that in spite of myself I shan't be able to endure your unfaithfulness" (quoted in Rollyson, *Life* 76).

2. Orel's comment may refer to West's refusal to keep the money she received for any writing connected to her relationship with Wells. When she received royalties for consulting with Gordon Ray for his biography of the relationship, for example, she donated the money to the London Library (Glendinning, *West* 155).

3. For an analysis of West's depiction of her son in her unpublished novel and her ambivalent correspondence with and about him, see Felber, "Unfinished Business and Self-Memorialization."

4. In the play *Rosmersholm*, Ibsen's Rebecca West kills herself. According to Glendinning, West came to regret the associations of her assumed name (*West* 37–38).

5. Derived from Freud's familial Oedipal triangle, this triangulated model of human interaction provides the basic paradigm underpinning Girard's *Deceit, Desire, and the Novel,* Bloom's *Anxiety of Influence,* Gilbert and Gubar's *Madwoman in the Attic,* Eve Kosofsky Sedgwick's *Between Men,* and a plethora of critical offshoots.

6. West fictionalizes Beaverbrook in another unfinished, posthumously published novel, *The Only Poet.* All references to unpublished letters, notes, and manuscripts cited as "Tulsa" are to the major collection of West's papers in the McFarlin Library Special Collections at University of Tulsa. My work in this archive was made possible by a travel-to-collections grant from *Tulsa Studies in Women's Literature.*

7. Wells was equally ambivalent, and much less generous. In *Wells in Love,* he wrote: "I do not know if I loved Rebecca West, though I was certainly in love with her towards the latter part of our liaison. . . . Beyond that, all these women I have kissed, solicited, embraced and lived with, have never entered intimately and deeply into my emotional life" (60–61). In the same work he claims, "We loved each other in bright flashes; we were mutually abusive; we were fundamentally incompatible" (108).

8. The characterization of the lover in *Sunflower* as a selfish baby suggests—and justifies—the mother's resentment of her child, a depiction that may offer some support or explanation for Anthony West's persistent complaints of insufficient motherly love.

9. In her literary criticism West praises Wells, however, for "the novel of ideas" and defends him from the "cretinous butlers who make up the mass of respectable English critics" ("Novel of Ideas," 111).

10. Wells was similarly criticized by Dorothy Richardson, who rejects the limitations of a logic she clearly defines as masculinist in her fictional portrait of him as Hypo G. [God] Wilson in *Pilgrimage.* For an analysis of Richardson and Wells's literary liaison, see Felber, *Gender and Genre in Novels without End* (esp. 89–91), and Felber, "Mentors, Protégés, and Lovers."

11. Wells did strike the fiery Odette Keun, a subsequent mistress. According to Keun's own accounts to West, Wells "frequently hit her and gave her black eyes" (Rollyson, *Life* 134).

12. Rebecca West's short story "Indissoluble Matrimony" similarly opposes a strong, sensual woman to a weak male. In this story the male character seeks retribution for his own deficiency by attempting to murder his wife.

13. The technical virtuosity of this scene provides an example of a generalization by Gilbert and Gubar: "where male-authored descriptions of sexual conflict are generally quite straightforward and almost always feature literal duels, battles, or wrestling matches, women's works—though they sometimes include physical confrontations—frequently imagine female victory either through duplicity and subterfuge or through providential circumstance. In women's texts, men generally win tests of bodily strength, but women outwit or outlast men who fortuitously succumb to fatal mischances" (*No Man's Land* 1:66–67). West reveals that physical violence is the resource of the weak in spirit.

14. This passage seems to allude to the scene in Kate Chopin's *The Awakening* in which Edna Pontellier awakens from her nap in Madame Antoine's cottage: "She stretched her strong limbs that ached a little. She ran her fingers through her loosened hair for a while. She looked at her round arms as she held them straight up and rubbed them one after the other, observing closely, as if it were something she saw for the first time, the fine firm quality and texture of her flesh" (55–56). The allusiveness of West's passage is supported by the chapter's opening line, after Sunflower has broken with Essington: "This was the best awakening of all her life" (*Sunflower* 239). Although I can find no evidence that West had read Chopin, the parallels between the two protagonists—their fantasies about a romantic rescue from an abusive man, and their inevitable disappointment—are substantial.

15. West was never forthright about her relationship with Beaverbrook, but Glendinning hypothesizes they were unable to achieve satisfactory sexual relations ("Afterword" 272; *West* 95–99). This interpretation is supported by West's notes for the novel. In "The American Section" of the novel in New

York, Sunflower is told "about Francis Pitt's impotence" (Notes on novel; Tulsa). Impotence is also mentioned as a problem in the fictionalized relationship in her unfinished *The Only Poet*. Little is known definitively about their actual private relationship, in part because Beaverbrook "was careful to destroy virtually all the evidence of their affair with the help of his authorized biographer, A. J. P. Taylor" (Rollyson, *Life* 100).

16. Critics who see *Heritage* as an uninterrupted indictment of West as a mother overlook this insight. On the other hand it is probable that, as of one of West's friends commented, the "greatest lie" of the novel is that Anthony had come to peace with his relationship with his mother. If he had, writing this book would have been unnecessary (Rollyson, *Life* 306).

17. Anthony West's choice of name suggests "the subject of Samuel Johnson's famous biography. Savage, a bastard, claimed that his mother, Lady Macclesfield, had ruined his life, refusing to acknowledge him or to provide him with the place in society he deserved. She had persecuted him and connived to get him hanged" (Rollyson, *Life* 301).

18. Though West names only the author in *Sunflower,* the passage quoted is from *Drama and Life* by Arthur Bingham Walkley (102–4). In her manuscript notebooks, she transcribes the passage and identifies it as "What Sunflower reads in bed" (Tulsa).

CHAPTER 3

1. The epigraph is from Kristeva, "Interview," and is cited by Grosz (*Lacan* 165).

2. In this chapter I depart from the usual procedure of identifying authors by last names because of the Fitzgeralds' shared surname. I do not intend by this usage to suggest any special chumminess with the subjects, but their own practice seemed to provide no alternative. Zelda for the most part used the name Fitzgerald both personally and professionally from the time of their marriage. On one occasion her review of *The Beautiful and the Damned* was credited to "Zelda Sayre (Mrs. F. Scott Fitzgerald)" (Bruccoli et al. 100); on another occasion her byline was "Zelda Sayre Fitzgerald," but she made no consistent effort to assume an independent name for her professional writing. She seemed willing to capitalize on Scott's reputation when her novel was promoted by his publisher.

3. Their collaboration could have been facilitated by their complementary writing skills. Zelda wrote with extravagant language and metaphor; her granddaughter, Eleanor Lanahan, notes the visual quality of Zelda's prose: "for anyone who is acquainted with Zelda's writing, it should come as no surprise that she painted. Her prose, like her art, is lush, vibrant and original" (12). Scott wrote to their daughter on June 12, 1940, that Zelda was "a great original in her way, with perhaps a more intense flame at its highest than I ever had" but that she was not a "'natural story-teller' in the sense that I am, and unless a story comes to her fully developed and crying to be told she's liable to flounder around rather unsuccessfully among problems of construction" (quoted in Mellow, *Lives* 340). Scott quite correctly assesses his own skill at plotting narratives.

4. The sketch is reproduced in color in Lanahan 23, and in black and white in Bruccoli et al. 99.

5. Whereas Scott received as much as four thousand dollars per story in 1931 (Bruccoli et al. 185), Zelda was paid only three hundred by *McCall's* for the

article "Where Do Flappers Go?" and then, after requesting the essay, they decided not to publish it (Hartnett 128). Nancy Milford records a somewhat better remuneration in the previous decade: "During 1922–23 she sold two short stories, a review, and at least two articles, earning $1,300 for her efforts" (102).

6. Even their biographers and critics cannot agree about the Fitzgeralds' authorship. The story was written primarily by Zelda with "help" from Scott (according to Milford 102), or as a collaboration (according to Bruccoli, "Preface" 12).

7. Two of the covers from 1928 and 1930 publications are reproduced in Hartnett 102–3. One is that of "A Millionaire's Girl," published in the *Saturday Evening Post*.

8. The following biographical account is as succinct as possible because the focus here is on literary analysis of *Save Me the Waltz*. For the most detailed discussions of biographical material see Nancy Milford, Jacqueline Courbin-Tavernier, and Dale Spender (*Writing?* 175–92).

9. Courbin-Tavernier, Milford, and Spender offer the most detailed cultural-biographical readings of appropriation in the Fitzgeralds' relationship. My reading (as far as I know the only sustained Lacanian–French feminist reading of the novel) differs from theirs in that I use this approach as a jumping-off point for a more detailed literary analysis.

10. Lacan puns on the French homophones *nom* (name) and *non* (no). The authoritarian father occupies the third position in the family triangle, an outsider to the close mother-child dyad. Because he assumes the function of law and authority, he says "non" to prohibited desires; but because he represents society in issuing cultural prohibitions, he also names and assumes the authoritarian role of "Name-of-the-Father."

11. Simone Weil Davis traces this plastic self to a "trend dominant in the period's perfume advertising. Ad copy for the 1920s, especially for scents, banked on the notion of women's changeable nature" (336).

12. Zelda actually sold some of her paintings: two were bought by Dorothy Parker and two by Gertrude Stein (Hartnett 143). Her extant paintings are reproduced in *Zelda: An Illustrated Life*, edited by Eleanor Lanahan. Hartnett lists the exhibits and their dates (142).

13. Bruccoli (*Epic*) and Milford call it San Carlo, but in *Save Me the Waltz* Zelda either fictionalizes or misspells it as "San Carlos."

14. In a perceptive analysis of this character, Davis views Gibbs as "a woman addicted to the alluring performance," a woman in "disguise as a commodity" (341, 342).

15. The incident may have its origin in a photo of Lubov Egorova, printed in Bruccoli et al. (161), which Zelda kept.

16. After her first mental breakdown in 1930 Zelda asked Scott to write her teacher for an assessment of her potential as a dancer (*Collected Writings* 448). In her response Egorova defined Zelda as someone who could dance well in minor roles, as a significant dancer, but not one who could compete with her teacher's achievement. This answer was something less than Zelda hoped for, but more than Scott had anticipated.

17. Davis also argues that Alabama's dancing lacks "transcendence" because she "sweats far more than she soars. That same body that she struggles so hard to master succumbs ultimately to blood disease, and she must stop dancing" (349).

18. A handful of critics have made this connection. Mary E. Wood notes the affinity of this writing with an *écriture féminine*, though she attributes it to Zelda

rather than to any character within the novel: "I think Zelda Fitzgerald is working, if unconsciously, towards this kind of writing, which challenges the prescriptive sentences of male-generated discourse" (260). Janet M. Ellerby also attributes it to Zelda rather than to Alabama and argues that "Cixous (1981) unknowingly describes Zelda appropriately as the woman writer filled with an urge to inscribe in language her woman's style . . . by writing through her own dancer's body" (166).

19. The Fitzgeralds' homophobia remains a relatively unexplored area of their biography.

20. Tellingly, in *Tender Is the Night,* one of Doctor Diver's patients is brought to the clinic by his father to be cured of alcoholism and homosexuality.

21. Many paintings are reproduced in *Zelda: An Illustrated Life,* edited by Eleanor Lanahan. However, not all her work survives. Paintings that friends bought from her have disappeared, and a fire in a Montgomery shed after her death destroyed others (Bruccoli, *Epic* 365). Bruccoli and Smith claim that Zelda's mother destroyed many of Zelda's oil paintings after her death (Bruccoli, Smith, and Kerr 173). Livingston states that one of Zelda's sisters ordered them destroyed (Lanahan 78).

22. Sheilah Graham's account of her own relationship with F. Scott Fitzgerald mentions that he used the phrase "poor lost Zelda" as a sort of nostalgic refrain, to rationalize both his loyalty to Zelda and his reluctance to marry Graham (56).

CHAPTER 4

1. The epigraph description of the partners is from p. 238. Of the many texts I considered while conceptualizing this study, I selected *The Forge* as the only modernist auto/biographical fiction I could find centering on a lesbian writing couple. Although this novel provides provocative contrasts to the heterosexual liaison fiction, in no way do I present it as representative of a lesbian tradition.

2. One might specify a Caucasian focus as well; I found no modernist auto/biographical fiction depicting literary liaisons between women of color. Gilmore's wide-ranging *Autobiographics* fills in the field somewhat through her discussion of contemporary autobiographies by minority writers Sandra Cisneros, Jamaica Kincaid, Cherríe Moraga, and others, but Gilmore does not deal specifically with literary liaisons.

3. Woolf expressed reservations about Sackville-West as a writer, accusing her of writing "with complete competency, and with a pen of brass" (Leaska 38). The differences in their literary and financial successes were significant. When they met in 1922, Virginia Woolf was "already a writer of acknowledged importance, but had yet to become a commercial success. And by 1922, Vita [ten years younger than Virginia] had already published several volumes of poetry and fiction, and was also an established author" (Leaska 22).

4. One contemporary observer of this couple, Bryher (herself part of a lesbian writing couple), felt that Toklas sacrificed her "gifts" but not her self: "they never grew to resemble each other as often happens in such cases. Her [Alice's] personality was intact" (Mellow, *Circle* 290–91). See also Bryher's *Heart to Artemis* (211). Toklas was not a professional writer or artist, but she served as Stein's secretary, with a significant workload after the success of *The Autobiography of Alice B. Toklas.* She also contributed by correcting French grammar and spelling (Mellow, *Circle* 429). Some critics argue with considerable dexter-

ity that Stein gives Toklas "voice" through creating a discourse that resembles her lover's voice, but I find such arguments strained. To my mind, the process whereby Stein "ventriloquizes 'Alice'" (Sidonie Smith, *Subjectivity* 76), albeit playfully, is a process whereby Toklas, puppetlike, only appears to speak; its ultimate effect is to efface the partner's voice.

5. *The Forge* has received almost no critical attention and, as far as I know, none as a coded lesbian novel. It was completed in five months (Troubridge 78) but was "submitted to ten publishers before it was finally accepted by Cassells" (Franks 60). Published on January 25, 1924, it was initially well reviewed (Cline 188). The current neglect is all the more surprising given the recent interest in *The Well of Loneliness* as a lesbian breakthrough text. *The Forge* may have been ignored because of its apparent heterosexual focus. The one critic who devotes a short chapter to it in her study of Hall states it "does not really lend itself to detailed literary analysis" (Franks 61). Admittedly, *The Forge* has neither the multiplotted richness of a Victorian novel nor the innovative stream of consciousness of many modernist novels, but it gains interest when viewed as coded autobiography.

6. Critics who fault Hall's depiction of lesbianism as "inversion" in *The Well of Loneliness* fail to contextualize her work historically (there was no prior commercial lesbian literary tradition for her to develop) and to appreciate the extent of her innovation in the novels of the 1920s. Each of her three early novels (*The Unlit Lamp, The Forge,* and *The Well of Loneliness*) experiments with a different method to inscribe stories of lesbian love.

7. Richard Ormrod notes that John would be classified today as a "transsexual," "a genetic female . . . with a psychosexual male identity" (94).

8. The *Oxford English Dictionary* (1989) dates the first use of the adjective form of *queer* to denote homosexuality to 1922, but only for American usage. The *OED* describes the word in its current sexual sense as imported from America in 1937. The ninth edition of Webster's, published in 1991, gives the earliest date for the noun use as 1812, but I could find no evidence that our contemporary use of the term was current in England at the time Hall wrote the novel.

9. Somewhat in contrast to Cline's argument, Laura Doan argues that the relationship between the media image of the lesbian and Hall's cultivation of the image of the mannish lesbian is more complex, less individualistic, and less idiosyncratic than previous critics have suggested. Doan asserts that Hall's image was comprised largely of clothes that were, during the period, at the forefront of fashion and the Modern and only became publicly associated with the mannish lesbian after *The Well of Loneliness* was tried in 1928 under the British Obscene Publications Act of 1857. (Hall lost the case because of the novel's lesbian subject matter and the novel was censored in England.)

10. This image may be derived not only from the conventional image of women as caged birds but also from biographical experience. While in Italy both Hall and Troubridge were disturbed by the "local custom of keeping birds in tiny cages" and they bought the birds to liberate them (Cline 181).

11. Jack Seymour's portrait of Hall and Troubridge, which Castle reproduces in her text, was created as a composite from two separate portraits of the partners.

12. Romaine Brooks was not happy with her depiction in *The Forge*. She told Natalie Barney that Hall saw her "with the eye of a sparrow who sees no further than the window pane. I find myself . . . chirping, pecking, hopping, just as she would do herself" (Cline 195). Franks notes that in the novel,

"Romaine appears as an utterly egocentric, artificial creature, who cares nothing for people and everything for art. Romaine was obviously not pleased when, upon John and Una's arrival in Paris in the summer of 1926, Natalie rather foolishly asked Una to read *The Forge* aloud" (33).

13. Romaine Brooks was well established as an artist by the time the novel was composed. Her first exhibit in 1910 had been a "big success" (Weiss 110).

14. Andrea Weiss describes the relations between the real-life prototypes, Brooks and Troubridge, to have been "permanently strained" by Brooks's caricatured painting of Una. Since the painting and the novel both date from 1924, it is difficult to know whether the visual or the verbal caricature came first (caption, Weiss 134).

15. Domna Stanton asks, "what would the elimination of the signature mean for women autobiographers, whose texts had yet to be explored, acknowledged, and included in the literary and critical canons [?]" (10).

16. Cline quotes from Hall's verse

> *Suppose we fetter our lives with love* . . .
> More fair than ocean, or skies above,
> And learn to dwell in each other's hearts,
> Safely where no harm parts. (85)

17. Cline claims that Hall fictionalized her conflict over personal freedom in the latter part of her relationship with Ladye through the relationship of Mrs. Ogden and her daughter Joan in Hall's first novel, *The Unlit Lamp* (95).

18. Case's discussion, she notes, is indebted to Teresa de Lauretis, *Technologies of Gender,* for this distinction.

CHAPTER 5

1. This passage from H.D.'s *The Gift* does not appear in the published book version but is quoted from the excerpt entitled "The Dream" published in *Contemporary Literature* 10.9 (1969): 605–26.

2. The three fictional texts that are the focus of my discussion are part of a sequence H.D. called the "Madrigal" cycle. DuPlessis explains: "Madrigal refers, of course, to *a capella* part singing in close harmony, offering various distinctive voices tracing intricate melodic and contrapuntal relations. It should be clear that 'madrigal' can be construed as forming horizontally what 'palimpsest' does vertically—a set of layered materials which intersect, through which one must read the interplay of present and past" (*That Struggle* 60). The novels do not comprise a straightforward chronological series because of the discrepancies between the times these novels were written, rewritten, and published. The publication dates do not reflect the order of composition. *HERmione,* set before World War I, was written in 1927 but was not published until 1981. *Bid Me to Live,* the World War I–era novel, was begun in 1918 (Guest 287) or 1921, according to a statement by H.D. (Spoo xi; Kloepfer 91); it was "roughed out" in 1939, and rewritten in 1950 (*Bid Me* 204, 210); but it was not published until 1960. H.D. wrote other autobiographical fictions. *Asphodel,* composed in 1921–1922 (Spoo x) and published in 1992, fills the gap in H.D.'s biography after *HERmione* and prior to *Bid Me to Live;* most notably it dramatizes her trip to Europe in 1911–1912 with Frances Gregg and her mother, and the beginnings

of her relationship with Aldington. "Hipparchia" was written prior to *Bid Me to Live* and after H.D.'s trip to Egypt with Bryher (Guest 91) and was published as part of *Palimpsest* in 1926. Another part of H.D.'s fictionalized life is told in *Paint It Today,* published in 1992 (Guest 34). Aldington is fictionalized in *Helen in Egypt;* Pound in *End to Torment, Helen in Egypt,* and *HERmione.*

3. My extensive treatment of *Bid Me to Live* is not intended to privilege the World War I period in H.D.'s development nor to privilege heterosexual liaisons (which this novel critiques). DuPlessis notes this novel's unique place in H.D.'s oeuvre; it "spans the four periods" she outlines in H.D.'s work (*That Struggle* 104).

4. Of those involved, only Dorothy Yorke and John Cournos (who play secondary and tertiary roles, respectively) complained that their portraits were unjust. However, as Aldington's mistress (Yorke) and the lover from whom Yorke was seduced (Cournos), they each had complex sentiments of guilt and resentment toward H.D. Indeed Cournos actually incorporated some of H.D.'s letters into his novel *Miranda Masters* to create a disparaging portrait (Hollenberg 129). For more on the Cournos-H.D. connection see Satterthwaite, "John Cournos and 'H.D.'"

5. A number of excellent studies have established feminist readings of *HERmione* as a lesbian romance and a story of the emerging writer. My interpretation of *HERmione* is heavily indebted to the foundational readings of Dianne Chisholm, Rachel Blau DuPlessis, and Susan Friedman.

6. Regarding H.D.'s sexuality and sexual preference, see Susan Friedman, who says: "With *Asphodel* and *Her,* it is difficult to determine where biographical fact gives way to requirements of artistic narrative. For example, *Her* ends with Fayne's double betrayal of Hermione; Fayne seduces George Lowndes and thereby ends both her relationship with Hermione and Hermione's engagement to George. Nowhere else does H.D. explain the end of her engagement to Pound in this way. Since H.D. was involved with both Bryher and Macpherson when she wrote *Her,* Fayne may represent a combination of Frances Gregg and Bryher. In addition, the ideal sister-love that Gregg represents in *Her* and *Asphodel* is well tempered by H.D.'s irritated references to her in her correspondence with Bryher and Macpherson" (*Psyche* 303n. 42).

7. This Lacanian interpretation is somewhat at odds with Susan Friedman's more celebratory reading of H.D.'s biography. In *Psyche Reborn* she argues that H.D.'s relationship with Gregg "led her to affirm a womanhood that fused her self as artist and lover into a single, whole identity" (39).

8. Claire Buck summarizes the critical debate on this issue: "On the one hand H.D.'s work provides ample possibilities for a reading in which she successfully empowers a female identity conceived in terms of unity and wholeness. This is the reading we find underpinning much of Friedman and DuPlessis' work . . . . Equally H.D.'s work supports a post-Lacanian psychoanalytic approach in which the female self is inescapably identified with lack and absence. This is the reading that Paul Smith, Joseph Riddel and I have all made. Both these readings, however, are enmeshed within the same terms and oppositions. Either the subject is unitary or divided and fragmentary. The former leaves out the relationship of subjectivity to representation. The meaning of the female subject is already assumed to be known. The latter reduces the operations of language to the phallic order of the Symbolic and all too easily opposes a masculine unity to a feminine lack and division" (163).

9. H.D.'s work has been the subject of much psychoanalytic criticism since Freud himself analyzed her. Buck states: "H.D.'s interest in psychoanalysis is not

confined to the analytic couch. It informs her writing as both a practical therapy and a theoretical paradigm" (41). Chisholm argues that "H.D.'s writing transcribes a Freudian poetics, that it displays such techniques as dream-analysis, reconstruction (of memory and fantasy), transference and counter-transference, and narrative speculation" ("Auto*hetero*graphy" 96).

10. Deborah Kelly Kloepfer points to the liberatory nature of this discovery: "Although many critics (and Freud himself) want to read H.D.'s relationship with the mother as pathological, it is this 'fixation' that begins to free H.D.'s work" (120).

11. For other readings of H.D. from a Lacanian perspective, or the Lacanian-inspired French feminists, see Christine Berni, in "The Recuperated Maternal," who argues that *HERmione* is "energized by a fantasy of maternal unity capable of obviating sexual division and restoring the speaking subject to wholeness" (52). By using Silverman rather than Kristeva or Lacan, Berni is able to find this wholeness, which Kristeva and Lacan view as illusory. Also see S. Travis, "A Crack in the Ice." Several feminist critics have tried to avoid the pessimism of the Lacanian model. Berni follows Silverman in a reading that allows her to find the development of a (nonessential) woman's identity at the end of *HERmione*. In her Lacanian study of H.D.'s works, Buck contends (and I agree) that "the links between subjectivity, sexual difference and language are already present in H.D.'s writing." Buck, however, specifies "that they are also made in recent critical theory does not mean that they are made in the same way or that they serve the same purpose. . . . Likewise, H.D.'s models of femininity and language are both similar to and different from those of recent French feminist theory" (5, 6).

12. Frances Gregg had, according to Spoo, a "minor career as a writer, publishing poetry and prose in *Poetry, The Forum,* and *The New Freewoman*" (Appendix to *Asphodel* 213).

13. Critics do not agree on what stage this fictionalization represents in the writer's development—whether it is a stage she must pass through or an end in itself (see Friedman, "Rescriptions" 41n. 25). I agree with Travis that the novel depicts a transitional stage Hermione must experience in her progression toward becoming an artist, and I do not see this argument as being at variance with the idea that the novel depicts "*revelations* of an ideal" (Friedman, "Rescriptions" 41n. 25; my emphasis).

14. See DuPlessis, "The object case, used in subject place, exactly locates the thematics of the self-as-woman" (*That Struggle* 61); and Susan Friedman, "Modernism of the 'Scattered Remnant'" (105). See also Friedman and DuPlessis: "Hermione's nickname . . . signifies her object status within conventional heterosexuality. With Fayne, however, the nickname signals a fusion, one that gives birth to two selves, subject and object indistinct" ("Two Loves" 12); also Buck, *H.D. and Freud.* For H.D.'s use of the linking verb, see Friedman, "Rescriptions"; regarding H.D.'s recurrent litany, "Love is writing," Friedman explains: "*HER* is full of such impossible formulae. Yoking two abstract and grammatically unbalanced nouns, the linking verb 'is' oscillates between the metaphoric and the literal" ("Rescriptions" 23). Friedman calls the technique H.D. uses in *HERmione* a "syntactical balance," which "underscores the identification" of the lovers Fayne and Hermione (*Psyche* 42).

15. H.D.'s ambiguous variation on the Philomela myth breaks down the subject-object distinction in other ways as it suggests that both Fayne and Hermione could be artists, unlike H.D.'s treatment of the Pygmalion myth

(discussed later). Fayne is both Philomela and Itylus; Hermione is both Procne ("married" to George-Tereus) and Philomela, the artist weaving an autobiographical story into her art.

16. Collecott argues that the performance would probably not have been one of Shaw's play but rather of the 1871 *Pygmalion and Galatea* by W. S. Gilbert ("Images" 351n. 68).

17. For other discussions of the circle pattern of imagery, see Linda Welshimer Wagner, "Culmination"; A. Kingsley Weatherhead, "Style in H.D.'s Novels," 552; and Joseph Milicia, "Within the Storm," 287.

18. A letter from H.D. to John Cournos, written around 1918, suggests that a lack of self-confidence resulting from Aldington's affair provoked a passive response in the author: "I am not able to think of myself as a *person* now. I must move, act, & do as it is *moved* upon me to do & act" (quoted in Zilboorg, *Aldington* 41).

19. Although H.D. and Aldington were not legally divorced until 1938, the determining event in ending the marriage was, according to Zilboorg, the "formal and symbolic act of registering the child," Perdita, which Aldington refused to do since he was not her father (*Aldington* 208). It was apparently H.D.'s decision to leave Aldington (Zilboorg, "Influence" 40).

20. Kloepfer sees a progression in H.D.'s work, from her use of a male "twin" to the use of homoeroticism: "By twinning herself with a male, she calls upon the early incestuous dyad on which she relied before the appearance of the sister motif in her work; through this heterosexual incest, which is later replaced by homoeroticism, she attempts thematically to rupture the tenets of discourse, based on the incest taboo, and to find a more comfortable entry into the space of language" (119). Although doubling devices are clearly evident in H.D.'s texts, I find this description of progression troubling because of the discrepancies between biographical chronology and the chronology of composition. *HERmione* is the biographical predecessor of *Bid Me to Live*, though following it in date of composition. The prolonged revision of *Bid Me to Live* from 1918 to 1950 also complicates generalizations about a progression to homoeroticism. In her life, H.D. vacillated between male and female lovers, and in her fiction, she alternates between the gendered solutions they represent.

21. Janice Robinson is alone in hypothesizing that H.D. and D. H. Lawrence were physical lovers, a controversial premise of her biography. Susan Friedman refutes this hypothesis with evidence from papers at the Beinecke and from H.D.'s daughter ("Rescriptions" 40n. 16).

22. Buck, for instance, distinguishes between Woolf's androgyny and H.D.'s bisexuality, claiming that the former focuses on a genderless creative mind whereas in "H.D.'s writing bisexuality is mobilized to support the new woman" (79–80).

23. Teresa Fulker also finds Rico a poetic muse figure who poses an alternative to Rafe, who is associated with the world of war in the novel (63–64).

24. There is indeed considerable parody in Lawrence's brief portrait of H.D. as Julia Cunningham in *Aaron's Rod*: "His sister Julia was bunched up in a low chair between him and his father. She, too, was a tall stag of a thing, but she sat hunched up like a witch. She wore a wine-purple dress, her arms seemed to poke out of the sleeves, and she had dragged her brown hair into straight, untidy strands. Yet she had real beauty" (23).

25. Emily Hahn concludes that H.D. "never did realize . . that he and Frieda had only been playing their old game that evening, irritating each other at her expense" (148). Hahn quotes Cecil Gray's assessment from his memoir, *Musical Chairs* (137–38): "Lawrence could not brook equals. . . . I am naturally not so well qualified to speak of his relations with women; but from what I do know of them which is not inconsiderable[,] I am sure that they must have been equally unsatisfactory. . . . He was definitely not attractive to women in himself, as apart from the seductive magic of his pen. His physical personality was puny and insignificant, his vitality low, and his sexual potentialities exclusively cerebral" (148).

26. Also named Vane in *Asphodel,* Gray receives similar characterization in that text: "now she knew better what love was[,] for Cyril Vane was tall and gentle and not heavy and not domineering like her husband." The protagonist claims that "it was partly that he helped me, seeing that it was all lop-sided, it was brotherly of him" (*Asphodel* 148).

27. The genre classification of "Hipparchia" is debatable. It might be termed a novella or a story. It appears in a collection of three short fictional pieces, *Palimpsest,* which Bryher had published privately (McNeil v). H.D.'s 1922 comment on the work then in progress is suggestive, though inconclusive: "I have another 'impressionistic' bit, not a story, not long enough for a novel. But the three would make a moderately solid prose work" (Hollenberg 150–51).

28. Although he sees a similarity between the Rico/Lawrence figures and Philip insofar as they represent "a kind of ideal," Peter E. Firchow claims that "*Palimpsest* contains no equivalent to the figures of Rico/Lawrence" (62 and n.19). It is, however, the substitution of the brother for Lawrence that most significantly illustrates the value of this poet-double figure for H.D. The imagery associated with Philip, who is "flaming" (*Palimpsest* 101), offers the best evidence that Philip is the Lawrence character, distilled to his symbolic significance.

29. King is also, however, one of the few critics to note H.D.'s parodic treatment of sexual encounters (see "HERmione").

30. Aldington receives a similar parodic treatment through the character of Darrington: "Let it be daggers drawn she wasn't one to clutch at that hulk of flesh that had been Darrington. Hulk of something that was like a bloated great zeppelin but women seemed to like it. Rent him out, lend him about, military stallion" (*Asphodel* 145).

31. Buck argues that "the category of the untranslatable becomes significant since it is this which allows H.D. to sustain the fantasy of another language for sexual difference. . . . This concept of an irreducible element to language which resists translation becomes increasingly important in H.D.'s work. . . . The renunciation of the possibility of translation enables H.D. to represent a knowledge of the 'woman' which challenges the definition of her as lacking" (9).

32. According to Marek's account, each woman contributed a variety of skills to joint projects: H.D. solicited contributions for the *Egoist* and worked on editing (105). In their work on *Close Up,* Bryher underwrote the financing of the publication (118); she managed correspondence, payment for contributions, layout, and proofreading (121); they both edited, solicited material, and contributed articles (129, 218n. 41). Bryher's "life as well as her published articles expressed a belief in cooperative intellectual work that seemed particularly needful at that time and in that place" (121).

33. I am indebted to a most generous anonymous reader for this suggestion.

Works Cited

Aldington, Richard. *Life for Life's Sake: A Book of Reminiscences*. New York: Viking, 1941.

Aldrich, Elizabeth Kaspar. "'The Most Poetical Topic in the World': Women in the Novels of F. Scott Fitzgerald." *Scott Fitzgerald: The Promises of Life*. Ed A. Robert Lee. London: Vision, 1989. 131 56.

Andersen, Margret. "Critical Approaches to Anaïs Nin." *Canadian Review of American Studies* 10 (1979): 255–65.

Anon. "Brief Reviews." *Atlantic* (1987): 94.

Anzaldúa, Gloria. *Borderlands/La Frontera*. San Francisco: Spinsters/Aunt Lute, 1987.

Bair, Deirdre. *Anaïs Nin: A Biography*. New York: Putnam, 1995.

———. *Simone de Beauvoir: A Biography*. New York: Summit, 1990.

Baker, Michael. *Our Three Selves: The Life of Radclyffe Hall*. New York: Morrow, 1985.

Benstock, Shari. *Women of the Left Bank, Paris, 1900–1940*. Austin: U of Texas P, 1986.

Benveniste, Emile. *Problems in General Linguistics*. 1966. Trans. Mary Elizabeth Meek. Coral Cables: U of Miami P, 1971.

Berni, Christine. "The Recuperated Maternal and the Imposture of Mastery in H.D.'s *HERmione*." *Women's Studies* 25.1 (1995): 51–71.

Bloom, Harold. *The Anxiety of Influence*. New York: Oxford UP, 1973.

Bobbitt, Joan. "Truth and Artistry in the *Diary of Anaïs Nin*." *Journal of Modern Literature* 9 (1982): 267–76.

Bovenschen, Silvia. "Is There a Feminine Aesthetic?" *New German Critique* 10 (1977): 111–37.

Brennan, Karen. "Anaïs Nin: Author(iz)ing the Erotic Body." *Genders* 14 (1992): 66–86.

Brewer, Maria Minich. "A Loosening of Tongues: From Narrative Economy to Women Writing." *MLN* 99.5 (1984): 1141–61.

Bruccoli, Matthew J. *The Composition of* Tender Is the Night: *A Study of the Manuscripts*. Pittsburgh, Pa.: U of Pittsburgh P, 1963.

———. "Preface." *Bits of Paradise: Twenty-one Uncollected Stories by F. Scott and Zelda Fitzgerald*. New York: Scribner's, 1973.

———. *Some Sort of Epic Grandeur: The Life of F. Scott Fitzgerald*. New York: Harcourt, 1981.

Bruccoli, Matthew J., Scottie Fitzgerald Smith, and Joan P. Kerr, eds. *The Romantic Egoists*. New York: Scribner's, 1974.

Bryher [Annie Winifred Ellerman]. *The Heart to Artemis: A Writer's Memoirs*. New York: Harcourt, Brace, 1962.

———. *Two Selves.* Paris: Contact, 1923.

Buck, Claire. *H.D. and Freud: Bisexuality and a Feminine Discourse.* New York: St. Martin's, 1991.

Butler, Judith. *Gender Trouble: Feminism and the Subversion of Identity.* New York: Routledge, 1989.

Caramello, Charles. *Henry James, Gertrude Stein, and the Biographical Act.* Chapel Hill: U of North Carolina P, 1996.

Case, Sue-Ellen. "Toward a Butch-Femme Aesthetic." *Discourse* 11.1 (1988–1989): 55–73.

Castle, Terry. *Noel Coward and Radclyffe Hall: Kindred Spirits.* New York: Columbia UP, 1996.

Chadwick, Whitney, and Isabelle de Courtivron, eds. *Significant Others: Creativity and Intimate Partnership.* London: Thames and Hudson, 1993.

Chisholm, Dianne. "H.D.'s Auto*heter*ography." *Tulsa Studies in Women's Literature* 9.1 (1990): 79–106.

———. *H.D.'s Freudian Poetics: Psychoanalysis in Translation.* Reading Women Writing Series. Ed. Shari Benstock and Celeste Schenck. Ithaca: Cornell UP, 1992.

Chodorow, Nancy. *The Reproduction of Mothering: Psychoanalysis and the Sociology of Gender.* Berkeley: U of California P, 1979.

Chopin, Kate. *The Awakening.* 1899. Ed. Nancy A. Walker. Case Studies in Contemporary Criticism. Ed. Ross Murfin. Boston: Bedford, 1993.

Cixous, Hélène. "Castration or Decapitation?" Trans. Annette Kuhn. *Signs: Journal of Women in Culture and Society* 7 (1981): 41–55.

———. "The Laugh of the Medusa." *Signs* 1.4 (1976): 875–93.

Clemens, Anna Valdine. "Zelda Fitzgerald: An Unromantic Revision." *Dalhousie Review* 62.2 (1982): 196–211.

Cline, Sally. *Radclyffe Hall: A Woman Called John.* London: John Murray, 1997.

Collecott, Diana. "Bryher's *Two Selves* as Lesbian Romance." *Romance Revisited.* Ed. Lynne Pearce and Jackie Stacey. New York: New York UP, 1995. 128–42.

———. "Images at the Crossroads: The 'H.D. Scrapbook.'" King, *Woman and Poet* 319–67.

Cook, Blanche Wiesen. "'Women Alone Stir My Imagination': Lesbianism and the Cultural Tradition." *Signs: Journal of Women in Culture and Society* 4.1 (1979): 718–39.

Courbin-Tavernier, Jacqueline. *Southern Literary Journal* 11.2 (1979): 22–42.

Crawford, Fred D. "Approaches to Biography: Two Studies of H.D." *Review* 7 (1985): 215–38.

Davis, Simone Weil. "'The Burden of Reflecting': Effort and Desire in Zelda Fitzgerald's *Save Me the Waltz.*" *Modern Language Quarterly* 56.3 (1995): 327–61.

de Lauretis, Teresa. *Alice Doesn't: Feminism, Semiotics, Cinema.* Bloomington: Indiana UP, 1984.

———. "The Essence of the Triangle or, Taking the Risk of Essentialism Seriously: Feminist Theory in Italy, the U.S., and Britain." Schor and Weed 1–39.

———. *The Practice of Love: Lesbian Sexuality and Perverse Desire.* Bloomington: Indiana UP, 1994.

———. *Technologies of Gender: Essays on Theory, Film, and Fiction.* Bloomington: Indiana UP, 1987.

Demetrakopoulos, Stephanie A. "Archetypal Constellations of Feminine Consciousness in Nin's First Diary." *Mosaic* 11.2 (1978): 121–37.

DeSalvo, Louise. *Conceived with Malice.* New York: Dutton, 1994.

Dickson, Lovat. *Radclyffe Hall at the Well of Loneliness: A Sapphic Chronicle.* New York: Scribner's, 1975.

Doan, Laura. *Fashioning Sapphism: The Origins of a Modern English Lesbian Culture.* New York: Columbia UP, 2001.

Doane, Mary Ann. *Femmes Fatales: Feminism, Film Theory, Psychoanalysis.* New York: Routledge, 1991.

DuBow, Wendy M. "The Elusive Text: Reading 'The Diary of Anaïs Nin, Volume 1, 1931–1934.'" *Anaïs: An International Journal* 11 (1993): 22–38.

DuPlessis, Rachel Blau. "Family, Sexes, Psyche: An Essay on H.D. and the Muse of the Woman Writer." King, *Woman and Poet* 69–90.

———. "For the Etruscans." Showalter 271–91.

———. *H.D.: The Career of That Struggle.* Key Women Writers Series. Ed. Sue Roe. Bloomington: Indiana UP, 1986.

———. "Romantic Thralldom in H.D." *Contemporary Literature* 20.2 (1979): 178–203.

———. *Writing beyond the Ending: Narrative Strategies of Twentieth-Century Women Writers.* Bloomington: Indiana UP, 1985.

Eakin, Paul John. *Fictions in Autobiography: Studies in the Art of Self-Invention.* Princeton: Princeton UP, 1985.

Edel, Leon. *Writing Lives: Principia Biographica.* New York: Norton, 1984.

Ekberg, Kent. "Studio 28: The Influence of Surrealist Cinema on the Early Fiction of Anaïs Nin and Henry Miller." *Lawrence Durrell Newsletter* 4.3 (1981): 3–12.

Ellerby, Janet M. "Conversation and the Fitzgeralds: Conflict or Collaboration?" *The Text and Beyond: Essays in Literary Linguistics.* Ed. Cynthia Goldin Bernstein. Tuscaloosa: U Alabama P, 1994. 157–76.

Evans, Oliver. *Anaïs Nin.* Carbondale: Southern Illinois UP, 1968.

Faderman, Lillian. *Surpassing the Love of Men: Romantic Friendship and Love between Women from the Renaissance to the Present.* New York: Morrow, 1981.

Felber, Lynette. *Gender and Genre in Novels without End: The British* Roman Fleuve. Gainesville: UP of Florida, 1995.

———. "Mentors, Protégés, and Lovers: Literary Liaisons and Mentorship Dialogues in Anaïs Nin's *Diary* and Dorothy Richardson's *Pilgrimage.*" *Frontiers* 15.3 (1995): 167–85.

———. "The Three Faces of June: Anaïs Nin's Appropriation of Feminine Writing." *Tulsa Studies in Women's Literature* 14.2 (1995): 309–24.

———. "Unfinished Business and Self-Memorialization: Rebecca West's Aborted Novel, *Mild Silver, Furious Gold.*" *Journal of Modern Literature.* Forthcoming.

Felski, Rita. *The Gender of Modernity.* Cambridge: Harvard UP, 1995.

Fetterley, Judith. "Who Killed Dick Diver? The Sexual Politics of *Tender Is the Night.*" *Mosaic* 17.1 (1984): 111–28.

Fink, Bruce. *The Lacanian Subject: Between Language and Jouissance.* Princeton: Princeton UP, 1995.

Firchow, Peter E. "Rico and Julia: The Hilda Doolittle–D.H. Lawrence Affair Reconsidered." *Journal of Modern Literature* 8.1 (1980): 51–76.

Fitch, Noël Riley. *Anaïs: The Erotic Life of Anaïs Nin.* Boston: Little, Brown, 1993.

———. "The Literate Passion of Anaïs Nin and Henry Miller." Chadwick and de Courtivron 155–71.

Fitzgerald, F. Scott. *Correspondence of F. Scott Fitzgerald.* Ed. Matthew J. Bruccoli and Margaret M. Duggan, with Susan Walker. New York: Random House, 1980.

Fitzgerald, Zelda. "Friend Husband's Latest." *Collected Writings* 387–89.

———. *Save Me the Waltz.* 1932. Carbondale: Southern Illinois UP, 1967.

————. "What a 'Flapper Novelist' Thinks of His Wife." Bruccoli et al. 112.

————. *Zelda Fitzgerald: The Collected Writings.* Ed. Matthew J. Bruccoli, introd. Mary Gordon. New York: Scribner's and Macmillan, 1991.

Fleishman, Avrom. *Figures of Autobiography: The Language of Self-Writing in Victorian and Modern England.* Berkeley: U of California P, 1993.

Foster, Jeannette. *Sex Variant Women in Literature.* 1956. Baltimore, Md.: Diana P, 1975.

Foucault, Michel. "What Is an Author?" *Textual Strategies: Perspectives in Post-Structuralist Criticism.* Ed. and introd. Josué V. Harari. Ithaca: Cornell UP, 1979.

Franks, Claudia Stillman. *Beyond the Well of Loneliness: The Fiction of Radclyffe Hall.* Wellingborough, England: Avebury, 1982.

Freedman, Estelle B., Barbara C. Gelpi, Susan L. Johnson, and Kathleen M. Weston, eds. *The Lesbian Issue: Essays from SIGNS.* Chicago: U of Chicago P, 1985.

Friedman, Ellen G. "Anaïs Nin." *Modern American Women Writers.* Ed. Elaine Showalter and A. Walton Litz. New York: Scribner's, 1991. 339–51.

————. "Looking Back on Nin Criticism." Rev. of *The Critical Response to Anaïs Nin,* ed. Philip K. Jason. *Anaïs: An International Journal* 13 (1997): 122–23.

Friedman, Ellen G., and Miriam Fuchs, eds. *Breaking the Sequence: Women's Experimental Fiction.* Princeton: Princeton UP, 1989.

Friedman, Susan Stanford. "H.D.'s Rescriptions of Joyce, Lawrence, and Pound." *Writing the Woman Artist: Essays on Poetics, Politics, and Portraiture.* Ed. Suzanne Jones. Philadelphia: U Penn P, 1991. 23–42.

————. "'I Go Where I Love': An Intertextual Study of H.D. and Adrienne Rich." *Signs* 9.2 (1983): 228–45. Rpt. in Freedman et al. 111–28.

————. "Modernism of the 'Scattered Remnant': Race and Politics in the Development of H.D.'s Modernist Vision." King, *Woman and Poet* 91–116.

————. *Penelope's Web: Gender, Modernity, H.D.'s Fiction.* Cambridge: Cambridge UP, 1990.

————. *Psyche Reborn: The Emergence of H.D.* Bloomington: Indiana UP, 1981.

————. "Women's Autobiographical Selves: Theory and Practice." *The Private Self: Theory and Practice of Women's Autobiographical Writings.* Ed. Shari Benstock. Chapel Hill: U of North Carolina P, 1988. 34–62.

Friedman, Susan Stanford, and Rachel Blau DuPlessis, "'I Had Two Loves Separate': The Sexualities of H.D." *Montemora* 8 (1981): 7–30.

Frye, Northrop. *Anatomy of Criticism: Four Essays.* 1957. Princeton: Princeton UP, 1971.

Fryer, Sarah Beebe. *Fitzgerald's New Women: Harbingers of Change.* Ann Arbor: UMI Research P, 1988.

Fulker, Teresa. "Not-War and the Inspiration of the *Gloire* H.D.'s *Bid Me to Live.*" *Sagetrieb* 12.2 (1993): 51–82.

Fuss, Diana. *Essentially Speaking: Feminism, Nature, and Difference.* New York: Routledge, 1989.

————. "Reading like a Feminist." Schor and Weed 98–115.

Gallop, Jane. *Reading Lacan.* Ithaca: Cornell UP, 1985.

Genette, Gerard. *Narrative Discourse: An Essay in Method.* Trans. Jane E. Lewin. Ithaca: Cornell UP, 1980.

Gilbert, Sandra, and Susan Gubar. *Masterpiece Theatre: An Academic Melodrama.* New Brunswick: Rutgers UP, 1995.

————. *No Man's Land: The Place of the Woman Writer in the Twentieth Century.* Vol. 1. *The War of the Words.* New Haven: Yale UP, 1988. Vol. 2. *Sexchanges.* New Haven: Yale UP, 1989.

Gilmore, Leigh. *Autobiographics: A Feminist Theory of Women's Self-Representation.* Reading Women Writing Series. Ithaca: Cornell UP, 1994.

Girard, René. *Deceit, Desire, and the Novel: Self and Other in Literary Structure.* Trans. Yvonne Freccero. Baltimore: Johns Hopkins UP, 1961, 1965.

Glendinning, Victoria. Afterword. West, *Sunflower* 268–76.

———. *Rebecca West: A Life.* New York: Knopf, 1987.

Goldman-Price, Irene C., and Melissa McFarland Pennell, eds. *American Literary Mentors.* Gainesville: UP of Florida, 1999.

Gordon, Mary. Introduction. Zelda Fitzgerald, *Collected Writings* xv–xxvii.

Graham, Sheilah. *College of One.* New York: Viking, 1967.

Graham, Sheilah, and Gerald Frank. *Beloved Infidel: The Education of a Woman.* New York: Bantam, 1959.

Griffin, Gabriele. "*What Is [Not] Remembered:* The Autobiography of Alice B. Toklas." *Women's Lives/Women's Times: New Essays on Auto/Biography.* Ed. Trev Lynn Broughton and Linda Anderson. Albany: State U of New York P, 1997. 143–56.

Grosz, Elizabeth. *Jacques Lacan: A Feminist Introduction.* New York: Routledge, 1990.

———. *Sexual Subversions: Three French Feminists.* Wellington: Allen and Unwin, 1989.

Gubar, Susan. "Sapphistries." *Signs* 10.1 (1984): 43–62. Rpt. in Freedman et al. 91–110.

Guest, Barbara. *Herself Defined: The Poet H.D.* Garden City: Doubleday, 1984.

H.D. [Hilda Doolittle]. *Asphodel.* Ed. with introd. Robert Spoo. Durham: Duke UP, 1992.

——— —. *Bid Me to Live.* Redding Ridge, Conn.: Black Swan, 1983.

———. *Collected Poems, 1912-1944.* Ed. Louis L. Martz. New York: New Directions, 1983.

——— —. "The Dream." *Contemporary Literature* 10.4 (1969): 605–26.

———. *End to Torment: A Memoir of Ezra Pound.* Ed. Norman Holmes Pearson and Michael King. Foreword Michael King. New York: New Directions, 1979.

———. *The Gift.* New York: New Directions, 1982.

——— —. *Helen in Egypt.* Introd. Horace Gregory. New York: New Directions, 1961.

———. *HERmione.* New York: New Directions, 1981.

———. "Hipparchia." H.D., *Palimpsest.* 3–131.

———. *Palimpsest.* Boston: Houghton Mifflin, 1926.

———. *Tribute to Freud.* Boston: Godine, 1974.

Hahn, Emily. *Lorenzo: D. H. Lawrence and the Women Who Loved Him.* Philadelphia: Lippincott, 1975.

Hall, Radclyffe. *The Forge.* London: Arrowsmith, 1924.

———. *The Well of Loneliness.* Garden City: Blue Ribbon, 1928.

Hammond, J. R. *H. G. Wells and Rebecca West.* New York: St. Martin's P, 1991.

Harmes, Valerie. "Interaction and Cross-Fertilization: Notes on the Influence of Henry Miller on Anaïs Nin's Early Fiction." *Anaïs: An International Journal* 4 (1986): 109–15.

Hartmann, Heidi. "The Unhappy Marriage of Marxism and Feminism: Towards a More Progressive Union." *Women and Revolution: A Discussion of the Unhappy Marriage of Marxism and Feminism.* Ed. Lydia Sargent. Boston: South End P, 1981. 1–41.

Hartnett, Koula Svokos. *Zelda Fitzgerald and the Failure of the American Dream for Women.* Vol. 22 of American Literature Series 24. New York: Peter Lang, 1991.

Henke, Suzette. "Life-Writing: Art as Diary, as Fiction, as Therapy." *Anaïs: An International Journal* 16 (1998): 79–87.

———. *Shattered Subjects: Trauma and Testimony in Women's Life-Writing.* New York: St. Martin's, 1998.

Henriques, Julian, et al. *Changing the Subject: Psychology, Social Regulations, and Subjectivity.* London: Methuen, 1984.

Herd, David. "Collaboration and the Avant-Garde." *Critical Review* 35 (1995): 36–63.

Hinz, Evelyn. *The Mirror and the Garden: Realism and Reality in the Writings of Anaïs Nin.* New York: Harcourt, 1973.

———. "Recent Nin Criticism: Who's on First?" *Canadian Review of American Studies* 13.3 (1982): 373–88.

Hoberman, Ruth. *Gendering Classicism: The Ancient World in Twentieth-Century Women's Historical Fiction.* Albany: SUNY, 1997.

Hollenberg, Donna. "Art and Ardor in World War One: Selected Letters from H.D. to John Cournos." *Iowa Review* 16.3 (1968): 126–55.

Hutcheon, Linda. *A Theory of Parody.* New York: Methuen, 1985.

Hutcheon, Linda, and Michael Hutcheon. "'All Concord's Born of Contraries': Marital Methodologies." *Tulsa Studies in Women's Literature* 14.1 (1995): 59–64.

Ian, Marcia. *Remembering the Phallic Mother.* Ithaca: Cornell UP, 1993.

Irigaray, Luce. "And the One Doesn't Stir without the Other." Trans. Hélène Vivienne Wenzel. *Signs* 7.1 (1982): 60–67.

———. "Any Theory of the 'Subject' Has Always Been Appropriated by the 'Masculine.'" *Speculum of the Other Woman.* Trans. Gillian C. Gill. 1974. Ithaca: Cornell UP, 1985. 133–46.

———. "The Power of Discourse and the Subordination of the Feminine." Irigaray, *This Sex* 68–85.

———. *This Sex Which Is Not One.* Trans. Catherine Porter with Carolyn Burke. Ithaca: Cornell UP, 1986.

———. "This Sex Which Is Not One." Irigaray, *This Sex* 23–33.

Jason, Philip K., ed. *The Critical Response to Anaïs Nin.* Critical Responses in Arts and Letters 23. Westport, Conn.: Greenwood P, 1996.

———. "Dropping Another Veil: Anaïs Nin's *Henry and June.*" Jason, *Critical Response* 199–214.

Jeffreys, Sheila. *The Spinster and Her Enemies: Feminism and Sexuality 1880–1930.* London: Pandora, 1985.

Jones, Ann Rosalind. "Inscribing Femininity: French Theories of the Feminine." *Making a Difference.* Ed. Gayle Greene and Coppelia Kahn. New York: Routledge, 1985. 80–112.

Jong, Erica. "A Story Never Told Before—Reading the New, Unexpurgated Diaries of Anaïs Nin." Jason, *Critical Response* 205–14.

Kamboureli, Smaro. "Discourse and Intercourse, Design and Desire in the Erotica of Anaïs Nin." *Journal of Modern Literature* 11.1 (1984): 143–58.

King, Michael J., ed. *H.D.: Woman and Poet.* Orono, Me.: National Poetry Foundation, 1987.

———. "*HERmione* by H.D." Rev. in *Paideuma* 11.2 (1982): 339–44.

Kloepfer, Deborah Kelly. *The Unspeakable Mother: Forbidden Discourse in Jean Rhys and H.D.* Ithaca: Cornell UP, 1989.

Koestenbaum, Wayne. *Double Talk: The Erotics of Male Literary Collaboration.* New York: Routledge, 1989.

Kram, Kathy. *Mentoring at Work.* Glenview, Ill.: Scott, Foresman, 1985.

Kristeva, Julia. "Freud and Love: Treatment and Its Discontents." Trans. Léon S. Roudiez. *The Kristeva Reader.* Ed. Toril Moi. New York: Columbia UP, 1986. 238–71.

———. "Interview—1974." *m/f* 5–6 (1981): 164–68.

———. *Revolution in Poetic Language.* 1974. Trans. Margaret Waller. New York: Columbia UP, 1984.

Lacan, Jacques. *Écrits: A Selection.* Trans. Alan Sheridan. New York: Norton, 1977.

———. *Feminine Sexuality: Jacques Lacan and the Ecole Freudienne.* Ed. Juliet Mitchell and Jacqueline Rose. New York: Norton, 1982.

———. "From Love to Libido." *Four Fundamental Concepts of Psycho-Analysis.* Ed. Jacques-Alain Miller. Trans. Alan Sheridan. New York: Norton, 1978. 187–200.

Laird, Holly. *Women Coauthors.* Urbana: Illinois UP, 2000.

Lanahan, Eleanor, ed. *Zelda, an Illustrated Life: The Private World of Zelda Fitzgerald.* With essays by Peter Kurth and Jane S. Livingston. New York: Harry Abrams, 1996.

Lang, Candace. "Autobiography in the Aftermath of Romanticism." *Diacritics* 12 (1982): 2–16.

Laplanche, Jean, and J.-B. Pontalis. *The Language of Psycho-Analysis.* 1967. Trans. Donald Nicholson-Smith. Introd. Daniel Lagache. New York: Norton, 1973.

Lawrence. D. H. *Aaron's Rod.* London: Heinemann, 1922.

Leaska, Mitchell A. Introduction. *The Letters of Vita Sackville-West to Virginia Woolf.* Ed. Louise DeSalvo and Mitchell A. Leaska. New York: Morrow, 1985. 11–46.

Lee, Jonathan Scott. *Jacques Lacan.* Boston: Twayne, 1990.

Lejeune, Philippe. *On Autobiography.* Trans. Katerine Leary. Foreword Paul John Eakin. Theory and History of Literature 52. Minneapolis: U of Minnesota P, 1989.

Levinson, Daniel. *The Seasons of a Man's Life.* New York: Knopf, 1978.

London, Bette. *Writing Double: Women's Literary Partnerships.* Ithaca: Cornell UP, 1999.

Luftig, Victor. *Seeing Together: Friendship between the Sexes in English Writing from Mill to Woolf.* Stanford: Stanford UP, 1993.

Lunsford, Andrea, and Lisa Ede. *Singular Texts/Plural Authors: Perspectives on Collaborative Writing.* Carbondale: Southern Illinois UP, 1990.

MacCannell, Juliet Flower. *Figuring Lacan: Criticism and the Cultural Unconscious.* Lincoln: U of Nebraska P, 1986.

MacKinnon, Catherine A. "Feminism, Marxism, Method, and the State: An Agenda for Theory." *Signs* 7.3 (1982): 515–44.

Makward, Christiane. "To Be or Not to Be . . . a Feminist Speaker." Trans. Marlene Barousm, Alice Jardine, and Hester Eisenstein. *The Future of Difference.* Ed. Hester Eisenstein and Alice Jardine. New Brunswick: Rutgers UP, 1985. 95–105.

Mallon, Thomas. "A Groupie for Greatness." *New York Times Book Review,* 15 Feb. 1987, 26.

Marcus, Jane. "A Wilderness of One's Own: Feminist Fantasy Novels of the Twenties: Rebecca West, Sylvia Townsend Warner." *Women Writers and the City.* Ed. Susan Merrill Squier. Knoxville: U of Tennessee P, 1984. 134–60.

Marek, Jayne E. *Women Editing Modernism: "Little" Magazines and Literary History*. Lexington: UP of Kentucky, 1995.

Markus, Julia. *Dared and Done: The Marriage of Elizabeth Barrett and Robert Browning*. New York: Knopf, 1995.

Martin, Shelby. "Winifred Bryher: A Checklist." *Bulletin of the New York Public Library* 79 (1976): 459–71.

Mason, Mary. "The Other Voice: Autobiographies of Women Writers." Miller, *Life/Lines* 19–44.

Mayfield, Sara. *Exiles from Paradise: Zelda and Scott Fitzgerald*. New York: Delacorte, 1971.

McAlmon, Robert, and Kay Boyle. *Being Geniuses Together, 1920–1930*. Garden City: Doubleday, 1968.

McNeil, Helen. Introduction. H.D., *Her*. London: Virago, 1984. v–xi.

Mellow, James R. *Charmed Circle: Gertrude Stein and Company*. New York: Praeger, 1974.

———. *Invented Lives: F. Scott and Zelda Fitzgerald*. Boston: Houghton Mifflin, 1984.

Milford, Nancy. *Zelda: A Biography*. New York: Harper, 1970.

Milicia, Joseph. "*Bid Me to Live:* Within the Storm." King, *Woman and Poet* 279–98.

Miller, Henry. "The Diary of Anaïs Nin." *Anaïs: An International Journal* 14 (1996): 14–18.

———. "Un Être Étoilique." *The Cosmological Eye*. Norfolk, Conn.: New Directions, 1939. 269–91.

———. "Into the Night Life." *Black Spring*. New York: Grove, 1963. 151–81.

———. *Tropic of Capricorn*. New York: Grove, 1961.

———. "Walking Up and Down in China." *Black Spring*. New York: Grove, 1963. 185–211.

Miller, Nancy K. *Life/Lines: Theorizing Women's Autobiography*. Ed. Bella Brodzki and Celeste Schenck. Ithaca: Cornell UP, 1988.

———. "Writing Fictions: Women's Autobiography in France." Miller, *Life/Lines* 45–61.

Mitchell, Juliet. *Psychoanalysis and Feminism*. New York: Random House, 1974.

Mizener, Arthur. *The Far Side of Paradise*. Boston: Houghton Mifflin, 1965.

Mulock, Dinah Maria Craik. *A Woman's Thoughts about Women*. Ed. Elaine Showalter. Washington Square: New York UP, 1993.

Nalbantian, Suzanne. *Aesthetic Autobiography: From Life to Art in Marcel Proust, James Joyce, Virginia Woolf, and Anaïs Nin*. Basingstoke, England: Macmillan, 1994.

Newton, Esther. "The Mythic Mannish Lesbian: Radclyffe Hall and the New Woman." Freedman et al. 7–25.

Niemeyer, Doris. "How to Be a Woman and/or an Artist: The Diary as an Instrument of Self-Therapy." *Anaïs: An International Journal* 6 (1988): 67–74.

Nin, Anaïs. *Delta of Venus*. New York: Harcourt, 1976.

———. *The Diary of Anaïs Nin, 1931–1934*. Ed. Gunther Stuhlmann. New York: Harcourt, 1966.

———. "Djuna." Nin, *Winter of Artifice* 9–108.

———. "Hans and Johanna." *Anaïs: An International Journal* 7 (1989): 3–22.

———. *Henry and June: From the Unexpurgated Diary of Anaïs Nin*. Preface Rupert Pole. New York: Harcourt, 1986.

———. *House of Incest*. 1936. Athens: Ohio UP, 1958.

———. *A Literate Passion: Letters of Anaïs Nin and Henry Miller, 1932–1953.* Ed. with introd. Gunther Stuhlmann. New York: Harcourt, 1987.

———. *Nearer the Moon: The Unexpurgated Diary of Anaïs Nin, 1937–1939.* Preface Rupert Pole. Biographical notes and annotations Gunther Stuhlmann. New York: Harcourt, 1996.

———. "Notes on Feminism." *Massachusetts Review* 13.1–2 (1972): 25–28.

———. *The Novel of the Future.* New York: Collier, 1968.

———. *Winter of Artifice.* Paris: Obelisk P, 1939.

Norton, Ann V. *Paradoxical Feminism: The Novels of Rebecca West.* Lanham: International Scholars, 2000.

Orel, Harold. *The Literary Achievement of Rebecca West.* London: Macmillan, 1986.

Ormrod, Richard. *Una Troubridge: The Friend of Radclyffe Hall.* London: Cape, 1984.

Parkes, Adam. "Lesbianism, History, and Censorship: *The Well of Loneliness* and the Suppressed Randiness of Virginia Woolf's *Orlando.*" *Twentieth-Century Literature* 40.4 (1994): 434–60.

Payne, Michelle. "Zelda Fitzgerald, Anorexia Nervosa, and *Save Me the Waltz.*" *Bucknell Review* 39.1 (1995): 39–56.

Perry, Ruth, and Martine Watson Brownley, eds. *Mothering the Mind: Twelve Studies of Writers and Their Silent Partners.* New York: Holmes and Meier, 1984.

Pétrequin, Marie-Line. "The Magic Spell of June Miller." Trans. Gunther Stuhlmann. *Anaïs: An International Journal* 6 (1988): 43–57.

Petry, Alice Hall. "Women's Work: The Case of Zelda Fitzgerald." *Literature, Interpretation, Theory* 1.1–2 (1989): 69–83.

Philip-Jones, Linda. *Mentors and Proteges: How to Establish, Strengthen and Get the Most from a Mentor/Protege Relationship.* New York: Arbor House, 1982.

Piper, Henry Dan. *F. Scott Fitzgerald: A Critical Portrait.* New York: Holt, 1965.

Pireddu, Nicoletta, "H.D.'s Palimpsests Texts: Scratching the Parchment of Male Writing." *Rohwedder: International Journal of Literature and Art* 7 (1992): 59–64.

Pondrom, Cyrena N. "Marianne Moore and H.D.: Female Community and Poetic Achievement." *Marianne Moore: Woman and Poet.* Ed. Patricia C. Willis. Orono, Me.: National Poetry Foundation, 1990. 371–402.

Radford, Jean. "An Inverted Romance: *The Well of Loneliness* and Sexual Ideology." *The Progress of Romance: The Politics of Popular Fiction.* Ed. Jean Radford. London: Routledge, 1986. 97–111.

Ragland-Sullivan, Ellie. "The Sexual Masquerade: A Lacanian Theory of Sexual Difference." *Lacan and the Subject of Language.* Ed. Ellie Ragland-Sullivan and Mark Bracher. New York: Routledge, 1991. 49–80.

Rank, Otto. *The Myth of the Birth of the Hero; and Other Writings.* Ed. Philip Freund. New York: Vintage, 1964.

Raoul, Valerie. "Women and Diaries: Gender and Genre." *Mosaic: A Journal for the Interdisciplinary Study of Literature* 22–23 (1989): 57–65.

Ray, Gordon N. *H. G. Wells and Rebecca West.* New Haven: Yale UP, 1974.

Richard-Allerdyce, Diane. *Anaïs Nin and the Remaking of Self: Gender, Modernity, and Narrative Identity.* DeKalb: Northern Illinois UP, 1998.

Richardson, Dorothy. "Seen from Paradise." *Journey to Paradise: Short Stories and Autobiographical Sketches.* Introd. Trudi Tate. London: Virago, 1989. 88–95.

———. *Windows on Modernism: Selected Letters of Dorothy Richardson.* Ed. Gloria G. Fromm. Athens: U of Georgia P, 1995.

Rivière, Joan. "Womanliness as Masquerade." Ed. Victor Burgin, James Donald, and Cora Kaplan. *International Journal of Psychoanalysis* 10 (1927): 303–13.

Robinson, Janice. *H.D.: The Life and Work of an American Poet.* Boston: Houghton Mifflin, 1982.

Rolley, Katrina. "Cutting a Dash: The Dress of Radclyffe Hall and Una Troubridge." *Feminist Review* 35 (1990): 54–66.

Rollyson, Carl. *The Literary Legacy of Rebecca West.* San Francisco: International Scholars, 1998.

———. *Rebecca West: A Life.* New York: Scribner, 1996.

Roof, Judith. *A Lure of Knowledge: Lesbian Sexuality and Theory.* New York: Columbia UP, 1991.

Rose, Jacqueline. "Introduction II." Lacan, *Feminine Sexuality* 27–57.

Rose, Phyllis. "Biography as Fiction." *Triquarterly* 55 (1992): 111–24.

Sackville-West, Vita. *The Edwardians.* Garden City: Doubleday, 1930.

Satterthwaite, Alfred. "John Cournos and 'H.D.'" *Twentieth-Century Literature* 22.4 (1976): 394–410.

Sayre, Gary. "*House of Incest:* Two Interpretations." *Anaïs, Art and Artists: A Collection of Essays.* Ed. Sharon Spencer. Greenwood, Fla.: Penkevill, 1986. 45–58.

Schaffner, Perdita. "A Profound Animal." Afterword. H.D., *Bid Me* 185–94.

Scheick, William, ed. *The Critical Response to H. G. Wells.* Critical Responses in Arts and Letters, 17. Westport, Conn.: Greenwood, 1995.

Schor, Naomi, and Elizabeth Weed, eds. *the essential difference.* Bloomington: Indiana UP, 1994.

Scott, Bonnie Kime. "Refiguring the Binary, Breaking the Cycle: Rebecca West as Feminist Modernist." *Twentieth-Century Literature* 37.2 (1991): 169–91.

———. *Refiguring Modernism.* Vol. 1. *The Women of 1928.* Bloomington: Indiana UP, 1995.

Sedgwick, Eve Kosofsky. *Between Men: English Literature and Male Homosexual Desire.* New York: Columbia UP, 1985.

Sheehy, Gail. "The Mentor Connection: The Secret Link in the Successful Woman's Life." *New York Magazine,* 5 April 1976, 37.

Showalter, Elaine, ed. *The New Feminist Criticism: Essays on Women, Literature, and Theory.* New York: Pantheon, 1985.

Silverman, Kaja. *The Acoustic Mirror: The Female Voice in Psychoanalysis and Cinema.* Bloomington: Indiana UP, 1988.

———. *The Subject of Semiotics.* New York: Oxford UP, 1983.

Simmons, Thomas. *Erotic Reckonings: Mastery and Apprenticeship in the Work of Poets and Lovers.* Urbana: U of Illinois P, 1994.

Simon, Linda. *The Biography of Alice B. Toklas.* Garden City: Doubleday, 1977.

Smith, Frederick James. "Fitzgerald, Flappers and Fame: An Interview with F. Scott Fitzgerald." 1921. Bruccoli et al. 79.

Smith, Sidonie. *Subjectivity, Identity and the Body: Women's Autobiographical Practices in the Twentieth Century.* Bloomington: Indiana UP, 1993.

Smith, Sidonie, and Julia Watson, eds. *Women, Autobiography, Theory.* Madison: U. of Wisconsin P, 1998.

Souhami, Diana. *The Trials of Radclyffe Hall.* London: Weidenfeld and Nicolson, 1998.

Speizer, Jeanne J. "Role Models, Mentors, and Sponsors: The Elusive Concepts." *Signs: Journal of Women in Culture and Society* 6.4 (1981): 692–712.

Spencer, Sharon. "Anaïs Nin's 'Feminine' Writing." Friedman and Fuchs 161–73.

Spender, Dale. *The Writing or the Sex? or Why You Don't Have to Read Women's Writing to Know It's No Good*. New York: Pergamon P, 1989.

Spengemann, William. *The Forms of Autobiography: Episodes in the History of a Literary Genre*. New Haven: Yale UP, 1980.

Spoo, Robert. Introduction. H.D., *Asphodel* ix–xxi.

Stanley, Julia Penelope, and Susan J. Wolfe (Robbins). "Toward a Feminist Aesthetic." *Chrysalis* 6 (1978): 57–71.

Stanton, Domna. *Female Autograph: Theory, Practice, of Autobiography*. Chicago: U of Chicago P, 1987.

Stephenson, Gregory. "From Psychic Myth to Mind-Movie: Anaïs Nin's 'The House of Incest' and Henry Miller's 'Scenario'." Ed. note by Gunther Stuhlmann. *Anaïs: An International Journal* 16 (1998): 88–91.

Stern, Daniel. "The Novel of Her Life: *The Diary of Anaïs Nin*, Volume IV (1944–47)." Zaller 153–56.

Stetz, Margaret Diane. "Rebecca West and the Visual Arts." *Tulsa Studies in Women's Literature* 8 (1989): 43–62.

Stewart, Grace. *A New Mythos: The Novel of the Artist as Heroine, 1877–1977*. Monographs in Women's Studies. Ed. Sherri Clarkson. St. Albans, Vt.: Eden P, 1979.

Stillinger, Jack. *Multiple Authorship and the Myth of the Solitary Genius*. New York: Oxford UP, 1991.

Stuhlmann, Gunther. "Should the Real June Please Stand Up?" *Anaïs: An International Journal* 18 (2000): 119–26.

Thomas, Sue. "Questioning Sexual Modernity: Rebecca West's *Sunflower*." *Journal of the Australasian Universities Modern Language Association* 89 (1998): 99–120.

———. "Rebecca West's Second Thoughts on Feminism." *Genders* 13 (1992): 90–107.

Travis, S. "A Crack in the Ice: Subjectivity and the Mirror in H.D.'s *HER*." *Sagetrieb* 6.2 (1987): 123–40.

Troubridge, Una. *The Life and Death of Radclyffe Hall*. London: Hammond, 1961.

Turnbull, Andrew. *Scott Fitzgerald*. New York: Scribner's, 1962.

Tytell, John. *Passionate Lives: D. H. Lawrence, F. Scott Fitzgerald, Henry Miller, Dylan Thomas, Sylvia Plath—In Love*. Secaucus, N.J.: Carol, 1991.

Vanacker, Sabine. "Stein, Richardson and H.D.: Women Modernists and Autobiography." *Bête Noire* 6 (1988): 111–23.

Wagner, Linda Welshimer. "*Helen in Egypt*: A Culmination." *Contemporary Literature* 10 (1969): 523–36.

———. "*Save Me the Waltz*: An Assessment in Craft." *The Journal of Narrative Technique* 12.3 (1982): 201–9.

Wagner-Martin, Linda W. "H.D.'s Fiction: Convolutions to Clarity." Friedman and Fuchs. 148–60.

Walkley, Arthur Bingham. *Drama and Life*. London: Methuen, 1907.

Wandor, Michelene. "Submissive Women and Ugly Men." *The Listener*, 10 July 1986, 27.

Watson, Julia. "Unspeakable Differences: The Politics of Gender in Lesbian and Heterosexual Women's Autobiographies." *De/Colonizing the Subject: The Politics of Gender in Women's Autobiographies*. Ed. Sidonie Smith and Julia Watson. Minneapolis: U of Minnesota P, 1992. 139–68.

Weatherhead, A. Kingsley. "Style in H.D.'s Novels." *Contemporary Literature* 10.4 (1969): 537–56.

Webster's Ninth New Collegiate Dictionary. Springfield, Mass.: Merriam-Webster, 1991.

Weiss, Andrea. *Paris Was a Woman: Portraits from the Left Bank.* San Francisco: HarperCollins, 1995.

Wells, H. G. *Boon.* New York: Doran, 1915.

———. *H. G. Wells in Love: Postscript to* An Experiment in Autobiography. Ed. G. P. Wells. Boston: Little, Brown, 1984.

West, Anthony. *H. G. Wells: Aspects of a Life.* New York: Random House, 1984.

———. *Heritage.* New York: Random House, 1955.

———. "Life with Aunty Panther." *Observer,* 4 Jan. 1976, 15.

West, Rebecca. "The Art of Skepticism." *Vogue,* 1 Nov. 1952.

———. *Family Memories.* London: Virago, 1987.

———. *Henry James.* New York: Holt, 1916.

———. "Marriage." Rev. of *Marriage* by H. G. Wells. Rpt. in *The Young Rebecca: Writings of Rebecca West, 1911–17.* Ed. and introd. Jane Marcus. Bloomington: Indiana UP, 1982. 64–69.

———. "The Novel of Ideas." Scheick 111–13.

———. *The Only Poet and Short Stories.* Ed. and introd. Antonia Till. London: Virago, 1992.

———. Papers. The Rebecca West Collection. Special Collections, McFarlin Library, U of Tulsa, Tulsa, Oklahoma.

———. *Selected Letters of Rebecca West.* Ed. and introd. Bonnie Kime Scott. New Haven: Yale UP, 2000.

———. *Sunflower.* Afterword Victoria Glendinning. London: Virago, 1986.

———. "Uncle Bennett." *The Strange Necessity: Essays and Reviews.* Introd. G. Evelyn Hutchinson. London: Virago, 1987. 199–213.

White, Hayden. *Metahistory: The Historical Imagination in Nineteenth-Century Europe.* Baltimore: Johns Hopkins UP, 1973.

Winegarten, Renee. "Rebecca West: The Art of Betrayal." *American Scholar* 53 (1984): 225–31.

Wolfe, Susan J., and Julia Penelope. "Sexual Identity/Textual Politics: Lesbian {De/Com}positions." Wolfe and Penelope, *Sexual Practice* 1–24.

———, eds. *Sexual Practice/Textual Theory: Lesbian Cultural Criticism.* Cambridge, Mass.: Blackwell, 1993.

Wood, Mary E. "A Wizard Cultivator: Zelda Fitzgerald's *Save Me the Waltz* as Asylum Autobiography." *Tulsa Studies in Women's Literature* 11.2 (1992): 247–64.

Zaller, Robert, ed. and introd. *A Casebook on Anaïs Nin.* New York: NAL, 1974.

Zilboorg, Caroline. "H.D.'s Influence on Richard Aldington." *Richard Aldington: Reappraisals.* Ed. Charles Doyle. English Literary Studies. ELS Monograph Series. Victoria, Can.: U of Victoria, 1990. 26–44.

———, ed. *Richard Aldington and H.D.: The Early Years in Letters.* Bloomington: Indiana UP, 1992.

Zimmerman, Bonnie. "Perverse Reading: The Lesbian Appropriation of Literature." Wolfe and Penelope, *Sexual Practice* 135–49.

———. "What Has Never Been: An Overview of Lesbian Feminist Literary Criticism." Showalter 200–24.

Index